ARCHAEOLOGY AS A TOOL
OF CIVIC ENGAGEMENT

ARCHAEOLOGY AS A TOOL OF CIVIC ENGAGEMENT

Edited by
Barbara J. Little and Paul A. Shackel

A Division of
ROWMAN & LITTLEFIELD PUBLISHERS, INC.
Lanham • New York • Toronto • Plymouth, UK

AltaMira Press
A division of Rowman & Littlefield Publishers, Inc.
A wholly owned subsidiary of The Rowman & Littlefield Publishing Group, Inc.
4501 Forbes Boulevard, Suite 200, Lanham, MD 20706
www.altamirapress.com

Estover Road, Plymouth PL6 7PY, United Kingdom

British Library Cataloguing in Publication Information Available

Library of Congress Cataloging-in-Publication Data

Archaeology as a tool of civic engagement / edited by Barbara J. Little and
Paul A. Shackel.
    p. cm.
  Includes bibliographical references and index.
  ISBN-13: 978-0-7591-1059-5 (cloth : alk. paper)
  ISBN-10: 0-7591-1059-X (cloth : alk. paper)
  ISBN-13: 978-0-7591-1060-1 (pbk. : alk. paper)
  ISBN-10: 0-7591-1060-3 (pbk. : alk. paper)
 1. Archaeology--Social aspects. 2. Archaeology--Political aspects.
3. Archaeology--Philosophy. 4. Archaeology--Case studies. 5. Social
participation. 6. Social justice. 7. Political participation. 8. Community life.
9. Public history. 10. Cultural policy. I. Little, Barbara J. II. Shackel, Paul A.

  CC175.A73 2007
  930.1--dc22
                                    2006101549

Printed in the United States of America

♾ ™ The paper used in this publication meets the minimum requirements
of American National Standard for Information Sciences—Permanence of
Paper for Printed Library Materials, ANSI/NISO Z39.48-1992.

Contents

Illustrations

Table

Figures

Chapter 1

Archaeology and Civic Engagement

Barbara J. Little

Our goal for this book is to encourage archaeologists to think about effective ways to participate in the civic renewal movement. The goals of this somewhat loosely defined, yet quite real, movement include community building, the creation of social capital, and active citizen engagement in community and civic life. Although archaeology per se is not usually seen as an explicit part of this movement, there is a role for the discipline to play, particularly as archaeological projects increasingly involve the communities in which they occur and the descendants of the peoples whose lives are the subject of study.

There is a great deal of public interest in the past and even trust in the lessons learned from historic places and remnants of historic places (e.g., Ramos and Duganne 2000, Rosenzweig and Thelen 1998). The contributors to this volume are interested in making the stories told at those places and about the past fully inclusive. A strong thread runs through the volume about raising consciousness about the past and connecting it with the present, particularly with the intention of using archaeological histories as pathways toward restorative justice. The authors here are each intensely interested in helping to create a useable, broadly conceived past that is civically engaging, that calls a citizenry to participate in debates and decisions about preservation and development but also, more importantly, to appreciate

1

the worthiness of all people's histories and to become aware of historical roots and present-day manifestations of contemporary social justice issues. A socially useful heritage can stimulate and empower both local community members and visitors to make historically informed judgments about heritage and the ways that we use it in the present. Such work is done in a variety of settings using many different methods.

Definitions of civic engagement vary somewhat, but they have in common the essential elements of involvement and participation in public life. According to Thomas Ehrlich in *Civic Responsibility and Higher Education* (2000:vi), "Civic engagement means working to make a difference in the civic life of our communities and developing the combination of knowledge, skills, values and motivation to make that difference. It means promoting the quality of life in a community, through both political and non-political processes." When archaeology is a tool for civic engagement, the emphasis is not usually on the political system in any formal way, although local politics will likely be involved. In addition, meaningful historical awareness coupled with varying degrees of empowerment can develop.

Social capital is a term that describes good will, fellowship, and the social interactions that count in the daily lives of people who make up a social unit. Social capital gives rise to connections of trust, reciprocity, shared values, and networks among individuals. It's been picked up by the World Bank and other international organizations as they have come to realize it as necessary to the efficient functioning of modern economies (e.g., Fukuyama 1999). One of the principles of social capital is that, unlike economic capital, it grows when it is spent. That is, drawing upon social capital generates more.

It is important to distinguish between social capital that is bonding, that is, exclusive and homogenizing, and that which is bridging, that is, inclusive and acting across social divides. There is an important caveat about bonding social capital. Strong communities with abundant social capital can coalesce around values that are not targeted toward the greater good. Group solidarity is often purchased at the cost of hostility toward outsiders.

There is a place for both types of social capital in every community, including in the archaeological community. The very idea that archaeologists can speak of an archaeological community stems from the bonding derived from common intellectual legacy, interest, and training. The extent to which archaeology can create bridging social capital with others varies greatly.

One widely read study of the trends in civic society is Robert Putnam's *Bowling Alone: The collapse and revival of American Community.* In 1996, Putnam started the Saguaro Seminar on Civic Engagement in America at the John F. Kennedy School of Government at Harvard University. This project works to expand knowledge about trust and community engagement and to develop strategies to increase civic engagement. The seminar's multiyear dialogue on building bonds of civic trust is summarized in the report "BetterTogether," available online at http://www.bettertogether.org/. The Saguaro Seminar comments on the blending of each kind of social capital:

> This bridging social capital helps to forge a common ground and promote citizen responsibility and engagement . . . mixed forms of bridging and bonding social capital may represent the most practical way of meeting our twin goals of greatly increasing community connectedness while multiplying our interactions with people unlike ourselves . . . In sum, we support all social capital strategies, as long as groups that are privileged or advantaged do not demonize those who don't or can't belong. We seek strategies that will raise the aggregate level of trustworthiness and trust in society. (2000:97)

In *Better Together,* the seminar participants consider five areas of life and identify efforts and potential for rebuilding civic bonds and connections. The areas they consider are the Workplace; the Arts; Politics and Government; Religion; and Schools, Youth Organizations, and Families. History and historic preservation appear briefly under "the Arts." This placement is interesting because it may give archaeology another place to enter the process. Frederick Turner discusses the role of the arts in healing the social fabric. He writes (2005:8), "Perhaps art has the complexity and ambiguity to heal the breach, to include and accept different worldviews. . . . Traditionally, that space for a healing art has been provided by ritual." His father, the anthropologist Victor Turner, wrote about *communitas* as the sense of common humanity and shared experience. Frederick Turner writes about the ritual process of passing through something together and creating *communitas*. In the less elegant language of civic engagement, that resultant bonding is social capital. Turner (2005:10) counsels that the work of "ritual-making must always be local, idiosyncratic, tailored to the special history and circumstances of the community," and he reminds us that rituals also allow a space for people to disagree without being shunned by the community. Particularly in the experience of fieldwork, archaeology can serve a nearly ritual function as it bonds people together in doing something a little strange. In that way, it is a sort of performance art, albeit with results beyond the performance. A re-visioned approach to museums and the use of archaeological collections, particularly in the way Moyer (this volume) discusses, could also create such ritual space.

The Saguaro Seminar did not adequately consider the role of the past in civic engagement. However, other organizations, such as the American Association of Museums, the U.S. National Park Service (NPS), and the International Coalition of Historic Site Museums of Conscience, actively use the past as a tool of civic engagement. As historian John Hope Franklin (2000), in his role as chair of the National Park System Advisory Board, succinctly states, inclusive history is relevant to citizenship:

> The places that commemorate sad history are not places in which we wallow, or wallow in remorse, but instead places in which we may be moved to a new resolve, to be better citizens. . . . Explaining history from a variety of angles makes it not only more interesting, but also more true. When it is more true, more people come to feel that they have a part in it. That is where patriotism and loyalty intersect with truth.

In the NPS, civic engagement refers to a long-term effort to build and sustain relationship with communities of stakeholders. It includes interpretive and educational programming as well as the planning process.

It is worth asking why the NPS as a federal agency cares about engaging communities and how this process may be different from legal compliance requirements such as public involvement. Public involvement is a legal requirement of the planning process that is required by environmental law and typically ends when the planning process is complete. Civic engagement is committed to a long-term sustained relationship with communities. It requires ongoing effort and some sharing of power.

The explicit reason for undertaking civic engagement is to keep national parks relevant to the American people, to transform these historic sites by making them active centers of democracy and citizen engagement. Parks and other historic places can be centers for democracy as places to reflect about identity and citizen responsibilities. Where the NPS is committed to bringing difficult and complex issues into the sunshine, civic engagement becomes a phrase to describe inclusive interpretation or engagement in difficult histories. The socially conscientious dialogue that results has a purpose, and that is to build, through both intellectual and emotional connections, civic consciousness and democratic values.

Civic engagement through history provides the gateway for archaeology to research and tell stories that are more complete and more accurate. The fullness of the nation's history and culture connects heritage to contemporary environmental, social, and cultural issues in order to move beyond a history packaged to be of interest only to related groups and move toward an inclusive history where experience is contextualized and people can relate to the lives and histories of others.

Of course, the NPS is following a number of trends here, including the museum community's self-examination over many years. In a very influential article, Ed Chappell (1989:265) wrote fifteen years ago something that remains pertinent: "At their worst, they [historical museums] make evil in the past seem romantic and inequality in the present seem inevitable. At their best, museums [and historic sites] help people to understand the rifts that separate us from one another. The time has come to stop adjusting the furniture and begin reforming our essential presentations of the past." The new museology calls for civic engagement, a commitment far beyond that of public education.

That call is answered by the International Coalition of Historic Site Museums of Conscience, founded in 1999. On its website, the coalition states,

> We hold in common the belief that it is the obligation of historic sites to assist the public in drawing connections between the history of our site and its contemporary implications. We view stimulating dialogue on pressing social issues and promoting humanitarian and democratic values as a primary function" (International Coalition of Historic Site Museums of Conscience:n.d.).

Such locations seek to provide an environment wherein visitors can have a civic engagement experience that teaches more holistic versions of the past and allows them to make linkages between that past and contemporary America. Commemorated historic site museums are not the only such places. At many archaeological sites, archaeologists can contribute to these opportunities through the unique and long-term perspective that archaeology brings to understandings of the past.

Adopting a Framework for Civic Engagement

In approaching civic engagement, I want to offer a framework constructed by Caryn McTighe Musil (2003). She is writing as an academician about what she characterizes as a "quiet revolution" in the academy over the last twenty years, where education for citizenship is increasingly valued. She distinguishes kinds of learning spurred by different kinds of civic engagement. Because so much of what archaeologists do in public work might be thought of as informal education, the perspective of a formal educator can help public archaeologists think about the ways that we structure projects. In addition, many colleges and universities integrate the concepts and tools of civic engagement with student service-learning requirements and sometimes use civic engagement to forge better relationships with their surrounding communities. There are enough archaeologists working as formal educators in institutions promoting civic engagement and service learning that Musil's categorization is helpful there as well.

Musil sets up her categories based on the kinds of citizen education that students may receive in the United States, which means that most of the situations are those in which relatively privileged students are challenged to work with less privileged communities. This juxtaposition works in thinking about archaeological outreach because of the ways in which the discipline is situated in academia and government. Clearly, the parallels are not strict, but they may be useful.

Six levels of civic scope correspond with phases of citizenship, levels of knowledge, definition of community, and benefits (see table 1.1). The lowest level and narrowest scope is exclusion-

Table 1.1. Educational phases leading to civic engagement and civic prosperity.

Phase	Community Is:	Civic Scope	Levels of Knowledge	Benefits
Exclusionary	only your own	civic disengagement	one vantage point(yours); monocultural	a few and only for a while
Oblivious	a resource to mine	civic detachment	observational skills; largely monocultural	one party
Naïve	a resource to engage	civic amnesia	no history; no vantage point; acultural	random people
Charitable	a resource that needs assistance	civic altruism	awareness of deprivations; affective kindliness and respect; multicultural but yours is still the norm center	the giver's feelings and the sufferer's immediate needs
Reciprocal	a resource to empower and be empowered by	civic engagement	legacies of inequality; values of partnering; intercultural competency; arts of democracy; multiple vantage points; multicultural	society as a whole in the present
Generative	an interdependent resource filled with possibilities	civic prosperity	struggles for democracy; interconnectedness; analysis of interlocking systems; intercultural competencies; arts of democracy; multiple interactive vantage points; multicultural	everyone now and in the future

Source: Musil 2003:8.

ary, wherein the community is only one's own, there is just one vantage point that is monocultural, the civic scope is "civic disengagement," and the benefits are few and temporary. The next two levels characterize student involvement as "oblivious" and then "naïve," which correspond respectively to civic detachment (one step up from civic disengagement) and civic amnesia.

In the lowest three levels of this six-level characterization Musil, as an educator interested in educating for citizenship, sees students as effectively disconnected and without knowledge of a historical perspective or any cultural vantage point that is not their own. There are probably examples of archaeological outreach that could be categorized along these same lines. The exclusionary phase could be considered analogous to the overly caricatured ivory tower, where archaeologists have no interest in sharing and no incentive to share their research or expertise with the uneducated public. Similarly, in the oblivious or naïve phases, there is—counterintuitive though it may be for archaeological projects—little consideration of historical context or cultural differences. The bandwagon effect that applauds public outreach because it is the "thing to do" because it supposedly meets public involvement goals for compliance-driven projects can generate efforts to supply the public with accessible information that is of very little benefit except to the self-selected curious few.

The next three levels are more promising. Next is the charitable phase, where the community is seen as a resource that needs assistance and the civic scope is one of civic altruism. The level of knowledge is awareness of deprivations within a community and of multiculturalism, although the giver's culture is seen as the normal center. The benefits of civic altruism are the sufferer's immediate needs and the giver's feelings. In the case of students' education, an example may be charitable work in a homeless shelter. In the case of archaeology, an example may be an archaeologist coming to the aid of the scientifically illiterate public by providing education about the best way to look at evidence of the past.

In the penultimate phase, the reciprocal phase, the community is a resource to empower and be empowered by. The benefits are seen as accruing to society as a whole in the present. This scope is that of civic engagement. The levels of knowledge are an awareness of the legacies of inequality, intercultural competency, multiculturalism and multiple vantage points, the values of partnering, and the arts of democracy. There are more and more examples of this type of project in archaeology across the globe; some of them are described by the contributors in this volume.

It is a matter of critical mass and creating a disciplinary expectation that will take archaeologists to the generative level, where the civic scope is that of civic prosperity and the benefits accrue not just in the present, but in the future as well. Just as recognition of the legacies of inequality cannot exist without broad historical and cultural perspectives, successful struggles for true participatory democracy cannot occur without reciprocity and mutual empowerment. Civic prosperity cannot occur without civic engagement.

Civic Engagement in Community Archaeology

Yvonne Marshall (2002) could say in her introduction to a recent issue of *World Archaeology* that community archaeology was a relatively new development, while acknowledging that community-based and community-controlled projects have been conducted over the course of decades. Marshall is referring to public archaeology in which there is community involvement in all parts of a project as a phenomenon that has reached a critical mass. Indeed, there are community archaeology projects all over the world and an increasing number specifically identifying community building and social capital. In addition to the contributors in Marshall's volume, see, for example, the following, including the individual contributions to edited volumes: Anyon and Ferguson 1995; Baram et al. 2001; Derry and Malloy 2003; Dongoske et al. 2000; Hantman 2005; Hodder 2000; Klesert and Downer 1990; LaRoche 2005; LaRoche and Blakey 1997; McDavid 1997; Mortensen 2005; Muckle 2002; Nassaney 2004; Nicholas and Andrews 1997; Shackel 2005; Shackel and Chambers 2004; Stottman 2004; Swidler et al. 1997; Uunila 2005; and Williams and Pope n.d.

Although the economy of heritage tourism is often a motivator for community involvement, community archaeology is about more than heritage tourism: "It is a specific approach to all aspects of archaeological practice and, as such, looks to transform the nature of our discipline in fundamental ways" (Marshall 2002:215).

Both local communities and descendant communities have varying and at times competing interests. I want to raise a caution in thinking about what communities *want* and the sentimentality we may inadvertently attach to whatever that is. I am thinking in particular about a very recent example close to my home, but unfortunately there are many examples and such challenges are ongoing.

The city of Manassas in northern Virginia, like many places, is undergoing a demographic shift as the composition of the neighborhood changes from largely homogeneous Euro-American or "white" to one mixed with Hispanic immigrants. In December 2005 the city council passed an ordinance to define what constitutes a legal family suitable for cohabitation. This law outlawed households consisting of family members outside of nuclear families, so cousins, nephews or nieces, aunts, uncles, and grandparents were forbidden from living in a household, even when the total number of persons was below the occupancy limit. The locality wanted to limit the number of immigrants in its community. Because complaints were almost invariably about Hispanic households, the city's chief building official told the *Washington Post* that the idea in changing the law's definition of a family was "to make sure these peripheral people start to be winnowed out." In a strongly worded editorial shortly thereafter, the *Post* condemned the city's actions and rightly observed that "America was built on diversity, and to mount a campaign of harassment against it, as Manassas has done, dishonors the nation's immigrant tradition as well as constitutional protections" (*Washington Post*, 2005).

Manassas rescinded this particular law when it became clear that the ACLU and fair housing advocates would bring suit, but such actions are not unique occurrences, nor is the feeling of the established residents of Manassas an isolated sentiment. Communities of all sizes make bad judgments as easily as they make good ones. The "people" speaking may speak egregious error.

This incident highlights for me one of the danger zones of exactly the sort of community-engaged work we demonstrate and advocate with this volume. What is valid community action? How do we respond to points of view that hold that the described action in Manassas was an attempt to "improve" city life by "winnowing out *peripheral* [emphasis added] people?" What is the basis for our judgments? When heritage places get identified, their stories told, the future of their past ensured, who is at the table? Who gets invited back? listened to? derided? dismissed? We can think of our own self-defined activism as intentional action to bring about social or political change, but we must be vigilant and continually self-critical and questioning about the types of changes we advocate. If we aim our activism at progressive social change and social justice, we should understand that we may be aiming at a moving target.

For all the potential pitfalls, however, such work is worth doing. As Marshall (2002:218) summarizes,

> Community archaeology encourages us to ask questions of the past we would not otherwise consider, to see archaeological remains in a new light and to think in new ways about how the past informs the present. . . . It is the only way that indigenous people, descendant communities and other local interest groups will be able to own the pasts archaeologists are employed to create . . . community archaeology can be extremely time consuming, deeply frustrating, humbling and challenging in unanticipated ways—but it is also rewarding in ways that transcend narrow academic accolades.

Because of the nature of the work, archaeologists tend to be relatively comfortable with ambiguity, but adding a sense of social responsibility, justice, and service to community adds additional layers of uncertainty and discomfort to our already difficult work. The added difficulty and complexity is appropriate and worth our best efforts. Some thinking from the European-

American Collaborative Challenging Whiteness (ECCW 2005:1) may help us balance the need to act with confidence against a willingness to understand that we may be wrong and need to change our approaches and ideas. This group advocates "critical humility," which they define

> as the practice of remaining open to discovering that our knowledge is partial and evolving while at the same time being committed and confident about our knowledge and action in the world. The two parts of this definition capture the paradox with which we struggle. If we are to hold ourselves accountable for acting, we must have confidence that our knowledge is valid enough to shape actions that are appropriate. At the same time, knowing that our knowledge is distorted by hegemony and possible self-deception, we need to be on constant alert about limits to the validity of our knowing.

As its name implies, the European-American Collaborative Challenging Whiteness is a group of scholars consciously and self-consciously challenging racialized categories. An increasing number of archaeologists are confronting racism explicitly in their work. One highly publicized and important project has raised the consciousness of historical archaeologists in ways similar to the impact of the Native American Graves Protection and Repatriation Act (NAGPRA) (see Colwell-Chanthaphonh, this volume). The African Burial Ground project in New York City provides a dramatic case study for civic engagement.

In the early 1990s, the U.S. General Services Administration (GSA) contracted for routine investigations to comply with the National Historic Preservation Act in advance of a new federal building at Foley Square in lower Manhattan. GSA did not anticipate the storm of public controversy that would be unleashed and continue for over a decade. Historical maps indicated the location of an eighteenth-century "Negroes Burying Ground," but consultants working in advance of the construction assumed that any cemetery would have been long since destroyed by subsequent construction. Excavations, beginning in the summer of 1991 and continuing through July 1992, eventually disinterred more than four hundred burials.

As Cheryl LaRoche and Michael Blakey (1997:84) describe, "The dynamics of the relationship and the shape of the project have been determined to a large extent by the relentless determination of the African-American descendent community to exercise control over the handling and disposition of the physical remains and artifacts of their ancestors." Concerned citizens, including journalists, religious leaders, artists, architects, lawyers, and many others, came together. The "constant barrage of petitions, angry rhetoric and community dissension, congressional hearings, professional meetings, lobbying, and political action" (LaRoche and Blakey 1997:86) changed the project completely and forced the continuing public engagement aspects of the project, from research design through reinterment through memorialization and ongoing public outreach.

"Think Globally, Dig Locally"

In his influential book *A Historical Archaeology of the Modern World*, Charles Orser (1996, 183ff) encourages archaeologists to "Think Globally, Dig Locally." That saying is a reminder of the balancing act required in all archaeological projects that are community-based (not only community-placed: see McDavid, this volume). The contributions to this volume range from global to local in their focus, from broad prescriptions to detailed case studies. Each considers its work in the context of archaeology as a tool for civic engagement.

Restorative justice is one of the themes that runs most strongly through all of these contributions. Chip Colwell-Chanthaphonh provides a contemporary context for an archaeology of reconciliation. He ties the search for justice to the search for the past, emphasizing that communities must face the truth and facts of history before conflict can be truly resolved. Starting with the lessons of South Africa's Truth and Reconciliation Commission, Colwell-Chanthaphonh reviews archaeology's role in the process of healing traumas caused by violence and dislocation such as unearthing mass graves in Guatemala, revealing the lives of Holocaust victims in Eastern Europe, and searching for the remains of American soldiers lost in Vietnam. He connects the role of archaeology to discerning the truth in the violent past, tying it specifically to Native rights in the wake of colonialism.

Martin Gallivan and Danielle Moretti-Langholtz collaborate with Indian tribes in Virginia to challenge historical narratives about the region that tend to leave them out. The legacy of the color line drawn between black and white left tribes caught in the middle. Archaeology at Werowocomoco, the seventeenth-century Powhatan center, balances collaboration, public engagement, and homeowner privacy (the site is on private land) while producing research results and opportunities for Virginia Indians to reconnect with the past and reinforce current identity. As the authors emphasize, civically engaged archaeology goes beyond public outreach as it promotes social justice.

Carol McDavid is explicitly concerned with successfully challenging anti-Black racism, a legacy confronted by most of the work in the volume. She is in favor of strategies that aim to create open, reciprocal, collaborative, mutually respectful interactions but calls for more explicit challenges to racism. Drawing on critical race theory, pragmatism, and related activist writing, McDavid shares insights gleaned from her archaeology outreach work in the Houston, Texas, area, including participation in the Levi Jordan Plantation Project in Brazoria, the Yates Community Archaeology Project in Freedmen's Town in Houston, and the Houston Heritage Society.

Motivated by the invisibility of inequality to many Americans, Paul Mullins suspects that there are many different ways engaged scholars can convince Americans to care about and contribute to a struggle against racism, poverty, and systemic inequalities. In the Ransom Place project on the campus of Indiana University–Purdue University, Indianapolis (IUPUI), he collaborates with members of the local African American community displaced when their neighborhood was cleared as a slum to make way for university expansion. He is interested in raising consciousness about present-day inequalities and working alongside existing community politics to address long-standing social justice issues like color line inequalities. Mullins was able to tap into the stewardship felt both on and off campus for the complex history of the area, succeeding in encouraging a new level of historical consciousness and public dialogue.

Mary Praetzellis, Adrian Praetzellis, and Thad Van Bueren describe their work with an African American community in West Oakland, whose neighborhood was severely damaged by the excesses of urban renewal. After a section of the Cypress Freeway collapsed in the Loma Prieta earthquake, the State Department of Transportation (Caltrans) made plans to rebuild the freeway. The local community organized to reroute the freeway so that it would no longer bisect this historic African American neighborhood. By working with the community to define an alternative route and in designing and implementing the cultural resource study that followed, Caltrans not only replaced a vital freeway corridor but embarked on an environmental justice project that partially redressed prior impacts to the community and restored a sense of pride in its history.

Lori Stahlgren and Jay Stottman describe two facets of their work in Louisville, Kentucky. They challenge the culture that has developed within the historic house museum community, which has consciously and unconsciously accentuated some voices from the past while silencing others. They describe how archaeology provides a wedge to change long-established interpretations. Discovering new information through excavation helped push a wedge into received history and changed the portrayal of slavery at Farmington. At the relatively new historic house museum of Riverside, archaeology has been integral since its establishment. Located in a neglected part of the city, Riverside uses archaeology as a focal point of community renewal and pride.

Kelly Britt explores the initial impact of an archaeological project on the civic nature of a community immersed in its own revitalization and the role of the archaeologist or heritage professional in this process. Her work at the Thaddeus Stevens and Lydia Hamilton Smith Historic Site in Lancaster, Pennsylvania, reclaims a local story of abolitionism and seeks to share it through an outreach program geared toward county schools. She explores the difficulties of top-down heritage management and the potential of historic sites and museums both as places for heritage tourism and as "new town halls."

Patrice Jeppson reassesses the archaeology of Franklin Court, the site of Benjamin Franklin's Philadelphia mansion, and describes the challenges of reclaiming an abolitionist history that involves reframing the national story of Benjamin Franklin. In addition, her research reclaims the untold history of African American workers in early excavations; but she worries whether through such work she is inadvertently co-opting minority history by reifying traditional power relationships. That is, by creating a new metanarrative is she negating an alternative history? Through such questions, Jeppson highlights the need for self-reflection by all archaeologists working toward new historical interpretations.

Meagan Brooks works with an ethnic community in Saskatchewan. The Doukhobors, a religious minority who emigrated from Russia in the late nineteenth century, initiated the project as part of an effort to reconnect with their heritage. In addition they were interested in contrasting their heritage as they understood it with the media coverage of an extremist group of the same ethnicity elsewhere in Canada. Brooks describes the participation of descendants in the Doukhobor Pit House Public Archaeology Project. She collected qualitative data, including questionnaires, daily journals, and interviews, to examine the impact the archaeological experience had upon the changing Doukhobor community. She also analyzes her own role as the heritage professional to better understand the contributions of archaeology to Canadian communities.

David Gadsby and Robert Chidester held public history workshops in Hampden, a working-class neighborhood in Baltimore, Maryland, as the first phase of an ongoing public archaeological project. They are working with the Hampden community, where Gadsby lives, to restore a sense of community being lost in the face of gentrification. Gadsby and Chidester want the research design of archaeology to reflect the needs and interests of the community, not merely the research agenda of the researchers. They and the community are aware of Hampden's explosively racist past and understand it as an issue that must be dealt with.

In his call for archaeology to work in the service of social justice, Paul Shackel ranges widely across the -isms that plague modern life through prejudices based on perceived differences of race, class, gender, sexual preference, ethnicity, religion, language, and other characteristics. He points out the omissions of history that make some people and their contributions less visible than others and ties civically engaged archaeology to the broader field of applied anthropology. Shackel is particularly interested in issues of labor and race as topics for civic dialog where an archaeology can contribute.

Teresa Moyer discusses the use and potential of exhibits and collections in helping people connect with difficult and often racist histories, including those directed against Chinese Americans. She calls for a shift in approach in the ways that we exhibit and otherwise use collections. Archaeologists and community members often focus on fieldwork and "exhibits as usual" because they are operating with certain models of what archaeology is. Looking at museums and their roles differently can reintegrate those whose stories are untold and make museums places where our work is useful and relevant.

Those who work with heritage in any arena find that one of the challenges is to sustain public participation. This challenge emerges from the perceived usefulness of heritage. Participation continues only as long as people find heritage useful. "Useful" is not limited to economic terms through tourism or paid admissions (although economic benefits are often legitimate goals and concerns). What is useful can be weighed in terms of public meaning and in political and social inclusion and action. Civically engaged archaeologists and their community partners face a challenge to broaden personal and community histories to both wider communities and the human family that stands to benefit from bridging connections with the past and among one another through shared history. Archaeologist Lawrence Moore (2006) analyzes the growth and development of Cultural Resource Management (CRM) and its relationship with the overall field of archaeology, tracking the ascendance of CRM's preservation ethic over academic scholarly research. He describes how something new is developing as ethics replace preservation as the central value of the discipline. He also predicts that "today, CRM is declining and Public Archaeology is on the horizon" (2006:33). Given the critical mass of community archaeology, it is

likely that the type of public archaeology that will come to pre-
dominate is the community-engaged, broad-thinking, and civically responsible type exemplified by the authors in this book.

References Cited

Anyon, Roger, and T. J. Ferguson
  1995 Cultural Resources Management at the Pueblo of Zuni, New
      Mexico, USA. *Antiquity* 69(266):913–930.
Baram, Uzi, Susan Lynn White, and Erin Westfall
  2001 Historical Archaeological Investigations of Site #8S0585 in
      Venice, Florida: The Venice Train Depot (VTD) Excavations of
      2001. Produced for Sarasota County Area Transit.
Chappell, E. A.
  1989 Social Responsibility and the American History Museum.
      Winterthur Portfolio 24(4):247–265.
Derry, Linda, and Maureen Malloy (editors)
  2003 *Archaeologists and Local Communities: Partners in Exploring the
      Past.* Society for American Archaeology, Washington, D.C.
Dongoske, Kurt, Mark Aldenderfer, and Karen Doehner (editors)
  2000 *Working Together: Native Americans and Archaeologists.* Society
      for American Archaeology, Washington, D.C.
Ehrlich, Thomas (editor)
  2000 *Civic Responsibility and Higher Education.* Oryx Press, Wesport,
      Connecticut.
European-American Collaborative Challenging Whiteness
  2005 Critical Humility in Transformative Learning When Self-Iden-
      tity Is at Stake. *Presented at the Sixth International Transformative
      Learning Conference, Michigan State University.* Note from the
      Collaborative: Collective authorship under one name reflects
      our understanding of the way knowledge is constructed. Mem-
      bers came together originally through a cultural consciousness
      project at the California Institute of Integral Studies in San
      Francisco; members are Carole Barlas, Elizabeth Kasl, Alec Ma-
      cLeod, Doug Paxton, Penny Rosenwasser, and Linda Sartor.
Franklin, John Hope
  2000 Keynote Address: Cultural Resource Stewardship. Discovery
      2000: The National Park Service General Conference, Septem-
      ber 11–15, 2000. St. Louis, MO. Electronic document, http://

www.nps.gov/discovery2000/culture/keynote.htm, accessed September 29, 2005.

Fukuyama, Francis
  1999 Social Capital and Civil Society. International Monetary Fund Conference on Second Generation Reforms. Electronic document, www.imf.org/external/pubs/ft/seminar/1999/reforms/fukuyama.htm, accessed January 19, 2007.

Hantman, Jeffrey L.
  2005 Colonial Legacies and the Public meaning of Monacan Archaeology in Virginia. *The SAA Archaeological Record* 5(2): 31–33.

Hodder, Ian (Editor)
  2000 *Towards Reflexive Method in Archaeology: The Example at Catalhoyuk*. McDonald Institute for Archaeological Research and British Institute of Archaeology at Ankara, Cambridge.

International Coalition of Historic Site Museums of Conscience
  n.d. International Coalition of Historic Site Museums of Conscience. www.sitesofconscience.org, accessed March 30, 2007.

Klesert, Anthony L., and Alan S. Downer (Editors)
  1990 *Preservation on the Reservation: Native Americans, Native American Lands, and Archaeology*. Navajo Nation Papers in Anthropology No. 26. Window Rock, Arizona.

LaRoche, Cheryl J.
  2005 Heritage, Archaeology, and African American History. *The SAA Archaeological Record* 5(2): 34–37.

LaRoche, Cheryl J., and Michael L. Blakey
  1997 Seizing Intellectual Power: The Dialogue at the New York African Burial Ground. *Historical Archaeology* 31(3):84–106.

Marshall, Yvonne (Editor)
  2002 Community Archaeology. Thematic Issue of *World Archaeology* 34(2).

McDavid, Carol
  1997 Descendants, Decisions, and Power: The Public Interpretation of the Archaeology of the Levi Jordan Plantation. *Historical Archaeology* 31(3):114–131.

Moore, Lawrence E.
  2006 CRM: Beyond Its Peak. *The SAA Archaeological Record* 6(1): 30–33.

Mortensen, Lena
  2005 The Local Meaning of International Heritage at Copan, Honduras. *The SAA Archaeological Record* 5(2):28–30.

Muckle, Bob (editor)
  2002   Community Archaeology. *Teaching Anthropology: Society for Anthropology in Community Colleges Notes* 9(1).
Musil, Caryn McTighe
  2003   Educating for Citizenship. *Peer Review* 5(3):4–8. Electronic document, www.aacu-edu.org/peerreview/pr-sp03/index.cfm, accessed September 29, 2005.
Nassaney, Michael S.
  2004   Implementing Community Service Learning through Archaeological Practice. *Michigan Journal of Community Service Learning* (Summer):89–99.
Nicholas, George P., and Thomas D. Andrews (Editors)
  1997   *At a Crossroads: Archaeology and First Peoples in Canada.* Publication No. 24, Archaeology Press, Department of Archaeology, Simon Fraser University, Burnaby, British Columbia.
Orser, Charles E., Jr.
  1996   *A Historical Archaeology of the Modern World.* Plenum, New York.
Putnam, Robert D.
  2000   *Bowling Alone: The Collapse and Revival of American Community.* Simon and Schuster, New York.
Ramos, Maria, and David Duganne
  2000   Exploring Public Perceptions and Attitudes about Archaeology. Department of the Interior, National Park Service. Prepared by Harris Interactive for the Society for American Archaeology, Washington, DC. Electronic document, www.cr.nps.gov/aad/pubs/Harris/index.htm, accessed January 15, 2006.
Rosenzweig, Roy, and David Thelen
  1998   *The Presence of the Past: Popular Uses of History in American Life.* Columbia University Press, New York.
Saguaro Seminar of Civic Engagement in America. John F. Kennedy School of Government, Harvard University
  2000   Better Together. Electronic document, www.bettertogether.org/pdfs/FullReportText.pdf, accessed August 30, 2006.
Shackel, Paul A.
  2005   Memory, Civic Engagement, and the Public Meaning of Archaeological Heritage. *SAA Archaeological Record* 5(2):24–27.
Shackel, Paul A. and Erve Chambers (editors)
  2004   *Places in Mind: Public Archeology as Applied Anthropology.* Routledge, New York.

Stottman, Jay
    2004   Can Archaeology Save the World? The Benefits of Archaeology. Session organized for Society for Historical Archaeology, St. Louis, Missouri.
Swidler, Nina, K. Dongoske, R. Anyon, and A. Downer (editors)
    1997   *Native Americans and Archaeologists: Stepping Stones to Common Ground.* AltaMira, Walnut Creek, CA.
Turner, Frederick
    2005   Civic Ritual and Political Healing. *American Arts Quarterly* 22 (1): 8–13.
Uunila, Kirsti
    2005   Using the Past in Calvert County, Maryland: Archaeology as a Tool for Building Community. *The SAA Archaeological Record* 5(2): 38–40.
Washington Post
    2005   Editorial, 30 December
Williams, Susan, and Peter Pope
    c. 2005   Findings: How Community Archaeology Creates Social Capital and Builds Community Capacity. Produced for the Newfoundland Archaeological Heritage Outreach Program (2000–2005). Electronic document, www.arts.mun.ca/nahop/SocialCapital.html, accessed January 19, 2007

Resources

Civil Practices Network http://www.cpn.org/
The Civic Practices Network (CPN) is a collaborative and nonpartisan project that brings together a diverse array of organizations and perspectives within the civic renewal movement.

Diversity Resources (National Park Service)
http://www.nature.nps.gov/helpyourparks/diversity/general.cfm, accessed September 30, 2005. See *Diversity Connections: A National Inventory* (Winter 2004–2005) for examples of how cultural resource programs, including archaeology, include the diverse population of America.

Environmental Protection Agency (EPA)
http://www.epa.gov/evaluate/toolbox/index.htm, accessed September 30, 2005.

This site contains summaries of nearly forty evaluations and reports focused on the public involvement activities of EPA and other agencies.

Each summary is searchable by environmental topic, and describes the focus of the evaluation, data collection methods, and key findings and recommendations.

The George Wright Society: http://www.georgewright.org/

The "Forum" Journal 2002, Volume 19, Number 4, *Civic Engagement at Sites of Conscience* (Guest Editor: Martin Blatt), is available here for free downloading.

Articles include

Introduction: The National Park Service and Civic Engagement (Martin Blatt).

Interpreting Slavery and Civil Rights at Fort Sumter (John Tucker).

Frankly, Scarlett, We Do Give a Damn: The Making of a New National Park (Laura Gates).

Civic Engagement with the Community at Washita Battlefield National Historic Site (Sarah Craighead).

The National Park Service: Groveling Sycophant or Social Conscience? Telling the Story of Mountains, Valley, and Barbed Wire at Manzanar National Historic Site (Frank Hays).

Activating the Past for Civic Action: the International Coalition of Historic Sites of Conscience (Liz Sevcenko).

Dialogue Between Continents: Civic Engagement and the Gulag Museum at Perm–36, Russia (Louis P. Hutchins and Gay E. Vietzke).

International Coalition of Historic Site Museums of Conscience http://www.sitesofconscience.org/, accessed September 29, 2005.

This site interprets history through historic sites that stimulate dialogue on pressing social issues and promote humanitarian and democratic values. It also shares opportunities for public involvement in issues raised at the sites.

National Park Service Civic Engagement website

http://www.nps.gov/civic/index.html, accessed September 29, 2005.

National Park Service Community Tool Box

http://www.nps.gov/civic/resources/toolbox.html, accessed September 29, 2005.

Learn about working in and with communities to accomplish shared goals with the Community Tool Box developed by the Northeast Region's Rivers, Trails and Conservation Assistance (RTCA) Program.

The Public Benefits of Archaeology (National Park Service)

http://www.cr.nps.gov/aad/PUBLIC/benefits/index.htm, accessed September 29, 2005.

Highlights various publics and how they may benefit from archaeology.

Chapter 2

History, Justice, and Reconciliation

Chip Colwell-Chanthaphonh

In *The Drowned and the Saved*, his last book before his suicide in 1987, Holocaust survivor Primo Levi begins by writing about the power of history. Levi tells us how the SS soldiers taunted the Lagers, concentration camp prisoners, by saying that the history of the Holocaust would be the Nazis' to tell. "However this war may end, we have won the war against you," the soldiers would say. "None of you will be left to bear witness, but even if someone were to survive, the world will not believe him. There will perhaps be suspicions, discussions, research by historians, but there will be no certainties, because we will destroy the evidence together with you" (Levi 1988:11).

When the war was going well for Germany the Nazis showed little concern about the evidence they left behind; however, toward the fall of 1944, when victory became less sure, the Nazis began destroying records, razing crematoria and gas chambers, and forcing the Lagers to dig up any buried victims and burn them on open pyres (Levi 1988:12–13). As Allied forces closed in on the German empire in 1945 and defeat became inevitable, rather than freeing the Lagers, the Nazis continued their brutal campaign of genocide unabated. The Nazis transferred prisoners, seemingly without reason, forcing them to walk hundreds of miles day and night with little food, water, clothing, or shelter. But Levi knew that a perverse logic fueled this violence. "It did not matter that they [the Lagers] might die along the way; what really mattered was that they should not tell their story," he (1988:14) writes. The point was to erase the possibility of history.

During moments of extreme violence, much is lost as part of the assault on human life and dignity. The past itself becomes a form of propaganda, an illusion of truth, and a political tool because, as Bettina Arnold (1999:1) has written, "the past legitimates the present." How societies understand the past is thus manipulated to justify violence, the politics of appropriation, and genocide. Truth is also a victim of violence and the regimes of power that seek to bend societies to their own malevolent ends. Few, perhaps, have explained this phenomenon better than George Orwell, who described in *1984* the repercussions of a Ministry of Truth that could convince the masses that "War is Peace," "Freedom is Slavery," and "Ignorance is Strength." And of course any notion of justice is lost immediately in a genocide or massacre, which by definition is haphazard, gratuitous, and excessively cruel.

If history and its attendant truths were without force in society, then governments would care little about their conditions. The scores of studies over the last several decades that document the manipulation of the past—for the better and worse—are persuasive evidence that the past is not inconsequential, because it is used to shape people's identities and their perceptions of others (Abu el-Haj 1998; Diaz-Andreu and Champion 1996; Herzfeld 1991; Kammen 1991; Meskell 1998; Plumb 1970; Trigger 1984). The battle between Druids and English authorities over Stonehenge, the debate over the Enola Gay and the atomic bombing of Japan, and the struggle over the Ancient One from Kennewick are just several recent examples to show that controversies putatively about the past are in fact often about control and power in the present (Bender 1998; Linenthal and Engelhardt 1996; Thomas 2000).

Despite the best efforts of the Nazis, some physical traces of the Holocaust endure; some victims survived to tell their tale (Levi 1985; Milton 1991; Wiesel 1982). The question remains, however, after any major conflict, how the victims can receive compensation and the whole society restore a sense of equilibrium. When an episode or era of violence was extreme, the restitution of money or objects or land may not be enough. How can we sufficiently punish someone who may have killed thousands? How can we repay someone who has been tortured, who lost her entire family, her home, her community? Instead of wanting things, people often want to reclaim the past, to re-establish the truth of what happened. When a torn society does not fully and honestly confront its past, when the truth about the past remains buried and obscured, the perpetrators of violence in a very real sense remain triumphant. When neo-Nazis deny the Holocaust, they aim to achieve the goals of history's erasure embarked upon by their nefarious predecessors (Lipstadt 1993).

In this chapter, I explore the philosophical basis of claiming history is fundamental to reconciliation, survey the role of archaeology in discerning the truth in the violent past, and argue that archaeologists should play an active role in the pursuit of justice. I contend that an essential aspect in the search for justice is the search for the past. Before communities and individuals can resolve conflict, they must first confront what has come to pass. The role of history in social justice has been widely recognized in Truth and Reconciliation Commissions created throughout the world—to uncover the past to achieve atonement and move society forward (Hayner 1994). Over the last decade, archaeology too has contributed to the process of confronting the traumas caused by violence and dislocation—unearthing mass graves in Rwanda, revealing the lives of Holocaust victims in Eastern Europe, searching for the remains of American soldiers lost in Vietnam. These investigations sometimes involve legal prosecution, but more often they are a kind of restorative justice that aspires to rehabilitate an entire society. This chapter looks at the ways in which archaeologists have been—and can become still more—civically engaged in the search for reconciliation and social justice.

A Question of Justice

The relationship between personal stories and justice can be seen most clearly in South Africa's extraordinary Truth and Reconciliation Commission (TRC). After decades of terrible violence, the post-apartheid government concluded that it could best heal its wounds through an open and transparent accounting of the past. The TRC's chair, Desmond Tutu (1999:20), understood that Nuremberg-like trials would be untenable for South Africans because, unlike the Allied victors after World War II, "neither side could impose victor's justice because neither side won a decisive victory." The institutionalized violence of apartheid meant that punishments could not focus on just a few individuals. Yet the victims could not forget or forgive, and a national amnesia would "in effect be to victimize the victims of apartheid a second time around" (Tutu 1999:29). The TRC instead sought to "rehabilitate and affirm the dignity and personhood of those who for so long had been silenced, and had been turned into anonymous, marginalized ones" (Tutu 1999:30).

Nancy Scheper-Hughes and Philippe Bourgois (2004:27) are partly correct to say that the TRC was "a complicated political gamble in which justice is traded for truth," but they also miss the point that the truth revealed is itself a powerful form of justice. Truth *versus* justice is a false dichotomy (Rotberg and Thompson 2000). As several observers have noted, "Properly understood, a just and moral appraisal of the past is the true life-blood of reconciliation" (Asmal et al. 1997:14). Tutu suggests that with this approach justice is withheld principally if justice is conceived of as *retributive*. But this was unappealing for South Africans because then "the wronged party is really the state, something impersonal, which has little consideration for the real victims and almost none for the perpetrator" (Tutu 1999:54). The TRC instead sought a *restorative* justice that is deeply concerned with "the healing of breaches, the redressing of imbalances, the restoration of broken relationships, a seeking to rehabilitate both the victim and the perpetrator" (Tutu 1999:54). Although the proceedings of the TRC were at times uneven, it is clear from the twenty-one thousand statements from victims that the act of testifying publicly, revealing one's story, and ultimately trying to understand the truth, can lead to redemption (Krog 1998; Meredith 1999).

What, after all, would truly constitute a retributive justice after such horrid events? This is a question that is asked after every episode of terrifying violence, of genocide. The quick trial and hanging of Adolf Eichmann, who administered the deaths of millions during the Holocaust, could be interpreted as a charade of justice, not its realization (Arendt 2004:99 [1963]). Scholar Mona Sue Weissmark (2004:6)—whose family was killed in the Holocaust—wrote that watching Eichmann's trial as a young girl revealed retributive justice to be but fleeting: "Legal punishment gave me a brief satisfaction, but in the end my sense of justice was not fully appeased. Legal justice could not wipe away the stain of injustice as I experienced it, because more than legal or material violations were involved. The injustices of the Holocaust were of such magnitude and scale that the agencies of law seemed inadequate to address the wrongdoings." Harold Kaplan (1994:x) similarly remarked, "The accused at Nuremberg were more than slightly comic. The very size of their crimes reduced them and added a pain to memory that we hardly expected."

The TRC emphasized the importance of narratives and stories in helping victims move beyond sorrowful pasts. Torture and other modes of social violence imperil not only victims' dignity and autonomy but also their ability to articulate their sufferings. Any balancing of justice must therefore also be a restoration of language. Justice is an ongoing process and goes beyond storytelling—but giving voice to the voiceless is fundamental to reconciliation. "Justice requires a balancing (an accounting), that something taken from the victim of the injustice must be restored, be given back," Teresa Godwin Phelps (2004:123) has suggested. "The balancing that truth reports afford victims begins to put the world back in order. The victims retrieve the ability to speak and shape their own stories."

Reconciliation does not require one truth to which everyone must subscribe, nor does reconciliation, if achieved, mean that the anguished past should be forgotten. Instead, the multivocality that emerges from TRCs is a process of engaging with the past and the memories in the present that remain (Rotberg 2000:6). History in this form is a dialogue that critically approaches varying versions of the past while continually aspiring to uncover the truth. For some, the notion of multivocality in archaeological research contradicts the notion of "the truth." It may seem that if all voices must be heard, then they must all be interpreted as equal. However, while all narratives should be given *equal consideration*, they should not necessarily all be given *equal weight*. Framed as standpoint theory, this kind of multivocality requires scientific and historical "practice to be reconstructed so that it incorporates a requirement to assess knowledge claims from a range of standpoints, to discern their silences, limitations, and partialities" (Wylie 1995:271); multivocality in this way is not subjective, but rather "imposes a higher standard of objectivity on the sciences than is embodied in the 'neutrality' scientists hope to achieve by ignoring or excluding considerations of difference and context" (Wylie 1995:271). Allowing for multiple—overlapping and entangled—narratives does not devalue the truth, but in opposite terms often gets us closer to understanding people, events, processes, and structures—the very heart of anthropological analyses. Scholars need to be deeply concerned about what has transpired in the past, the truths of history (see Arnold 2002).

As we will see, some kinds of archaeology, particularly those informed by forensics, explicitly address retributive justice. They seek scientific answers about who committed what violence, where and when. Other archaeological projects, however, have goals that cannot deal with such particulars because of the temporal distance of the events or the moral ambiguities of the violence being studied. These projects, I suggest, are more concerned with a kind of restorative justice, which in Tutu's (1999:54) terms seeks "the healing of breaches, the redressing of imbalances, the restoration of broken relationships, a seeking to rehabilitate both the victim and the perpetrator." Archaeology can work in both ways, but all such endeavors are a form of social justice. These archaeologists are not merely telling stories about the past, but are profoundly concerned about justice in the present. In the same way that environmental justice involves reckoning with the past and resource conservation today, such archaeological projects do not merely want to punish people for mistakes in the past, but also want to see healing and atonement in the here and now.

Archaeologies of Justice and Reconciliation

Archaeology—as defined by behavioralists since the 1970s—aims "to describe and explain the multifarious relationship between human behavior and material culture in all times and places" (Schiffer 1995:ix). While archaeology has long focused on objects, behavioral archaeology has significantly helped shift the discipline toward a broader temporal view (e.g., Rathje and Murphy 1992). This conception of archaeology's unique contribution to the social sciences also underlines the rise of Cultural Resource Management in the 1970s (Green 1998). No longer restricted to King Tut and Cahokia, archaeology could focus on increasingly applied problems such as resource claims, agricultural technology, and economic development (Downum and Price 1999). Strengthening the field's engagement with applied research naturally entails working with the public, the people who benefit from or pay the costs of archaeological study (Jameson 1997). This work essentially means bringing the past into the present, "making archaeology an integral part of a community's heritage" (Shackel 2004:14). An archaeology of reconciliation is an extension of these trends, an attempt to bring resolution in the present based on the study of the past.

Although forensics has been tied to anthropology since the late 1800s, the two fields were not fully synthesized until the 1970s (Crist 2001; Snow 1982). The excavation and analytical methods of forensic archaeology and anthropological archaeology are identical while the goals are clearly distinct: "Evidence is not gathered to uncover the broad patterns of human behavior, but rather to reconstruct the specifics of single events" (Connor and Scott 2001:3). Both kinds of research "seek to protect the physical and spatial integrity of potential evidence and remains" (Haglund 2001:28), but for the forensic archaeologist "the site is the crime scene; the artifacts are the evidence" (Connor and Scott 2001:4).

In 1984 the government of Argentina began to search for those who disappeared during the "dirty war," the state-sponsored illegal and violent campaign against dissident citizens between 1976 and 1983. Forensic anthropology was put to use in this investigation, which garnered the field worldwide attention (Stover and Ryan 2001). An international group led by the American Association for the Advancement of Science, collaborating with Argentinean archaeologists, discovered important evidence through exhumations that offered physical proof of widespread murder. Following this work, other nations—Bolivia, Brazil, Columbia, Ethiopia, Haiti, Peru, to name a few—employed forensic science to substantiate legal claims, as in Honduras where archaeological "exhumations and identifications were essential to the initiation and advancement of trials in the Honduran court system" (Haglund 2001:30). The work is often macabre. Archaeologists recovered the remains of close to five hundred human beings in Rwanda only a year after they were murdered in the genocide of 1994 (Haglund et al. 2001). Nightmares haunt the archaeologists, as surely they haunt the survivors of such attacks (Stover and Ryan 2001:22). The work is also important. On December 11, 1981, government forces massacred the villagers of El Mozote in the Republic of El Salvador (Binford 1996). Nearly a decade later, criminal trials proceeded and the victims were exhumed. Archaeologists determined that at least 143 people were killed, 131 of them children under twelve years old; that the bullets were manufactured by the United States government; that at least twenty-four killers took part (Scott 2001). The evidence from the excavations aided the indictment of several El Salvadoran Army officers.

The archaeological study of the El Mozote victims was significant not only for its legal implications. It also revealed the truth of an event that had long been known but could not be openly discussed. The archaeological work in this way directly aided the Commission on the Truth in El Salvador, which was given its mandate in a 1992 peace agreement to investigate "serious acts of violence that have occurred since 1980 and whose impact on society urgently demands that the public should know the truth" (Scott 2001:79).

In an article by Eric Stover and Molly Ryan (2001), which discusses forensic work in Argentina, Guatemala, Iraqi Kurdistan, and the former Yugoslavia, the role of archaeology in bringing reconciliation is made clear. In Argentina, the authors note, a 1987 law meant that only thirty to fifty top officials could be prosecuted, yet the work of exhumation continued. "With most of the dirty war's perpetrators now effectively amnestied, why continue to dig up the disappeared?" Stover and Ryan (2001:10) ask. "From a humanitarian perspective, families would finally know the fate of their lost ones and be able to give them a proper burial. There was also the need to set the historical record straight." In Argentina, archaeologists were able to identify the remains of a young man named Nestor Fonseca; during the exhumation, the man's widow suddenly showed up, asking to see his body. When she saw his remains, she knelt by the grave for a time, then rose and thanked the archaeologists for their work. In Guatemala, "not just families, but entire villages would come to the exhumation sites. Before the scientists began their work, women from the surrounding villages would kneel next to the grave and pray for the deceased" (Stover and Ryan 2001:23). Explaining such powerful emotions, one of the Guatemalan archaeologists said,

> A clandestine grave is not so much hidden as it is officially nonexistent. There is no possibility for the families and their communities to ritualize death, as it is done in any society. The mere existence of these mass graves . . . terrorizes and oppresses the communities which have to live with them. The official exhumation of the victims is the first step toward peace for these communities. It is then that the survivors and victims of this mechanism of terror finally become activists for their rights. (Stover and Ryan 2001:14)

Collective memories of mass murder more distant in time are no less difficult to confront. This is apparent with the Holocaust of World War II, where places such as Dachau remain stigmatized for the past they symbolize (Ryback 1999). Archaeological excavations at Holocaust sites are one way for people to confront the past and recognize the individual victims in an event often only calculated in the millions of deaths. As one archaeologist expressed it at the extermination camp of Chełmno, in Poland, "When you say that 200,000 or 300,000 people were killed here, that doesn't really say much. . . . For me, when we find a small toy or a shoe, that represents a living person. Through these small things we re-create the history of people who had dreams and life plans" (Golden 2006:189). Such excavations are thus a way to tell the untold stories of the victims that would otherwise remain buried. Recognizing the humanity of victims is an important goal for such endeavors. As David E. Stannard (1992: xi) suggests in studying holocausts, "We must do what we can to recapture and to try to understand, in human terms, what it was that was crushed, what it was that was butchered. It is not merely enough to acknowledge that much was lost." The excavations at Chełmno further seek to redress the imbalances that resulted from the mass murder. When the victims were killed, they were cremated and put in giant pits; their possessions were sorted through, kept as booty or buried. These remains are recovered and given special honor and respect (Golden 2006:191). Any human remains found are reinterred at a nearby cemetery. People from around the world attend the reburial ceremonies.

In recent years, scholars have increasingly focused on the "contested past" (e.g., Bender 1993; J. Hill 1992; McGuire 2004; Pak 1999; van der Veer 1992), but archaeology also has the potential to quell conflict, to create a common ground (Dongoske et al. 2000). The recent collaboration of some Israeli and Palestinian archaeologists exemplifies the idea of using a shared historical landscape to achieve reconciliation (Scham and Adel 2003); this work exemplifies how even scholars from warring nations can collaborate through an archaeology anchored in goodwill and trust. The "working through" that ultimately transforms contested ground to common ground, Scham and Adel demonstrate, does not entail the construction of a shared and unified historical narrative, but rather a reflexive understanding of the past that embraces multivocality. Heritage in such work is the basis of a restorative justice, embodying Tutu's model of healing breaches, redressing imbalances, and restoring broken relationships.

While archaeology can bring the possibility of resolution at the community level, it can also serve to help individuals find peace. The Joint POW/MIA Accounting Command (JPAC), created in 2003, is a joint unit of the United States military; it uses archaeological survey and excavation and forensic anthropology to seek the recovery of 35,000 people missing from World War II, 8,100 from the Korean War, 1,800 from the Vietnam War, 120 from the Cold War, and 1 from the Gulf War (www.jpac.pacom. mil). Whatever one's political views of these wars might be, the missing soldiers are a continuing emotional strain in the lives of family and friends. From the numerous media reports about the JPAC, it is clear that the discovery and repatriation of these individuals bring a sense of resolution. As one man said about his friend who went missing in Vietnam in 1966, "Not knowing is far worse torture than a funeral" (Bulwa 2005). Similarly the daughter of a CIA pilot who died when she was three weeks old felt that having the remains of her father at last no longer meant she had to suffer as she grieved (Bolt 2005). "I'm not saying goodbye to him, because now I can visit him," she said. "Now I know where he's at forever."

In the context of MIA repatriations, the repatriation of American Indian remains collected over the last century can be understood as a powerful social process of healing for contemporary native descendents. As Rick Hill (1994) noted early in the Native American Graves Protection and Repatriation Act (NAGPRA) debate, since the taking of human remains and sacred objects deeply wounded many communities, the return of those same remains and objects can lead towards genuine reconciliation. "It fell to the living to make it right with the dead," as David Hurst Thomas (2000:215) wrote about the reburial of victims from the infamous Sand Creek Massacre, in which dozens of Cheyenne were slaughtered and collected for museums. It is significant that only fifteen years after NAGPRA, many institutions and archaeologists have come to recognize the historical unbalanced treatment of Native Americans and their heritage and cultural property. Many museum professionals, such as those at the University of Pennsylvania Museum of Archaeology and Anthropology, have radically changed how they view and deal with native peoples, engaging with them collaboratively through new kinds of exhibits, acquisitions, internships, publications, and programs for visiting artists (Preucel et al. 2005; Preucel et al. 2006). The curators suggest that the new way forward for both anthropologists and Native Americans is much like the Native

Hawaiian concept that "out of 'heaviness' (*kaumaha*) must come 'enlightenment' (*aokanaka*)" (Preucel et al. 2006:186).

Repatriation and reburial have provided specific platforms for anthropologists to work through a kind of restorative justice. NAGPRA, like many Truth and Reconciliation Commissions, was mandated by law. However, I suggest that scholars in North American can go still further, without legal mandates, using archaeology as a form of dialogue about difficult past events. Today many archaeologists are coming to recognize the impact of colonialism on native peoples in North America—and indeed suggest that colonialism, in contrast to "culture contact," is the proper frame by which discussions of these interactions should take place (Silliman 2005). And still, while archaeologists recognize the deleterious impacts of colonialism, little discussion unfolds about how the legacies of this history continue to be played out, how knowledge of this past might lead to Tutu's "redressing of imbalances" (e.g., Stein 2005). This is important, as Paul Farmer (2005:129–132) reminds us, because anthropologists are uniquely positioned to not merely document violence, but also reveal the mechanisms of violence. Archaeologists are not just builders of monuments, but they construct knowledge of the past, which is "an instrument that informs our capacity to analyze the present" (Todorov 1996:259).

A handful of archaeologists are already illustrating the possibilities of such an approach. One example is the work being done at Fort Apache in central Arizona, a place marked by conflict and difficult memories (Mahaney and Welch 2002; Welch 2000; Welch et al. 2000a). Built in 1869 by the U.S. government, Fort Apache was a military base, central in the control and subjugation of Apache peoples in the late 1800s. Some Apaches participated in this colonization as scouts for the U.S. Army; other Apaches were active resistors. In the twentieth century portions of the post later became an Indian boarding school, while other parts fell into disuse. However, in the late 1990s, the White Mountain Apache Tribe, in conjunction with archaeologists and cultural preservationists, decided to restore the fort's grounds and buildings and explicitly use the place to focus on the contentious history, to create a place of reconciliation. The community's strategy was simple but not easy:

How can Fort Apache be returned to active duty in service to the Apache community? The first step must be to acknowledge that Fort Apache either caused or symbolizes many of the problems and challenges faced by the Apache people, including diminished territory and cultural integrity. Such an acknowledgment will make possible a stepwise reconciliation among Fort Apache's many stakeholders and a cleansing of the personal and interpersonal wounds caused by the events and the processes of an earlier era. Once individuals and group representatives begin to focus on common ground and shared history and humanity, forgiveness and healing are within reach. (Welch et al. 2000b:5)

More than four thousand people attended the first annual Fort Apache Heritage Reunion on May 20, 2000. The event began with a procession of different tribes, followed by community leaders and government officials. There were songs, dances, and nonviolent historical reenactments. Different reconciliation programs were offered, such as "listening posts" where attendees shared their feelings and remembrances about the fort, which encouraged "Apaches and non-Apaches to confront their ambiguous, even hostile sentiments and to think about the relationship between memories, emotions, and the future" (Welch and Riley 2001:10–11). Although ambitious and hopeful, the White Mountain Apache Tribe's project is converting "a symbol of oppression and cultural erosion into a powerful symbol of hope, power, and self-determination" (Welch and Riley 2001:10–11). It is too soon to say if this project will achieve its goals of explaining Apache heritage to outsiders, perpetuating Apache heritage for tribal members, and maintaining a forum that honors Apache survival. But whatever the fate of Fort Apache, the White Mountain Apache Tribe is showing us the possibilities of dedicating archaeology to the goals of civic engagement and social justice.

Some Conclusions: The Justice of Things

The study of past violence is closely connected to the pursuit of justice, although few archaeologists often explicitly write about their labors in this regard. Archaeology, however, cannot contribute equally to all forms of justice.

Political philosophers have largely expressed skepticism about the role of history in distributive justice, which involves questions about how to resolve *present* inequalities, such as the unbalanced distribution of wealth, education, and health care in society. Jeremy Waldron (1992) is one prominent philosopher who contends that historical injustices cannot be fully compensated in the present (see also Lyons 1977; Sher 1980). To begin with, Waldron posits, is the consideration that when we offer recompense to the descendants of people who were wronged long ago, we engage in "counterfactual reasoning," which involves speculating on what might have happened if certain events had not occurred. That is, to ascertain how to distribute goods today while taking into consideration historical injustices, we would have to somehow calculate what losses people have suffered because of particular wrongs. However, Waldron argues that this line of thinking is fraught with difficulties because it is all but impossible to gauge what *might* have been at any given moment, much less over centuries. Waldron also discusses how modern circumstances may supersede past injustices. Imagine that a well located on a family's homestead plot was dishonestly appropriated. It seems right to try to return the family's well as long as there is enough water for everyone. But then, suppose a catastrophic drought comes. It now seems right that everyone must share the well the family formerly held—irrespective of the fact that it was unjustly taken—because otherwise many people will die of thirst. In other words, entitlements to resources shift over time because of changing circumstances and depend on the contexts of their use. Waldron (1992:27) recognizes the importance of symbolic gestures of reparation and that history may spur us to pursue justice in the present, but he writes that "it is the impulse to justice now that should lead the way in this process, not the reparation of something whose wrongness is understood primarily in relation to conditions that no longer obtain."

Historical considerations have a clearer and stronger role in questions of reparative justice. Within this category are two others, which as discussed throughout this chapter, archaeology can and should contribute to: retributive justice and restorative justice. Retributive justice involves applying punishment to those who have behaved wrongly. When archaeology is used as a forensic science, it can help uncover who committed what crimes, when, and where. This is the important work that has been done in Argentina, Honduras, Rwanda, El Salvador, and elsewhere to uncover the violence and to gather evidence that can be used in prosecutions. Other archaeological research, such as that used in land and water claims litigation, also falls into this category (e.g., Lilley 2000; Ross 1973). The uncovering of past thefts and violence often has a dual role, however, in part because crimes of such magnitude can never be fully prosecuted in courts. The eye-for-an-eye logic may work for a single murder but turns into a farce of justice when used to prosecute those who commit genocide.

Restorative justice is thus an important form of justice, a way for individuals and communities to seek healing when violence has suffused an entire society, when the magnitude of violence reaches a vast scale. Archaeology here too has played an important role to date, particularly in formal programs such as TRCs and legally mandated programs such as NAGPRA. I want to suggest, however, that archaeologists and historians can play a still greater role in developing projects like those at Fort Apache—projects that explicitly seek to engage in forms of *informal* restorative justice, projects without government sanction or coercive power. One of the key mechanisms of a program of informal restorative justice, I believe, is to realize the truth. The concept of "truth" here is by no means simple. Indeed, the very complexity of past events, their causes and consequences, is vital to address in this mode, as too often regimes of power seek to falsely reduce the truth to neat boundaries of good versus evil, us versus them. But restorative justice, whatever its methods, needs a clear commitment to the ideal of truth—that the past, however messy and complex, really happened and really can be understood. A restorative justice that obscures the truth performs the opposite of its express goal, to foster reconciliation by bringing to light what was previously and perversely hidden in the shadows of people's lives.

The work of anthropologists can play a particularly important role in addressing one of the shortcomings of formal TRCs,

which involves linking macrolevel and microlevel events, experiences, processes, and structures (Chapman and Ball 2001:7).
Researchers can provide insight for such an approach through
anthropological methods to reveal hidden truths, but also to
show how history itself is constructed and used as a cultural
strategy in particular political settings. As Paul Farmer (2005)
has written, it is essential to understand the relationship between
individuals and the structural violence that surrounds them. He
suggests that one of the best ways to demystify organized violence is to start with individual stories, for it is through personal
stories that some may "learn to see the connections between
personal experience, psychological experience, cognition, and
affect on the one hand, and the political economy of brutality on
the other" (Farmer 2005:133).

In this approach scholars are neither heroes nor saviors, but
only participants who can offer insights given their particular
disciplinary training while encouraging the larger community
to engage in positive dialogue. Importantly, every culture has its
own way of dealing with painful pasts, and restorative justice
should not supplant local remedies (Kelsall 2005). However,
because violence on the scale of massacres and genocides is
so often intercultural, restorative justice approaches reconciliation through dialogue that fosters cross-cultural conversation
and understanding. Whether by way of a museum exhibit on
American Indian boarding schools or a book on a massacre of
American Indians, the study of the traumatic past can be a vital
means to pursue informal restorative justice (e.g., Colwell-Chanthaphonh 2007; Hoerig 2002). These public artifacts—museum
exhibits or books—are a kind of collective "working through,"
a critical historiography that seeks to build or rebuild a sense of
community (LaCapra 2001:65).

Projects built around the idea of restorative justice share at
least three common features. One feature is that they are *multivocal* without eschewing the truth. More exactly, by incorporating
many voices and perspectives, these projects approach the truth
from multiple standpoints, instead of one privileged position
such as that of the state or ivory tower. In this way history should
be constructed not through a celebratory multivocality, but rather

through a critical multivocality in which the truth is constantly being questioned, debated, and desired. Another prominent feature is the way such work is *dialogical,* geared toward cultivating an exchange of knowledge, experiences, and opinions. As noted, dialogue seems the most obvious way to create affirmative interaction among disparate peoples. Because of this too, these conversations need to be democratic—evenhanded, open, and inclusive. A final feature is that they are deeply *historical,* meaning that they are genuinely diachronic, examining change through time from the distant past to the social and political present. This approach requires linking individual stories to structures of power, linking microtruths to macrotruths.

In this chapter I have argued that archaeologists should play an active role in the search for justice, whether participating in the identification of massacre victims, telling the stories of those whose past was erased, or bringing resolution among different people still in conflict. Forensic archaeology is ideally suited to such endeavors, but other kinds of archaeology can become engaged in dealing with a difficult past. I do not suggest that every project must take this approach, but rather I would encourage those who do study a contentious past to consider how their efforts can be used to address and overcome the injustices of the past. In this way Tutu's notion of restorative justice can be applied most fruitfully to the discipline, a dialogic approach that does not imply scholars must have all the answers. As many have observed, archaeology is inherently a social endeavor and so will be used, sometimes abused, by the people who are affected by the subjects of our studies, our roles as social actors. It is thus not a question of *whether* the material past will be used by society but *how* it will be used—a means to what end.

References Cited

Abu el-Haj, Nadia
  1998   Translating Truths: Nationalism, the Practice of Archaeology, and the Remaking of Past and Present in Contemporary Jerusalem. *American Ethnologist* 25(2):166–188.

Arendt, Hannah
  2004 [1963] From Eichmann in Jerusalem: A Report on the Banality
        of Evil. In *Violence in War and Peace,* edited by Nancy Scheper-
        Hughes and Philippe Bourgois, pp. 91–100. Blackwell, Ox-
        ford.
Arnold, Bettina
  1999 The Contested Past. *Anthropology Today* 15(4):1–4.
  2002 Justifying Genocide: Archaeology and the Construction of
        Difference. In *Annihilating Difference: The Anthropology of
        Genocide,* edited by Alex Hinton, pp. 95–116. University of
        California Press, Berkeley.
Asmal, Kader, Louise Asmal, and Ronald Suresh Roberts
  1997 *Reconciliation Through Truth: A Reckoning of Apartheid's
        Criminal Governance.* David Philip Publishers, Cape
        Town.
Bender, Barbara
  1993 Stonehenge—Contested Landscapes (Medieval to Present-
        Day). In *Landscape: Politics and Perspectives,* edited by Barbara
        Bender, pp. 245–279. Berg, Oxford.
  1998 *Stonehenge: Making Space.* Berg Press, Oxford.
Binford, Leigh
  1996 *The El Mozote Massacre: Anthropology and Human Rights.* Uni-
        versity of Arizona Press, Tucson.
Bolt, Greg
  2005 Pilot's Secret Mission Ends Five Decades Later. *The Register-
        Guard* 16 June.
Bulwa, Demian
  2005 Vietnam MIA Gets Funeral Rites for Remains of Airman—39
        Years Late. *San Francisco Chronicle* 2 June.
Chapman, Audrey R., and Patrick Ball
  2001 The Truth of Truth Commissions: Comparative Lessons from
        Haiti, South Africa, and Guatemala. *Human Rights Quarterly*
        23(1):1–43.
Colwell-Chanthaphonh, Chip
  2007 *Massacre at Camp Grant: Forgetting and Remembering Apache
        History.* University of Arizona Press, Tucson.
Connor, Melissa, and Douglas D. Scott
  2001 Paradigms and Perpetrators. *Historical Archaeology* 35(1):1–6.
Crist, Thomas A. J.
  2001 Bad to the Bone? Historical Archaeologists in the Practice of
        Forensic Science. *Historical Archaeology* 35(1):39–56.

Diaz-Andreu, Margarita, and Timothy Champion (editors)
1996   *Nationalism and Archaeology in Europe.* University College London Press, London.

Dongoske, Kurt E., Mark Aldenderfer, and Karen Doehner (editors)
2000   *Working Together: Native Americans and Archaeologists.* Society for American Archaeology, Washington, D.C.

Downum, Christian E., and Laurie J. Price
1999   Applied Archaeology. *Human Organization* 58(3):226–239.

Farmer, Paul
2005   The Banality of Agency: Bridging Personal Narrative and Political Economy. *Anthropological Quarterly* 78(1):125–135.

Golden, Juliet
2006   Remembering Chełmno. In *Archaeological Ethics,* edited by Karen D. Vitelli and Chip Colwell-Chanthaphonh, pp. 188–193. AltaMira Press, Walnut Creek.

Green, William
1998   Cultural Resource Management and American Archaeology. *Journal of Archaeological Research* 6(2):121–167.

Haglund, William D.
2001   Archaeology and Forensic Death Investigations. *Historical Archaeology* 35(1):26–34.

Haglund, William D., Melissa Connor, and Douglas D. Scott
2001   The Archaeology of Contemporary Mass Graves. *Historical Archaeology* 35(1):57–69.

Hayner, Priscilla B.
1994   Fifteen Truth Commissions—1974 to 1994: A Comparative Study. *Human Rights Quarterly* 16(4):597–655.

Herzfeld, Michael
1991   *A Place in History: Social and Monumental Time in a Cretan Town.* Princeton University Press, Princeton.

Hill, Jonathan D.
1992   Contested Pasts and the Practice of Anthropology. *American Anthropologist* 94(4):809–815.

Hill, Rick
1994   Repatriation Must Heal Old Wounds. In *Reckoning with the Dead: The Larsen Bay Repatriation and the Smithsonian Institute,* edited by Tamara L. Bray and Thomas W. Killion, pp. 184–186. Smithsonian Institute Press, Washington, D.C.

Hoerig, Karl A.
2002   Remembering Our Indian School Days: The Boarding School Experience. *American Anthropologist* 104(2):642–646.

Jameson, John H., Jr. (editor)
  1997   *Presenting Archaeology to the Public.* AltaMira Press, Walnut Creek.
Kammen, Michael
  1991   *Mystic Chords of Memory: The Transformation of Tradition in American Culture.* Vintage Books, New York.
Kaplan, Harold
  1994   *Conscience and Memory: Meditations in a Museum of the Holocaust.* University of Chicago Press, Chicago.
Kelsall, Tim
  2005   Truth, Lies, Ritual: Preliminary Reflections on the Truth and Reconciliation Commission in Sierra Leone. *Human Rights Quarterly* 27(2):361–391.
Krog, Antjie
  1998   *Country of My Skull.* Jonathan Cape, London.
LaCapra, Dominick
  2001   *Writing History, Writing Trauma.* Johns Hopkins University Press, Baltimore.
Levi, Primo
  1985   *Moments of Reprieve.* Summit Books, New York.
  1988   *The Drowned and the Saved.* Translated by Raymond Rosenthal. Vintage Books, New York.
Lilley, Ian (editor)
  2000   *Native Title and the Transformation of Archaeology in the Post-Colonial World,* vol. 50. Oceania Monographs. University of Sydney, Sydney.
Linenthal, Edward T., and Tom Engelhardt
  1996   *History Wars: The Enola Gay and Other Battles for the American Past.* Henry Holt, New York.
Lipstadt, Deborah E.
  1993   *Denying the Holocaust: The Growing Assault on Truth and Memory.* Free Press, New York.
Lyons, David
  1977   The New Indian Claims and Original Rights to Land. *Social Theory and Practice* 4(3):249–273.
Mahaney, Nancy, and John R. Welch
  2002   The Legacy of Fort Apache: Interpretive Challenges at a Community Historic Site. *Journal of the Southwest* 44(1):36–47.
McGuire, Randall H.
  2004   Contested Pasts: Archaeology and Native Americans. In *A Companion to Social Archaeology,* edited by Lynn Meskell and Robert W. Preucel, pp. 374–395. Blackwell, Oxford.

Meredith, Martin
  1999   *Coming to Terms: South Africa's Search for Truth.* PublicAffairs, New York.
Meskell, Lynn (editor)
  1998   *Archaeology Under Fire: Nationalism, Politics, and Heritage in the Eastern Mediterranean and Middle East.* Routledge Press, London.
Milton, Sybil
  1991   *In Fitting Memory: The Art and Politics of Holocaust Memorials.* Wayne State University Press, Detroit.
Pak, Yangjin
  1999   Contested Ethnicities and Ancient Homelands in Northeast Chinese Archaeology: The Case of Koguryo and Puyo Archaeology. *Antiquity* 73:613–618.
Phelps, Teresa Godwin
  2004   *Shattered Voices: Language, Violence, and the Work of Truth Commissions.* University of Pennsylvania Press, Philadelphia.
Plumb, John H.
  1970   *The Death of the Past.* Houghton Mifflin, Boston.
Preucel, Robert W., Lucy F. Williams, and William Wierzbowski
  2005   The Social Lives of Native American Objects. In *Objects of Everlasting Esteem: Native American Voices on Identity, Art, and Culture,* edited by Lucy F. Williams, William Wierzbowski, and Robert W. Preucel, pp. 1–26. University of Pennsylvannia Museum of Archaeology and Anthropology, Philadelphia.
Preucel, Robert W., Lucy F. Williams, Stacey O. Espenlaub, and Janet Monge
  2006   Out of Heaviness, Enlightenment: NAGPRA and the University of Pennsylvania Museum of Archaeology and Anthropology. In *Archaeological Ethics,* edited by Karen D. Vitelli and Chip Colwell-Chanthaphonh, pp. 178–187. AltaMira Press, Walnut Creek.
Rathje, William, and Colin Murphy
  1992   *Rubbish! The Archaeology of Garbage.* Harper Collins, New York.
Ross, Norman A.
  1973   *Index to the Expert Testimony before the Indian Claims Commission.* Clearwater Publishing Company, New York.
Rotberg, Robert I.
  2000   Truth Commissions and the Provision of Truth, Justice, and Reconciliation. In *Truth v. Justice: The Morality of Truth Commis-*

sions, edited by Robert I. Rotberg and Dennis Thompson, pp. 3–21. Princeton University Press, Princeton.

Rotberg, Robert I., and Dennis Thompson (editors)
2000 *Truth v. Justice: The Morality of Truth Commissions.* Princeton University Press, Princeton.

Ryback, Timothy W.
1999 *The Last Survivor: Legacies of Dachau.* Vintage Books, New York.

Scham, Sandra A., and Yahya Adel
2003 Heritage and Reconciliation. *Journal of Social Archaeology* 3(3):399–416.

Scheper-Hughes, Nancy, and Philippe Bourgois
2004 Making Sense of Violence. In *Violence in War and Peace,* edited by Nancy Scheper-Hughes and Philippe Bourgois, pp. 1–31. Blackwell, Oxford.

Schiffer, Michael B.
1995 *Behavioral Archaeology: First Principles.* University of Utah Press, Salt Lake City.

Scott, Douglas D.
2001 Firearms Identification in Support of Identifying a Mass Execution at El Mozote, El Salvador. *Historical Archaeology* 35(1): 79–86.

Shackel, Paul A.
2004 Working with Communities: Heritage Development and Applied Archaeology. In *Places in Mind: Public Archaeology as Applied Anthropology,* edited by Paul A. Shackel and Erve J. Chambers, pp. 1–16. Routledge, London.

Sher, George
1980 Ancient Wrongs and Modern Rights. *Philosophy and Public Affairs* 10(1):3–17.

Silliman, Stephen W.
2005 Culture Contact or Colonialism? Challenges in the Archaeology of Native North America. *American Antiquity* 70(1):55–74.

Snow, Clyde Collins
1982 Forensic Anthropology. *Annual Review of Anthropology* 11:97–131.

Stannard, David E.
1992 *American Holocaust: The Conquest of the New World.* Oxford University Press, Oxford.

Stein, Gil J. (editor)
2005 *The Archaeology of Colonial Encounters: Comparative Perspectives.* School of American Research Press, Santa Fe.

Stover, Eric, and Molly Ryan
  2001 Breaking Bread with the Dead. *Historical Archaeology* 35(1):7–25.
Thomas, David Hurst
  2000 *Skull Wars: Kennewick Man, Archaeology, and the Battle for Native American Identity.* Basic Books, New York.
Todorov, Tzvetan
  1996 *Facing the Extreme: Moral Life in the Concentration Camps.* Translated by Arthur Denner and Abigail Pollak. Henry Holt, New York.
Trigger, Bruce G.
  1984 Alternative Archaeologies: Nationalist, Colonialist, Imperialist. *Man (N.S.)* 19:355–370.
Tutu, Desmond
  1999 *No Future Without Forgiveness.* Doubleday, New York.
van der Veer, Peter
  1992 Ayodhya and Somnath: Eternal Shrines, Contested Histories. *Social Research* 59(1):85–109.
Waldron, Jeremy
  1992 Superseding Historical Injustice. *Ethics* 103(1):4–28.
Weissmark, Mona Sue
  2004 *Justice Matters: Legacies of the Holocaust and World War II.* Oxford University Press, Oxford.
Welch, John R.
  2000 The White Mountain Apache Tribe Heritage Program: Origins, Operations, and Challenges. In *Working Together: Native Americans and Archaeologists,* edited by Kurt E. Dongoske, Mark Aldenderfer and Karen Doehner, pp. 67–84. Society for American Archaeology, Washington, D.C.
Welch, John R., and Ramon Riley
  2001 Reclaiming Land and Spirit in the Western Apache Homeland. *American Indian Quarterly* 25(1):5–12.
Welch, John R., Nancy Mahoney, and Ramon Riley
  2000a The Reconquest of Fort Apache. *CRM* 9(5): 15–19.
Welch, John R., Nancy Mahoney, Ngozi Robinson, and Bambi Kraus
  2000b *Ndee La Ade: Gathering of the People.* White Mountain Apache Tribe and Commercial Graphics Inc., Pinetop, AZ.
Wiesel, Elie
  1982 *Night.* Translated by Stella Rodway. Doubleday, New York.
Wylie, Alison
  1995 Alternative Histories: Epistemic Disunity and Political Integ-

rity. In *Making Alternative Histories: The Practice of Archaeology and History in Non-Western Settings*, edited by Peter R. Schmidt and Thomas C. Patterson, pp. 255–272. School of American Research Press, Santa Fe.

Chapter 3

Civic Engagement at Werowocomoco: Reasserting Native Narratives from a Powhatan Place of Power

Martin D. Gallivan and Danielle Moretti-Langholtz

With its historic sites, house museums, and heritage parks presenting the early colonial era through the Civil War, Tidewater Virginia and the broader Chesapeake region are home to a number of places where the public may encounter historical recreations and interpretations of the American past. Every summer tourists flock to Jamestown, Colonial Williamsburg, Mount Vernon, Monticello, Yorktown, and the Civil War battlefields of northern Virginia. In recent years, interpreters at several of these sites have begun to expand their presentations to include discussions of difficult and complex histories. Incorporating such histories can be challenging and often requires a reworking of broader historical narratives.[1]

Despite these efforts to reach the public with more inclusive presentations of the past, discussions of the complex and at times discomforting history of American Indians in the Chesapeake region are generally quite limited. Where this history is included at heritage locations, it is often subsumed within an overarching national narrative of progress toward a pluralistic, democratic American present. This is partly the legacy of a heritage infrastructure built in earlier centuries around the public ownership, preservation, and celebration of houses and landscapes viewed as illustrative of a history in which Native societies presumably disappeared quite early (Thomas 2000).

Efforts to invoke the Virginia Indian past that do appear at public heritage sites often seem ungrounded and fleeting since former Native settlements are generally located elsewhere on private land. Discussions of precontact indigenous history at heritage locations in the region often center on subsistence and settlement with a nod to the theme that others were living here before the founders of the nation arrived on Virginia's shore. Contact-period histories typically emphasize the Powhatan celebrities, Pocahontas and Chief Powhatan, and present their stories as an intriguing backdrop to the survival of English settlers at James Fort. References to Virginia Indians during the colonial era often focus on the early seventeenth century and cease after Bacon's Rebellion in 1676 and the negotiation of the Treaty of Middle Plantation.

With the exception of the Pamunkey Indian Museum on the Pamunkey Reservation and a related exhibit at the National Museum of the American Indian, public places that link Native experiences in the past and present are largely absent from the major heritage sites in the region. As the premier living history museum for experiencing the Native past in the Virginia Tidewater, Jamestown Settlement's recreated "Powhatan Village" offers a vivid representation of Virginia Indian cultural practices, yet the emphasis on lifeways during a precontact ethnographic present distances the exhibit from colonialism and its postcolonial ramifications.[2]

The following discusses our efforts to make an archaeological research project in the Virginia Tidewater a starting point for civic engagement centered on the historical experiences of Native communities in the region. In this context, civic engagement refers to dialogue between archaeologists and various "publics" concerning the past, its contemporary consequences, and the potential for collective action that responds to these consequences. Our point of departure for this effort is a sense that Native history in the region is marked by a series of ruptures separating these communities from their lands, their identities, and their historical narratives (cf. Shackel 2001). Particularly over the past quarter century, Virginia's tribes have taken the initiative in drawing attention to these ruptures and to their implications for contemporary political realities. Whether fighting the destruction of environmental settings and sacred sites tied to the King William Reservoir Project, seeking federal recognition in the U.S. Congress, or demanding a role in planning for the 2007 quadricentennial of Jamestown's settlement, Virginia's Native communities have begun to reassert a strong and insistent voice in the public life of the commonwealth. A number of archaeologists, historians, and museum specialists have responded to this resurgence by including Virginia's Indian communities in research and heritage projects involving the Native past.

We have worked to join these efforts at collaborative research in the context of an archaeological investigation at a Native settlement in Gloucester County, Virginia. The project, currently in its fifth year, is predicated on close consultation with Virginia's tribes around excavations at the Werowocomoco site, the Contact-period political center of the Powhatan chiefdom. Like most Native American archaeological sites in the Chesapeake region, Werowocomoco is located on private property. Balancing public engagement, Native collaboration, and homeowner privacy is not simple in such locations, though the owners of the Werowocomoco site property have provided unwavering support for involving Native communities in every stage of the research. In partnership with the property owners and the other members of the Werowocomoco Research Group, we have worked to link our scholarly research to Virginia Indians' efforts to gain a voice in heritage issues.

Heritage work that preserves cultural traditions and updates relations to place can be a social process that strengthens Native claims to deep roots and a status distinct from that of other local interest groups (Clifford 2004). The Werowocomoco project as both community archaeology and academic research provides Virginia Indians a venue for reaffirming connections with place, with elders, and with ancient practices that are both substantial and invented. Borrowing language from Clifford's (2004:8–9) recent discussion of his work with Alaskan Native communities, we hope that the Werowocomoco research offers Virginia Indians an opportunity to reconnect with the past and to say to others: "We exist," "We have deep roots here," "We are different." As the early seventeenth-century seat of authority in the Powhatan chiefdom, the village of Werowocomoco represents a place of power and of history with lasting consequences for Virginia's Indian communities.

The following briefly summarizes Werowocomoco's Contact-period history and events of subsequent centuries that introduced ruptures between Virginia's Native communities and their lands and identities. We turn next to the structure of archaeological research in Virginia and related ruptures between Virginia Indians and their historical traditions. Finally, we discuss our efforts to build civic engagement between archaeologists and Virginia Indians in the context of the Werowocomoco research. The Werowocomoco project represents but a small step toward civic engagement and, perhaps, social justice for Virginia's Native communities. Nonetheless, the reemergence of the site and narratives drawn from its history occurs at a moment that is open to Virginia Indians' return to a powerful place as never before.

Werowocomoco in History and in Archaeology

Werowocomoco, located on the northeast shore of the York River, served as the political center of the Powhatan chiefdom that dominated much of Tidewater Virginia during the early seventeenth century. The village was the principal residence of Wahunsenacawh, generally known as Powhatan, the paramount chief of the Powhatan chiefdom. The polity and early colonial history involving Wahunsenacawh, his daughter Pocahontas, and his brother Opechancanough have received considerable attention from historians (e.g., Axtell 2001; Feest 1978; Townsend 2004), ethnohistorians (e.g., Gleach 1997; Gunn-Allen 2003; Rountree 1989), archaeologists (e.g., Gallivan 2003; Potter 1993; Turner 1976), and popular authors (e.g., Price 2003). Disney films about Pocahontas and the New Line Cinema film *The New World* have introduced versions of this history to a mass audience.

Prior to the recent excavations at the site, information regarding Werowocomoco's role in early colonial history came largely from Jamestown colonists' written accounts of events from 1607 through 1609. During this interval, Wahunsenacawh exercised considerable authority over Native communities in the Virginia Tidewater. Wahunsenacawh was known as the *Mamanatowick* or "great king" of Tidewater Indians referred to by the English collectively as Powhatans. The Powhatans included those Algonquian speakers of Tidewater Virginia who came under the political influence of the *Mamanatowick* during the late sixteenth century. Residing in dozens of settlements and grouped into about thirty political districts, approximately thirteen thousand Powhatans lived in dispersed villages along rivers of the coastal plain (Rountree and Turner 2002). The Powhatans' mixed horticultural-foraging-fishing subsistence economy was centered on such riverine communities. From Werowocomoco along the York (then the Pamunkey) River, Wahunsenacawh dominated a social network through which gifts, tribute, and power flowed.

The village also served as the scene of several early colonial encounters involving Wahunsenacawh and Jamestown's leaders. It is largely from John Smith's (1986a, 1986b, 1986c, 1986d) published accounts of his experiences in Virginia from 1607 to 1609 that scholars draw an understanding of these events. The first occurred in December 1607 when a large group of Powhatan men led by the paramount chief's brother Opechancanough captured Smith on the upper reaches of the Chickahominy River. In the following days Opechancanough took Smith to Werowocomoco. Upon meeting Smith, Wahunsenacawh urged that he and the colonists abandon James Fort in order to settle in a village closer to Werowocomoco under Wahunsenacawh's protection. Wahunsenacawh promised to provision the colonists if the English would reciprocate with copper objects and iron tools. Scholars disagree on the interpretation of the ensuing events reported by Smith involving Wahunsenacawh, Smith, and Pocahontas. However, common to all of these understandings is a sense that Wahunsenacawh sought to impress Smith with his wealth and power before remaking Smith as a Powhatan leader and incorporating the Jamestown colonists into the Powhatan paramountcy. In a later version of the 1607 events that took place at Werowocomoco, Smith added the well-known story in which

Powhatan's daughter Pocahontas reportedly saved Smith from death at her father's hand.

Smith and the colonists returned to Werowocomoco at least five times prior to Wahunsenacawh's departure from the village in 1609. A close reading of this history indicates that the village served as a central stage for early colonial political theater directed by the Mamanatowick and, at times, by the English colonists. Chief Powhatan orchestrated the colonists' exposure to Powhatan ritual, exchange, and the built environment such that Werowocomoco emerges from the documents as a place of considerable importance.

The fact that colonial-era events at Werowocomoco have entered the realm of American folklore increases the importance of civic engagement centering on the site's archaeology. Though the general location of the village site has been known for over a century (Brown 1890:151, 188; Mook 1943:379; Tyler 1901), large-scale archaeological investigations at the site awaited the twenty-first century. Excavations at the site beginning in 2003 have emphasized a landscape approach to this large, fifty-acre site (Gallivan et al. 2006). Our investigations thus far indicate that the site contains evidence of dispersed village communities at the location dating from A.D. 1250 through contact. Scrap copper, glass beads, and other metal objects dating to the first quarter of the seventeenth century highlight trade relations with the English.

The excavations have also identified a set of large features that reflect a spatial reorganization of the settlement landscape circa A.D. 1300. Two parallel ditch features that measure approximately 1 m. in plan and 0.5–0.7 m. in depth occur in an area located away from the residential core of the village. Stratified deposits within these features contained solely Native artifacts and returned radiocarbon dates ranging from A.D. 1300 to A.D. 1600. The ditches run for approximately 200 m. roughly north-south before turning eastward to form what appears to be an enclosure. Our preliminary interpretation of these features is that they represent an effort by Native communities at the site to reconfigure space within the village. Beginning roughly two centuries before Wahunsenacawh was born, prominent landscape features segregated an area of the site from the village community concentrated along the York River front.

The Virginia Tidewater after Werowocomoco

The colonists reported that Wahunsenacawh left Werowocomoco in 1609 to distance himself from Jamestown, located only fifteen miles away. Over the next four centuries, this disruption of the Powhatan political landscape was followed by ruptures between Virginia's Native communities and their traditional homelands, identities, and histories. The English refined their colonial policies by enlarging their trading relationships with Native communities outside the Chesapeake (Fausz 1988) and by expanding their occupation of Indian territories within the region (Rountree 1990). Throughout the century relations between the Powhatan Indians and the colonists fluctuated between strained acceptance of each other and intermittent warfare and armed conflict. By the beginning of the eighteenth century Virginia had witnessed a demographic collapse of Native people and a permanent rupture of the indigenous relationship with important places—villages, ossuaries, sacred sites, and areas where traditional subsistence activities took place. With a few exceptions (e.g., McCarthy 1985; Rountree 1990) the details of Powhatan land loss in the seventeenth and eighteenth centuries have not been documented or enumerated.

In addition to loss of access to former territories, travel for Powhatan Indians became increasingly restricted and controlled by colonial governance. In 1649, five years after a Powhatan uprising, the General Assembly passed legislative acts in an effort to stabilize and repair relations with the Indians in the colony (Rountree 1990:128–143). Though these laws were attempts to reduce the opportunity for conflict between settlers and the indigenous population, in practice they only furthered ruptures between Native communities, traditional places, and political sovereignty. Seventeenth-century legislative acts included those that outlawed the killing of Indians, except in cases of trespass on lands under colonial control. Another act required that Indians wear metal badges or "certificates" to identify those granted permission to enter fortified settlement areas or plantations (Hening 1969:323–326). These colonial decrees highlight the degree to which Native peoples had been relegated to occupying space in the borderlands of their former territories. In the span of a single generation the once powerful Powhatan people had become almost powerless in their own homeland. Destruction of the Powhatans' political power, subsistence base, language, and religious practices ensued at a rapid pace along with alienation from traditional places.

By the 1680s the labor force in the colony of Virginia had been transformed from indentured servants to slave labor (Kolchin 1993:11). As the colony, and later the Virginia Commonwealth, institutionalized a dichotomous black/white racial classification system, the Indian population was caught in the middle. Native descendants found it increasingly difficult to fit themselves into Virginia's ever narrowing definition of "Indian." The culmination of the commonwealth's imposition of a biracial dichotomy was the passage of the 1924 Racial Integrity Act, which subsumed Indian identity under the category of "colored persons" (Acts of Assembly 1924). The Racial Integrity Act included a ban on interracial marriage, made it a felony to file a false registration of race, and forced Native children to attend school for "colored persons." Proponents of the eugenics movement were a primary force behind the act, viewing the law as a preventive against the "amalgamation" of races (Virginia State Directives 1924:16). Walter Plecker, head of Virginia's Bureau of Vital Statistics, enthusiastically supported this movement and implemented the legislation with zeal. Plecker himself altered the racial designation on birth certificates of those descended from Virginia Indians by crossing out "Indian" and writing "Colored" in its place. The sting of the Racial Integrity Act, which remained in force until 1968, is still felt in Virginia's indigenous community. Native people were denied the right to self-identify as Native people, making it impossible for them to enter the civic arena as representatives of their respective communities. Despite the fact that the Pamunkeys and Mattaponis had long-held reservation lands within the commonwealth, official state policy maintained that there were no longer indigenous Indians in Virginia. An implicit historical narrative in which the Native presence ended late in the seventeenth century had taken hold.

Archaeological Practice in Virginia

Archaeological research in the Virginia Tidewater has considerable potential to recover culture histories that challenge the restrictive narratives under which Native history is often subsumed. Indeed, a number of studies conducted by avocational, academic, and cultural resource management archaeologists have generated nuanced understandings of the region's precontact archaeological record. However, such studies only rarely result in forms of civic engagement with the general public in which received narratives are discussed or challenged.

The history of Chesapeake archaeology involves a trajectory from nineteenth-century antiquarianism to avocational leadership through cultural resource management that is largely devoid of Native voices (Dent 1995:25–68; MacCord 1990). During much of the twentieth century the limited archaeological research conducted in the region was largely in the hands of avocational archaeologists, including those within the Archaeological Society of Virginia. Sporadic efforts by university-based researchers produced definitive cultural chronologies and artifact sequences, some still used today. Despite the potential that this research could serve as common ground for partnerships between archaeologists and Virginia Indians, we are not aware of any sustained interaction or collaboration between these groups.

Binford's (1991) landmark study of the archaeology and ethnohistory of Native societies in coastal Virginia and North Carolina, originally written as his dissertation (1964), contributed to changes in the ways American archaeologists conceived of Native culture history. The processual research model inspired by Binford and others eventually came to dominate the expanding array of academic and cultural resource management archaeology conducted in the Chesapeake by the late 1970s. Processual archaeology's emphasis on explanations rooted in the natural environment, cultural materialism, and demographic profiles often served to push proximate historical developments to the background. As Trigger (1980), among others, has noted, by limiting the role of agents in the negotiation of change, this approach to the archaeological record made connections to Native American societies appear somewhat distant. In Virginia, a new generation of archaeologists began producing sophisticated studies influenced by the "new" archaeology by the mid-1970s.

Roughly contemporaneously with the growing influence of processual archaeology, cultural resource management efforts driven by compliance requirements began to alter the landscape of archaeological practice throughout the nation. The 1966 National Historic Preservation Act's Section 106 requires that federal agencies "take into account" the potential effects of their undertakings on historic properties eligible for the National Register of Historic Places, including archaeological sites. Regulations for the act spell out a consultation process that includes parties with interests related to historic properties affected by development. The Section 106 process has resulted in a rapid expansion of high-quality archaeological research throughout the Chesapeake region. However, the meaningful civic engagement with various publics envisioned by the National Historic Preservation Act remains elusive. With several notable exceptions, the product of cultural resource management efforts is generally a technical report that remains part of a vast and largely inaccessible "gray" literature. Sustained dialogue between cultural resource management archaeologists and Native communities is still rather rare in Virginia.

In part, this is the product of a cultural resource management structure that places consultation responsibilities in the hands of federal agencies or their proxies. While cultural resource management archaeologists have begun to build ties to Virginia Indian leaders and those in other descendant communities, they are generally prevented from initiating consultation by regulations that place that role in the hands of government agencies. Even when compliance officials make concerted efforts to coordinate with descendant communities, the episodic nature of a process structured around individual construction projects limits their ability to create relationships of trust with Native communities. Such relationships take time to develop. Given the history of Native-government relations in Virginia over the last four hundred years, Virginia Indians are understandably wary of archaeologists and government officials unknown within their communities.

A greater diversity of archaeological practice emerged in the Chesapeake at the end of the twentieth century. Along with archaeological approaches that allow a wider range of interpretive possibilities, archaeologists have begun to widen the opening for meaningful engagement with Native communities. Starting in the 1970s experimental archaeologist Errett Callahan (2002) assisted the Pamunkey tribe with exhibits for their tribal museum, a first for Virginia Indians. Three decades later the Pamunkey tribe's exhibits at the National Museum of the American Indian are structured around a narrative of Pamunkey cultural persistence and rootedness to place. Jeffrey Hantman's partnership with the Monacan community (Hantman et al. 2000) represents for us a model of sustained collaboration in the region. Hantman has incorporated Monacan voices in his effort to write a seamless Monacan history linking "prehistory" to the recent Monacan past. Hantman started these efforts by developing close relationships with the Monacan community and by consulting with the Monacan Tribal Council about its priorities regarding the archaeological record.

Additionally, political developments at the end of the twentieth century set the stage for contacts between archaeologists and Native communities in Virginia. During the 1980s the Virginia Commonwealth officially recognized eight Indian tribes. State recognition of the Virginia tribes coincided with nationwide calls among Native activists for protection and repatriation of Native Americans' human remains. During the past decade the remains of more than one hundred individuals have been reburied in Virginia in cooperation with several state-recognized tribes (Moretti-Langholtz 1998; Rountree and Turner 2002). Each of these reburials involved significant cooperation between the Native and archaeological communities in conjunction with the Virginia Department of Historic Resources. In 1997 the Nansemond Tribe, under the leadership of Chief Emeritus Oliver Perry, oversaw the reburial of sixty-four remains on land set aside for this purpose in a state park within the Virginia Beach area. Though sporadic, such reburials have been the source of deep emotion in the community.

The Werowocomoco Research Project

These efforts to make engagement with descendant communities integral to archaeological practice serve as the foundations of the Werowocomoco research. From the beginning of the project we sought to develop an exacting and long-term study of a Native village site built around close partnerships with descendant communities of Virginia Indians. Mindful of the history of archaeological practice in the region and of the approaching quadricentennial anniversary of Jamestown in 2007, we have worked to broaden discussions of colonial Virginia by privileging the Native culture history that occurred at the site and within related Powhatan communities. By recovering evidence of long-term Native history at a location that played a prominent role in the precontact Powhatan world, we hope to encourage new forms of civic engagement that incorporate a broader range of historical narrative possibilities. Representations of a Native center within which consequential events occurred before and after 1607 may in fact serve as the starting point for understandings of the region's history that are less teleological (i.e., constructed around purposeful development toward a specific end). The site calls attention to the development of the Powhatan chiefdom and highlights events in which Jamestown's very survival was at risk and was heavily influenced by Native actors.

The current research at Werowocomoco began in 2001 with a survey of the site directed by Fairfield Foundation archaeologists Thane Harpole and David Brown in consultation with Randolph Turner of the Virginia Department of Historic Resources (Harpole et al. 2004). The survey was prompted by the property owner's identification of a remarkable array of Native artifacts and early colonial trade items on her farm. The following year researchers from the Fairfield Foundation, Virginia Department of Historic Resources, and the College of William and Mary joined to form the Werowocomoco Research Group (WRG).[3]

From its inception, the WRG has worked toward a model of archaeological research on Native sites in the Chesapeake that includes close Native collaboration at every stage. The research group met with the Virginia Council on Indians (VCI), the state-sanctioned advisory board on Indian affairs, in November of 2002 to inform the council that we had identified a site we believed to be Werowocomoco. The WRG requested that our presentation be received in a VCI executive session to ensure that information pertaining to the project would reach tribal leaders for each of the eight state-recognized tribes prior to any public announcement about the location of the site and plans to excavate. During the WRG presentation we discussed our survey results and assessment of the site's significance. We also sought the advice of the VCI in arranging a meeting with tribal leaders so that they would learn of the site directly from the research team and before any media coverage appeared. Additionally, we introduced the VCI to the members of the research group and the property owners before outlining a long-term plan to study Werowocomoco with the close involvement of the Native communities. Council members expressed their support for the project and offered important guidance on future Native involvement. These discussions included plans for a subsequent visit to the site and for the formation of an all-Native advisory board to the research team.

In February 2003, the Werowocomoco Research Group presented a detailed project proposal to tribal chiefs, members of the Virginia Council on Indians, and other representatives of Virginia's state-recognized tribes in meetings held at the College of William and Mary. Presentations to the community outlined current understanding of the site from an academic point of view. The research team discussed a multiyear research design for the site centered on William and Mary field schools. Together with the property owners, the WRG then hosted an event at the site, giving community representatives the chance to see the location firsthand. Representatives from the state-recognized tribes attended the meetings.[4] During these meetings the property owners asked that the Virginia Indians consider Werowocomoco as a place where members of their communities were always welcome. The research team listened carefully to the tribal representatives as they discussed their own perspectives on the site and its history. Though these perspectives varied, several tribal leaders expressed a powerful connection to

Werowocomoco as the historic center of the Powhatan chiefdom and as a modern place for renewing Virginia Indians' influence on representations of the Native past. Others encouraged us to pursue research that focuses on the power and social complexity of the Powhatan chiefdom during the years prior to 1607.

Representatives from six of the Powhatan descendent communities subsequently formed a Virginia Indian Advisory Board (VIAB) to guide WRG's efforts. The Virginia Indian Advisory Board has since met regularly with the WRG, receiving updates and reports on the research and advising the research team as we have formulated our research goals and policies. In keeping with the goals of our partnership the research team shares all information we have on the project with the advisory board, including minutes of all meetings and financial reports of all activities. Grant funding for the project from the National Endowment for the Humanities and the Virginia Foundation for Humanities has supported the advisory board's role in the form of honoraria. The advisory board has served as the critical linkage between the research team and the tribal communities. Among other decisions, the advisory board has been central to the creation of a policy for the accidental discovery of human remains on site, a policy that involves close coordination with the Native community. In response to the property owners' invitation, the advisory board has also facilitated regular Native visitation to the site. These visits have included a week-long open house for members of the Native community to visit the site during the archaeological field season. The advisory board was also instrumental in making visitation to the site by primary school educators a high priority. Opening the site to teachers, particularly those who cover early colonial history, has allowed the research at Werowocomoco to reach a larger audience.

More recently, Virginia Indians have broadened their involvement with the research at Werowocomoco by participating in the research firsthand. The Pamunkey representative to the advisory board joined the research team as a field technician during the 2005 and 2006 excavation seasons. Also a member of the Pamunkey Tribal Council, he is now prepared to review cultural resource management projects that affect the tribe with a better understanding of the archaeological research process. Another Pamunkey descendant enrolled in the William and Mary field school and also served as a Virginia Department of Historic Resources intern for the 2005 summer.

By opening spaces in the archaeological community for members of the Virginia Indian community, the WRG sought to encourage archaeological research that combines indigenous values with an academic research agenda. In opening their home to members of the Native community who resided on-site during the field season, the property owners allowed the Werowocomoco site to become a place where Virginia Indian visitors felt welcome. Our Pamunkey partners assumed a lead role in liaising with other members of tribal communities, a considerable number of whom visited the site. On days set aside for public visitation during the field season, our Pamunkey partners spoke with visitors about the excavations and about their own complicated feelings regarding archaeological research involving their ancestors. The Pamunkey members of the research team also discussed these issues with members of the press, whose coverage allowed the public to see another side of modern archaeological practice.

Civic Engagement, Social Justice, and Werowocomoco

Ultimately, civic engagement involving archaeological research must extend beyond "public outreach" toward descendant communities. New topics and forms of discourse should emerge from archaeologists' frank discussions of their research with a range of publics, and some of these discussions may contradict existing historical narratives. Taking archaeological practice from civic engagement and toward social justice, conceived of as equity, honesty, and tolerance across segments of a society, represents a difficult challenge that we have not begun to master. We do recognize that efforts to promote social justice must be structured around the particulars of a historical and cultural context (Miller 2001). To the extent that civic engagement centered on archaeology may promote social justice in Virginia, the restrictive narratives that have structured much heritage presentation in the region should be called into question. Given its place in history during the precontact, colonial, and modern eras, the Werowocomoco site has considerable potential to promote social justice understood this way.

Despite the promise of civic engagement at Werowocomoco, public reactions to the project make it clear that social justice as an outcome to the research is not guaranteed. Following our consultation with Virginia Indian communities at the beginning of the project, the Werowocomoco Research Group hosted a press conference in the spring of 2003 announcing our plans for the site. Interest in the story was considerably greater than we anticipated, with coverage in major national and foreign newspapers and televised reports on national network news. Some of the coverage mentioned Virginia Indians' involvement in the project, allowing the general public to learn more about the continued presence of Native communities in Virginia and the potential for civic engagement with these communities. However, much of the press coverage emphasized Pocahontas' relationship with John Smith. While certainly significant in its own light, Pocahontas' reported rescue of Smith has drawn attention away from the larger precontact and colonial-era history lived by Natives at the site and across Tidewater Virginia. Centering the Werowocomoco story on John Smith's experiences in December 1607 misses the opportunity to engage in Native-centered and more nuanced historical narratives.

Though civic engagement at Werowocomoco represents an incomplete project, the site has emerged as an appropriate place for such engagement to begin. Werowocomoco has become a location where Native narratives have begun to challenge the received stories of the past. By highlighting Werowocomoco's history and by giving descendant communities a central role in its recovery, the Werowocomoco research project has created a place for new discussions regarding the Native past—between tribes and between Indians and archaeologists. Research at the site may also play a role in the nascent movement toward an "indigenous archaeology" in which Native North American peoples become full partners in representations concerning their past (Watkins 2000). Drawing ideas from Little's introduction to this volume, we hope the Werowocomoco project will contribute to the creation of social capital that is bonding within the Virginia Indian community and bridging across the academic-Native divide.

Notes

1. Examples from Tidewater Virginia often relate to the history of enslaved Africans. Portrayals of slave auctions, beatings, and storytelling by reenactors at Colonial Williamsburg play a role in the living history museum's programs, upsetting some visitors. The Thomas Jefferson Foundation now includes discussions of Thomas Jefferson's relationship with Sally Hemings, an enslaved African with whom Jefferson fathered several children at Monticello.

2. The National Park Service and the Jamestown Settlement have constructed new visitor centers and exhibits for the 2007 commemoration of the founding of James Fort. Efforts to elicit Native commentary on the respective exhibits have been undertaken by each organization.

3. Werowocomoco Research Group members include Martin Gallivan, assistant professor at William and Mary; Randolph Turner, director of the Tidewater Regional Office of the Virginia Department of Historic Resources; Danielle Moretti-Langholtz, director of the William and Mary American Indian Resource Center; and David Brown and Thane Harpole, codirectors of the Fairfield Foundation. Bob and Lynn Ripley are the current owners of the Werowocomoco site property.

4. Virginia's state-recognized tribes are the Mattaponi, Pamunkey, Upper Mattaponi, Chickahominy, Eastern Chickahominy, Nansemond, Rappahannock, and Monacan.

References Cited

Acts of Assembly
   1924   *House Bill No. 311. An Act to Preserve Racial Integrity.*
Axtell, James
   2001   *Natives and Newcomers: The Cultural Origins of North America.*
          Oxford University Press, New York.
Binford, Lewis Roberts
   1991   *Cultural Diversity among Aboriginal Cultures of Coastal Virginia
          and North Carolina.* Garland, New York.

1964 Archaeological and Ethnohistorical Investigations of Cultural Diversity and Progressive Development among Aboriginal Cultures of Coastal Virginia and North Carolina. Ph.D. dissertation, University of Michigan. University Microfilms, Ann Arbor.

Brown, Alexander
1890 *The Genesis of the United States*. Houghton, Mifflin and Company, Boston.

Callahan, Errett
2002 The Pamunkey Indian Museum Displays. *The Bulletin of Primitive Technology* 23:12–17.

Clifford, James
2004 Looking Several Ways: Anthropology and Native Heritage in Alaska. *Current Anthropology* 45(26):5–30.

Dent, Richard J.
1995 *Chesapeake Prehistory: Old traditions, New Directions*. New York: Plenum Press.

Fausz, J. Frederick
1988 Merging and Emerging Worlds: Anglo-Indian Interest Groups and the Development of the Seventeenth-Century Chesapeake. In *Colonial Chesapeake Society*, edited by L. G. Carr, P. D. Morgan, and J. B. Russo, pp. 47–98. Published for the Institute of Early American History and Culture, Williamsburg, Virginia, by the University of North Carolina Press, Chapel Hill.

Feest, Christian F.
1978 Virginia Algonquians. In *Handbook of North American Indians*, edited by W. C. Sturtevant, pp. 235–270. Smithsonian Institution, Washington, D.C.

Gallivan, Martin D., Thane Harpole, David A. Brown, Danielle Moretti-Langholtz, and E. Randolph Turner, III
2006 *The Werowocomoco (44GL32) Research Project: Background and 2003 Archaeological Field Season Results*. Commonwealth of Virginia. Research Report Series, No. 17. Virginia Department of Historic Resources, Richmond.

Gallivan, Martin D.
2003 *James River Chiefdoms: The Rise of Social Inequality in the Chesapeake*. University of Nebraska Press, Lincoln.

Gleach, Frederic W.
1997 *Powhatan's World and Colonial Virginia: A Conflict of Cultures*. University of Nebraska Press, Lincoln.

Gunn-Allen, Paula
2003 *Pocahontas: Medicine Woman, Spy, Entrepreneur, Diplomat.*

Harper, San Francisco.

Hantman, Jeffrey L., Karenne Wood, and Diane Shields
  2000 Writing Collaborative History: How the Monacan Nation and Archaeologists Worked Together to Enrich Our Understanding of Virginia's Native Peoples. *Archaeology* 53(5):56–59.

Harpole, Thane, David A. Brown, and Anthony Smith
  2004 *Archaeological Survey of the Powhatans' Political Center, 44GL32, Gloucester County, Virginia.* DATA Investigations, Gloucester, Virginia.

Hening, William Waller
  1969 *The Statutes at Large; Being a Collection of All the Laws of Virginia, from the First Session of the Legislature in the Year 1619.* Published for the Jamestown Foundation of the Commonwealth of Virginia by the University Press of Virginia, Charlottesville.

Kolchin, Peter
  1993 *American Slavery, 1619–1877.* Hill and Wang, New York,

MacCord, Howard A.
  1990 *The Archaeological Society of Virginia — A Forty-Year History.* Archaeological Society of Virginia, Special Publication no. 21.

McCarthy, Martha W.
  1985 Seventeenth-Century Apartheid: The Suppression and Containment of Indians in Tidewater Virginia. *Journal of Middle Atlantic Archaeology* 1(1):1–80.

Miller, David
  2001 *Principles of Social Justice.* Harvard University Press, Cambridge.

Mook, Maurice A.
  1943 The Ethnological Significance of Tindall's Map of Virginia, 1608. *William and Mary College Quarterly* 23(4):371–408.

Moretti-Langholtz, Danielle
  1998 *Other Names I Have Been Called: Political Resurgence among Virginia Indians in the Twentieth Century.* Unpublished Ph.D. dissertation, University of Oklahoma, Department of Anthropology.

Potter, Stephen R.
  1993 *Commoners, Tribute, and Chiefs: The Development of Algonquian Culture in the Potomac Valley.* University Press of Virginia, Charlottesville.

Price, David
  2003 *Love and Hate in Jamestown: John Smith, Pocahontas, and the Heart of a New Nation.* Knopf, New York.

Rountree, Helen C.
  1989 *The Powhatan Indians of Virginia: Their Traditional Culture.* University of Oklahoma Press, Norman.

1990   *Pocahontas's People: The Powhatan Indians of Virginia through Four Centuries.* University of Oklahoma Press, Norman.

Rountree, Helen C., and E. Randolph Turner
2002   *Before and after Jamestown: Virginia's Powhatans and their Predecessors.* University Press of Florida, Gainesville.

Shackel, Paul A.
2001   Public Memory and the Search for Power in American Historical Archaeology. *American Anthropologist* 103(3):655–670.

Smith, John
1986a Generall Historie of Virginia. In *The Complete Works of Captain John Smith (1580–1631),* edited by P. L. Barbour, pp. 5–475, Vol. II. University of North Carolina Press, Chapel Hill.

1986b A Map of Virginia. In *The Complete Works of Captain John Smith (1580–1631),* edited by P. L. Barbour, pp. 119–189, Vol. I. University of North Carolina Press, Chapel Hill.

1986c The Proceedings. In *The Complete Works of Captain John Smith (1580–1631),* edited by P. L. Barbour, pp. 191–279, Vol. II. University of North Carolina Press, Chapel Hill.

1986d A True Relation. In *The Complete Works of Captain John Smith (1580–1631),* edited by P. L. Barbour, pp. 5–117, Vol. I. University of North Carolina Press, Chapel Hill.

Thomas, David Hurst
2000   *Skull Wars.* Basic Books, New York.

Townsend, Camilla
2004   *Pocahontas and the Powhatan Dilemma.* Hill and Wang, New York.

Trigger, Bruce G.
1980   Archaeology and the Image of the American Indian. *American Antiquity* 45(4):662–676.

Turner, E. Randolph
1976   *An Archaeological and Ethnohistorical Study of the Evolution of Rank Societies in the Virginia Coastal Plain.* Unpublished Ph.D. dissertation, Pennsylvania State University.

Tyler, Lyon G.
1901   Werowocomoco. *William and Mary College Quarterly* 10(1):1–4.

Virginia State Directives
1924   *Eugenics in Relation to the New Family and the Law on Racial Integrity,* Volume XVI. State Board of Health, Richmond.

Watkins, Joe
2000   *Indigenous Archaeology: American Indian Values and Scientific Practice.* AltaMira Press, Walnut Creek, CA.

Chapter 4

Beyond Strategy and Good Intentions: Archaeology, Race, and White Privilege

Carol McDavid

Like others in this volume, this paper will consider the topic of civic engagement in archaeology, and attempt to understand how archaeological work can lead to social justice. It will not address any benefit that this engagement might have *for archaeology*—stewardship, while not abandoned, is not the point of this volume, or of this paper. Instead, it will examine how archaeological work can lead to "community building, the creation of social capital, and active citizen engagement in community and civic life" (Little 2005 and this volume), especially with regard to one specific area of archaeological interest, African Diaspora archaeology.

Within contemporary African Diaspora research, a primary focus (almost by definition) is to examine the historical effects of racism—in particular, white racism. Our attention to racism should go farther than an academic understanding of it in the past, however. Racism is a thread that connects past and present, and it continues to be a major impediment to social justice in American society. Therefore, those of us who work in this area of archaeology have a responsibility, a mandate even, to do two things: to reflect upon how race and racism emerge in "everyday" public archaeology practice, and to find ways to discuss these difficult issues with our publics as we present our archaeological work. Drawing on writing in critical race theory, and related work about the issue of white privilege, in this paper I will attempt to do both. This will, I hope, push the ideas discussed in "Public Participation in African American Archaeology" (McDavid and Babson 1997) (and elsewhere) past our now-comfortable but still limited notions of public involvement, to far less comfortable levels of self-reflection and critique.

By white privilege, I refer to the taken-for-granted and largely unacknowledged (by white people[1], that is) advantages and benefits of being white. Whites are *taught* to think of their lives as normative, neutral, and ideal (Thandeka 1999). As described in the now-famous article by Peggy McIntosh, white privilege is the "invisible package of unearned assets which [we] can count on cashing in each day . . . about which [we] were meant to remain oblivious" (McIntosh 1988, 2). McIntosh lists forty-six ways that white privilege is enacted in everyday life; sadly, most have as much currency now as they did when she first listed them. Put in personal terms, it means not being followed by security as a potential shoplifter when I enter a fancy store, and not worrying whether I am being stopped because of my color when pulled over by a police officer. It means that an affirmative action employer can hire me without having my coworkers suspect I got it because of my race. It means *never* being asked to speak for all of the people in my racial group, and, in light of recent events with Hurricane Katrina, it means that if I am desperate to find food and water in the middle of a flood, I can be pretty sure that my skin color will not cause people to call me a looter. It means that someone of another color can be prejudiced toward me without this translating to the things that I need to survive—because in all likelihood, "a slur is as far as it's going to go" (Wise 2002). And, in the context of history, it also means that when I am told about "the founders" of my country, state, or city, most of the time I am being told about people of my own color—even when people of other colors are part of the story.

To discuss white privilege I must first be willing to claim my own whiteness. The comments I share here necessarily derive from that subject position, and from a personal belief that, as a white person, I may be able to broach these issues with other whites (students, publics, and colleagues) in unthreatening, and thus productive, ways. Indeed, *because of* white privilege, my comments to whites about my archaeological data and their connection to race and racism will likely be more readily accepted than they would if my identity were something else (McIntosh 1988, 8). However, I need to be aware that I enact white privilege, and run the risk of reproducing it (Marx 2003, 4), even as I ask others to identify it in their histories and lives, and ask them to disrupt its effects whenever possible. As McIntosh put it, "Describing white privilege makes one newly accountable . . . what will I do to lessen or end it?" (McIntosh 1988, 2).

This is an admittedly ideologically driven perspective, and, as other white scholars involved in antiracism activism have observed, writing about this issue can tend to be somewhat confessional and self-conscious (Marx 2003). I accept this, and I will therefore ground my theoretical musings with on-the-ground first-person examples. This level of reflexivity may be somewhat risky, especially in an academic forum like this volume. For one thing, I can be accused of essentializing "what white is," thus reifying whiteness and negating "the extent to which whiteness is multidimensional and contested" (Bonnett 1997). For another, in a discipline in which objectivity is still valorized, there is perhaps some measure of professional risk of declaring that I am one of "those whose passions drive their questions and methods" (Bergerson 2003, 57).

Pragmatist philosophy, which I have discussed elsewhere in terms of archaeology and its publics (McDavid 2000, 2002a, 2002b, 2004a), offers guidance here. The pragmatic move demands that we accept the risk of uncertainty and maintains that we cannot wait to talk about painful issues until we are certain that we are not being racist, classist, or otherwise oppressive. It asserts that truths will emerge *within the process of looking for them.* To be engaged in finding social justice, in a society infected with racism and white privilege, we cannot afford to be immobilized by fears that we are not being archaeological, academic, formal, sensitive, or correct enough (Eichstedt 2001). Time, and our interactions with each other, will tell us if our strategies (all of which are works in progress) are effective, or if we need to look elsewhere for answers.

Pragmatism also calls for using theories as tools, as situations and needs demand, and as mentioned above, critical race theory

(CRT) can be one of these tools. Introduced in archaeology by Epperson (Epperson 1999; Epperson 2004), CRT, also known as race-crit, has had limited application in archaeological writing to date. It began in the 1970s at the intersection of race and law, but has expanded in recent years to include critical race feminism, critical white studies, queer theory, asian crit, and lat-crit theory. CRT represents a wide body of legal and political research, mostly conducted by scholars of color, that critically examines the role of race as a social construct that organizes both everyday and institutional interactions. It arose as a response to the failure of U.S. jurisprudence to adequately address the effects of race and racism in society. Among its originators are Derrick Bell (Bell 1995; Bell 1992), Mari Matsuda (Matsuda 1995), Kimberley Crenshaw (Crenshaw 1995), and Richard Delgado (Delgado and Stefancic 2001). Over the last decade, CRT has also been used as a powerful theoretical and analytical framework in educational research, which in turn offers a valuable model for archaeologists who wish to use these ideas. This writing includes the work of Gloria Ladson-Billings and William F. Tate (Ladson-Billings and Tate 1995), who introduced Critical Race Theory to education, as well as later work (Bergerson 2003; DeCuir and Dixson 2004; Dixson and Rousseau 2005; Eichstedt 2001; Gorski 2000; Jensen 2002a, 2002b; Lloyd 2004; Marx 2003; Sleeter 2000/2001a).

A major tenet of CRT analysis is to center the study and understanding of racism as something that continues to be tightly knit into the fabric of society (Bell 1992)—it reminds us that racism is the common, everyday experience of most people who are not white. It analyses how it continues to operate both institutionally and individually, and how it is deeply embedded in all arenas—"legally, culturally, and even psychologically" (Ladson-Billings and Tate 1995, 52). It is enacted not just through individual acts of prejudice but, more insidiously, though the everyday taken-for-granted realities of white privilege (Jensen 2002a, 2002b; McIntosh 1988; Sleeter 2000/2001b; Wise 2002).

Because the ways that white privilege persists, racism is even more difficult to cure, and CRT maintains that only the most blatant forms of discrimination can be addressed by laws and rules that insist *only* on treatment that is the same across the board. Therefore, CRT rejects so-called "liberal" approaches to racism, such as neutrality and colorblindness. Neutrality implies that whiteness is the norm, and part of white privilege means having the luxury, in most situations, to simply not be aware of one's race. How often do whites refer to others as "my white friend," or "my white colleague"? Doing so would seem odd, because we usually assume whiteness unless stated otherwise. Colorblindness is equally problematic for race crits, who argue that, despite our best intentions, most *people* cannot practice true colorblindness. We notice each other's colors whether we want to or not, as I have noted elsewhere when reflecting upon the experience of being a white archaeologist speaking about African American archaeology with black audiences (McDavid 2003d, 2004b, 2005). The CRT critique points out that because colorblindness is *presumed* to fully incorporate racial justice ("justice for all"), it has not allowed American society to develop a concept of justice that takes account of racial difference.

Before closing this lengthy introduction, it is important to state that even though this discussion will deal primarily with race, it is arguably as important to confront class as well—not least because, as research as shown, the audiences for archaeology are inherently imbalanced with respect to both (Falk and Dierking 1992; Hooper-Greenhill 1994; McGuire and Walker 1999; Merriman 1991; Wallace 1996). In racialized capitalist America, these issues are not easily separated, as was shown all too clearly in the aforementioned Hurricane Katrina disaster, which clearly exposed the unacceptable inequities that run along race and class lines in the United States. Therefore, this paper should be read with a subtext of class, with analysis by others in mind (see Gadsby and Chidester, and Shackel, in this volume). I should also note that several CRT writers have attempted to analyze the ways that race intersects with class (and gender) (see Bell 1992 and Crenshaw 1995, among others).

Public Archaeology Contexts

Before moving to examples, I will describe the projects in which I participate. The first, the Levi Jordan Plantation project, in Brazoria, Texas, deals with the archaeology of slavery and tenancy, and has been under archaeological investigation by Kenneth L. Brown for almost twenty years (Brown and Cooper 1990; Brown 1994, 2000, 2001, 2004). My work with the project, which has taken place over fifteen years and been described in detail elsewhere (McDavid 1997, 1999, 2000, 2002a, 2002b, 2003a, 2004a, 2004d), has been to work with diverse descendant groups to use archaeology as a tool for community collaboration and reform.[2] Meaningful participation from all descendant groups began in the early 1990s and has continued despite recent changes in the ownership of the site that have made this more challenging (McDavid 2003b). I will discuss these challenges in more detail below.

The second project is the Yates Community Archaeology Project (YCAP), located in Freedmen's Town, an economically disadvantaged but historically rich urban African American neighborhood in Houston, Texas (McDavid 2004b, 2004c, 2005). My codirector David Bruner and I are both involved in all aspects of managing the project, including public archaeology. The neighborhood has been a major hub of black life in Houston since its founding, and it received a National Historical Register designation in 1986 (House, 1999). Our work takes place on house museum properties owned by our sponsor, the Rutherford B. H. Yates Museum, Inc. (RBHY), a preservation organization that hopes to save the few remaining historic properties in Freedmen's Town. We also do research, when invited, on properties owned by other members of the community.

The third project concerns the Heritage Society (THS) in Houston. I serve on the society's board and its Education and Collections committees, give talks to its docents on various aspects of archaeology, and provide input on public interpretation activities as needed. The Heritage Society (http://www.heritagesociety.org) operates Houston's only outdoor historic museum; the nine houses it owns and interprets are located in Sam Houston Park, a mile from Freedmen's Town. Until the last few years, the society has been mostly focused on the decorative arts; board members and volunteers are, typically, affluent, conservative Houstonians who appreciate antiques and architecture as well as history. When I was first asked to join the society two years ago, I initially hesitated because of the park's predominantly white approach to history [even though two of its houses were built and/or occupied by blacks and interpreted as such, it is still known by some local black activists as "slaveholder park" (Tanarka 2005)]. After some thought I decided to join and work from within, in order to support several like-minded volunteers and staff (including a new director) in their efforts to present more inclusive historical interpretations and programs.

Examples and Analyses:
Public Archaeology through a CRT Lens

I was recently asked to speak to the docents at the Heritage Society about "how to handle hurtful histories in a tour setting." This was a follow-up to a talk I had given earlier on African American archaeology, after which I had learned that many docents were uncomfortable discussing slavery and similar topics, especially with black audiences (the group is almost entirely composed of white women of middle age and older). I had also noticed, during other society work, that its house interpretations tended to compartmentalize black history, addressing it only in the "black" houses, rather than including it (and the histories of other groups) in the tours of all houses. My talk was aimed at helping them to be more comfortable presenting inclusive histories, and offering some confidence to those whose instincts were already leaning in that direction. I decided that the best approach would be to share my personal experiences—not to preach, but simply to encourage them to apply some new ideas to their individual situations and needs.

So, I discussed, with specific examples, how our individual identities affect our work, how we can be changed personally by the work, and how our work can change other people (McDavid 2004c). I then brought up the idea of white privilege, framing the acceptance of it as personal work that I had had to do in order to be more comfortable talking about racialized histories. I pointed out how whites are carefully taught not to recognize white privilege, drawing analogs between white privilege and male privilege (McIntosh 1988). A repeated theme was that the public interpretation of history can be one pathway to social change, and that they could be a part of this change. It was also important to demonstrate how acknowledging white privilege does not, necessarily, lead to self-loathing or guilt, and that what mattered was how they used their work to confront white privilege and challenge racial stereotypes (Jensen 2002b). My objective was to offer a framework within which the docents could not only become aware of their whiteness, but could also make it meaningful by choosing, in a more careful and race-conscious way, to publicly interpret history in different ways. The examples in the talk illustrated several CRT ideas: centering race, acknowledging white privilege, and rejecting colorblindness and neutrality.

The message was fairly strong, but given the responses during and afterward, it was well received by most. During the question/answer session, two questions in particular struck me as revealing. One questioner asked how she could talk about the lives of black people at all if she did not know "for sure" who lived in each particular house, and when, and so on; in reply I offered a few examples from other house museums that have attempted to address this concern. This question reinforced the huge disconnect between academic/professional writing about how to present more inclusive histories (which has figured prominently in museum, archaeology, and public history writing for almost twenty years; see Chappell 1989) and the everyday docent in some traditional house/history museums, where ideas from the new social history have not yet been adopted. Another question had to do with what terms whites should use when referring to other ethnic groups—fully ten minutes was devoted to discussing whether people in the past (or present) should be referred to as "black" or "African American." I first suggested that this sort of fear should not stop them from talking about black history, but also answered that in Houston, either "black" or "African American" would probably not offend—*if* the information being offered on the tour was inclusively and sensitively presented. I then encouraged them, with more examples, to use language in their tours that would invite audiences to enrich or even contest the information offered, rather than to present information about black (or any other) culture and history as "The Truth." They were very concerned that their tours should be, above all, factually accurate, so we then discussed the idea that historical truth could be seen as contingent, and that different people could see the facts differently, through the lens of their own experience (and that the language that they chose, as tour guides, could affect how people understood history).

After the talk, I was asked to provide input on some new house scripts for an upcoming event, which, with permission, I sent in turn to some of my (black and white) Yates Museum colleagues for review; the responses received were then incorporated into the final scripts. CRT offers a framework for this, in that it recognizes the experiential and the idea that the "knowledge of women and men of color is legitimate, appropriate, and critical to understanding, analyzing, and teaching about racial subordination" (Solorzano 1988, 122). It insists that our work must "reflect the perspectives of those who have experienced and been victimized by racism firsthand" (Ladson-Billings and Tate 1995, 52) and argues for new epistemologies that recognize that "people of color make sense of the world in ways that are different from the dominant, white view" (Bergerson 2003, 55).

In CRT, "counterstories," or narratives that challenge the dominant view (Delgado 1989), can be one way to obtain and use this type of experiential, first-person knowledge. Counterstories can come from interviews, oral histories, or other first-person accounts. As Bell has suggested, when white people do not want to listen to a direct opinion, they may respond well to a story in which they can "suspend their beliefs, listen to the story, and then compare their views" to the ones voiced in the story (Bell 1995, 902). Counterstories therefore allow the subversion of "dominant views of reality by expressing the experiences of people of color in ways that whites may be more willing and able to hear" (Bergerson 2003, 54). I will return to the possible role of archaeology in writing counterstories as I close this paper.

The point of describing the above talk is not to suggest it as an exemplar; I would say several things differently if the occasion repeated. Rather, it is to illustrate how we can, if we choose, include conversations about our social agendas—in this case race and white privilege—each time we discuss our work.

Another issue raised by race-crits is that of "false empathy," which Richard Delgado (Delgado 1997) points out is the mistake privileged people make when they believe they can discern the feelings, thoughts, or opinions of an underprivileged person. In the context of the YCAP project, this idea can be useful in examining what happens when well-meaning outsiders attempt to effect change—even good change—in a disadvantaged neighborhood.

As mentioned earlier, YCAP's work in Freedmen's Town is sponsored by a house museum with historic preservation as its main agenda. The museum's board members are mostly black, but the cofounder and major spokesperson—the de facto leader—is a white woman with a long and respected history of activism in support of the Freedmen's Town community. All members of the museum group are socially and politically progressive individuals who embrace principles of racial equity. Although a few have family connections, none live in Freedmen's Town (although the other cofounder, now deceased, was a lifelong resident and descendant of one of the community's founders).

Because of their preservation-first agenda, coupled with a sincere desire to help the neighborhood, the museum has sometimes pursued preservation objectives, which are at odds with the goals of some of the more important long-term community leaders. As one example, the museum has advocated restoring one particular historic building for use as an elite performing arts venue for African American artists, instead of a community center for elderly poor and Internet cafe, which some of the community's leaders preferred. The museum's preference was based in a preservationist-oriented best use perspective, as well as the feeling that using the building to showcase the talents of African American artists would be more in keeping with what the community's founders, who formed the core of Houston's early black professional community, would have wanted.

Another example was the museum's insistence that the best way to preserve the area's historic brick streets (which could be quite significant archaeologically) was to pedestrianize them. The local community had been fighting City Hall to preserve the streets,[3] but it also felt that certain infrastructure improvements needed *under* the streets—new water lines, and so on—were just as important. Therefore, it was willing to accept a city plan that would renovate—but not fully restore—the streets. Even though the museum people agreed that the infrastructure improvements were important, they argued that they could take place in another way, and campaigned for a preservation-first plan, which would close the streets to all vehicle traffic.

While some members of the community thought the museum's plan was acceptable, even desirable, some of the most vocal and powerful leaders did not. More to the point, some were insulted that the museum was campaigning, in public venues, for pedestrianization *without their stated support.* They maintained pedestrianization would affect *their* day-to-day lives in a significant way, whereas the museum people—though diverse in ethnic terms—all lived *outside* the community. Some characterized the museum's proposal as an elitist, even racist notion, and one that outsiders had no right to pursue. Some pointed out that since *their* African American ancestors had purchased and laid the bricks, outsiders should not take *any* public position that opposed theirs. The problem here was not only that the main museum spokesperson is white, but that the entire group was "read" as white because of the white museum leader's public efforts on behalf of the community, and because they were outsiders. The museum decided to back off from its pedestrianization plan, and attempts to repair the relationships involved have been ongoing.

Both examples illustrate what can happen when whites (or in this case, blacks who are perceived as outsiders, with a white leader) attempt to do work that is community *placed*, not community *based* (Ervin 2000), and when well-meaning, economically advantaged people attempt to make decisions about what is best for a disadvantaged community in which they do not live. The leaders of the museum group are, without doubt, empathetic toward the people who live in Freedmen's Town and do see their work as antiracist, even though this is packaged as historic preservation activity. As Linda Martín Alcoff put it, "White support for antiracism is often . . . an extension at times of the colonizer's privilege to decide the true, the just, and the culturally valuable" (Alcoff 1998, 2).

This critical analysis is not meant to denigrate the good work that our sponsors are doing; it is to point out how this same work has sometimes been *seen* as an attempt to colonize community discourses and reproduce racial power imbalances. The CRT caution about false empathy, as well as the mandate to develop alternative epistemologies that account for lived experiences of people of color, can help white advocates to find ways to ally themselves *productively* with those who are most likely to benefit from social, economic, and political change. For example, some community leaders recently invited the museum to coordinate funding efforts to preserve several historic churches in the area. What is notable in this case, however, is that the museum was *invited*; the museum's resources and skills are being used to support the community in something *it wishes to do.*

I will turn to the Jordan Plantation project for a final example. Over the years, this project has evolved from a traditional archaeology project with little public involvement (typical of most archaeological projects prior to the 1990s) to a grassroots public archaeology project controlled by members of ethnically diverse local descendant communities (Brown 2000; McDavid 2002a). In March 2002, primary control of the project shifted again, when the Texas Parks and Wildlife Department (TPWD), a large state agency, purchased the property from descendants of the founder. The purchase was predicated upon the written understanding that the TPWD would continue to involve the members of the original planning group (the Levi Jordan Plantation Historical Society, or LJPHS) in major decisions about the site's management and public interpretation. It is fair to say that members of both groups have been challenged while attempting to enact this involvement. The local group felt marginalized by the policies and culture of a large bureaucracy, and the agency had the difficult job of dealing with the desires of a mature community organization with a large, and vocal, stake in the project. Recently the situation has improved, with the (summer 2005) adoption of a formal Memorandum of Understanding outlining the responsibilities of both groups, although to some degree both sides are holding a collective breath to see what happens next.

One seemingly minor but revealing example will illustrate how CRT can be a useful analytic tool within this fraught relationship. After the sale took place, agency staff (all of whom were white, as is most of the agency) began a "Master Planning" process for the site. They employed their usual way of scheduling meetings and keeping people in the loop—e-mail. While understandable, this was unfortunate, because none of the African American members of LJPHS communicate with e-mail—and all European American members do. Whether this is coincidental or due to differential access based on race (or age, or other factors) is a difficult question, and not answerable in this short paper (see McDavid 2000, 2002b, 2003c, 2003d for discussion of the "digital divide" and new technologies). In any event, the agency people did not *intend* to exclude people, but it happened, and this exclusion played out along racial lines. Now, except for formal correspondence, when regular mail can be used, our white members notify the rest about meetings, as well as emerging problems and issues. This solution is obviously unsatisfactory because it means that all information goes—in both directions—through white filters.

In the case described here, exclusion was not "a race thing," but it plays out that way. CRT insists that race and *differential* privilege be taken seriously, not ignored or subsumed under "business as usual" institutional practices, which is what happened here. It foregrounds the problematics of privilege, even when it does not necessarily solve them.

Conclusion

In this paper I have suggested that public archaeology activities can be productively analyzed through a critical race theory lens, using this theory pragmatically—as a tool to think with. Even though it is clear that I have found it useful, a word of caution is also needed—it would be inappropriate to use CRT reductively. Not all situations apply, and even those that do can be analyzed, just as usefully, with other theoretical tools, as others and I have done elsewhere. The CRT-informed questions I have embraced here are: To what extent does our work contribute to or hinder the empowerment of oppressed people? To what extent can this work be used to confront and disrupt white privilege? To what extent can our study of the history of a people victimized by racism be used to eradicate racism now? I am not suggesting that archaeologists who are differently "raced" than I should not ask themselves these questions as well—but their answers will, necessarily, come from a perspective other than my own. And it is also true that individual efforts, mine or anyone else's, cannot answer these questions fully.

Therefore I return to pragmatism, and the notion proposed by William James and most pragmatists since: that theories provide instruments, not answers, and that our work must be evaluated less as a solution than as a program for more work. Evaluated in these terms, CRT does not offer easy solutions, though it does offer us different ways to think about race and white privilege. As we do this, it is important to remember that CRT was developed *by* people of color *for the purposes of* people of color, which leads me to another cautionary note: when whites center race in the manner that CRT suggests, does this have the effect of colonizing it to further our own interests? By foregrounding race, and acknowledging whiteness as a race, do we run the risk of foregrounding ourselves? Whites need to take care that our interest in CRT does not deflect the conversation away from CRT's original purpose—to address the issues of people of color (Bergerson 2003, 56).

I have suggested elsewhere that archaeology can be used to create alternate visions of the past, considering this from a pragmatic view that seeks historically situated, pluralist conversations about archaeology (McDavid 1997, 232). Pragmatism, which (like CRT and other theories) argues that reality is constructed by *individual* experience, led me to speculate whether archaeological data might also be used to write counterstories that Delgado describes; they do, after all, provide a glimpse into the ways that material culture was actually *used* by people in the past.

The problems with doing this as a white scholar within African American archaeology are evident. I do not need to call myself a critical race theorist, however, to use its ideas to reflect critically upon white privilege as part of the public archaeology experience, and thus to further the cause of social justice. This has to happen, however, within contexts of collaboration, shared power, openness, and reciprocated knowledge. I have also written elsewhere about how the act of participation in ethnically diverse projects can change how people of different races see and understand each other (McDavid 2004c). In CRT terms, can these projects cause whites to move from what is sometimes seen as *false* empathy, as described above, to embrace a more informed, genuine empathy? Can CRT be used to help us learn how to work *alongside* people of color, supporting or being directed *by* them, rather than helping from an outside, dominant position?

I believe that it can, but that we have to find new ways to ask for and offer help—that is, to promote involvement and participation—which are not in themselves tokenizing. Clearly, one way to avoid this (and to avoid asking black people to speak for everyone in their racial group) is to seek these sorts of conversations transparently, honestly, and most of all, often. It also, just as obviously, means working *purposefully* toward a future reality in which docents, board members, and staffs of the organizations with which we work are themselves representative of diverse groups. That is, we can use CRT to theorize about race and white privilege, but we also must think carefully and intentionally about how knowledge is created and controlled, and then act upon what we learn.

Even then, unless shared racial power is built in from the beginning, I suspect change will be very gradual. This highlights another insight from CRT: its critique of the liberal idea of incrementalism. As DeCuir and Dixson point out (2004, 29), "Those most satisfied with incremental change are those less likely to be directly affected by oppressive and marginalizing conditions." It is true that token change usually allows those in power to sidestep making real change. While I am in sympathy with the CRT rejection of liberal complacency, and agree that our efforts must be unceasing, I also realize that we have to choose our battles carefully. Therefore, the talk I gave to the Heritage Society docents was somewhat less frontal than a talk I might give to another group, such as the board of the Yates Museum. I do want the opportunity to speak again, after all—to keep the conversation going (McDavid 2000).

An important question, from a CRT perspective, is also whether whites can "be" critical race theorists at all. I tend to agree with white antiracism scholars Bergerson (2003), Alcoff (1998), and Eichstedt (2001), as well as some race-crits (Delgado 1997), that, in addition to doing the research our discipline demands, whites should do three things: to help other whites to acknowledge white privilege ("where our words may be heard in places where people of color are not"); to use CRT strategically, as I have tried to do here; and to encourage students and colleagues to find alternate epistemologies that draw as much from "the lived experiences of individuals who have traditionally been marginalized" (Bergerson 2003, 58–60) as they do from traditional scientific methods. The latter has direct implications for archaeological work, as discipline-wide experiments with more inclusive research and outreach methods continue.

Archaeology does have a useful role to play in the confrontation and deconstruction of white privilege—and, by extension, to be used in aid of a social justice that is truly "for all." Our experiments will continue, they will be messy, we will make mistakes, and we will be criticized for them. They also may not work; I do not believe that I will live long enough to see racism and white privilege disappear. Even so—especially so—I also believe that any efforts we can make now to diminish them are worth the effort. What matters, when considering the possibility of archaeology and civic engagement, is not which specific strategies we use. What matters is *how* we use them.

Notes

1. I use the terms white people/whites/European American, and black people/blacks/African American, to refer to those who are of European and African descent, respectively, while acknowledging that these terms are extremely problematic (Bonnett 1997). Like Hanel (2001) I dislike the term "non-white" because it implies that "white" is normative, and agree that the term "people of color" suggests that

white people lack color—although I use it, reluctantly, when nothing else seems to suit. The term "black" is also difficult, since it can refer not only to people of African descent, but also to Asians, Pacific Islanders, and Caribbean and Indigenous people who have been constructed as nonwhite or black in various historical and cultural circumstances. In addition, this nomenclature does not take proper account of multiracial people, who in practice may choose to claim one race or another—or, if they do not, are identified as such by others. The ramifications of this are, after all, one point of this paper. As Ladson-Billings and Tate point out, "discussions of race in America position *everyone* as either "white" or "nonwhite" (1995:63). I eagerly await a solution to this problem, although it will likely not emerge until the points made here are made moot by profound social change.

2. Even though recent comments about this project (Epperson 2004) reflect a misreading of the timeline described in (McDavid 1997), the main thrust of Epperson's critique, to propose the utility of CRT in archaeology was extremely useful, as can be seen by my remarks here.

3. At this writing, the streets are still more or less intact, although that could change at any time.

References Cited

Alcoff, L. M.
  1998   What Should White People Do? *Hypatia* 13(3).
Bell, D.
  1995   Who's Afraid of Critical Race Theory? *University of Illinois Law Review*:893–910.
Bell, D. A.
  1992   *Faces at the Bottom of the Well: The Permanence of Racism.* Basic Books, New York.
Bergerson, A. A.
  2003   Critical Race Theory and White Racism: Is There Room For White Scholars In Fighting Racism In Education? *Qualitative Studies in Education* 16(1):51–63.
Bonnett, A.
  1997   Antiracism and the Critique of "White" Identities. *New Communities* 22(1):97–110.
Brown, K. L.
  1994   Material Culture & Community Structure: The Slave and Tenant Community at Levi Jordan's Plantation, 1848–1892. In

Working Toward Freedom: Slave Society and Domestic Economy in the American South, edited by J. Larry E. Hudson, pp. 95–118. University of Rochester Press, Rochester, NY.

2000   From Archaeological Interpretation to Public Interpretation: Collaboration within the Discipline for a Better Public Archaeology (Phase One). Paper presented at the 65th Annual Meeting of the Society for American Archaeology, Philadelphia, Pennsylvania.

2001   Interwoven Traditions: Archaeology of the Conjurer's Cabins and the African American Cemetery at the Jordan and Frogmore Plantations. Paper presented at the Places of Cultural Memory: African Reflections on the American Landscape conference, Atlanta, Georgia.

2004   Ethnographic Analogy, Archaeology, and the African Diaspora: Perspectives from a Tenant Community. *Historical Archaeology* 38(1):79–89.

Brown, K. L. and D. C. Cooper
1990   Structural Continuity in an African-American Slave and Tenant Community. *Historical Archaeology on Southern Plantations and Farms, Historical Archaeology* 24(4):7–19.

Chappell, E. A.
1989   Social Responsibility and the American History Museum. *Winterthur Portfolio* 24(4):247–265.

Crenshaw, K.
1995   Mapping the Margins: Intersectionality, Identity Politics, and Violence Against Women of Color. In *Critical Race Theory: The Key Writings that Formed the Movement*, edited by K. Crenshaw, N. Gotanda, G. Peller, and K. Thomas, pp. 357–383. New Press, New York.

DeCuir, J. T. and A. D. Dixson
2004   "So When It Comes Out, They Aren't That Surprised That Is Is There": Using Critical Race Theory as a Tool of Analysis of Race and Racism in Education. *Educational Researcher* (June/July):26–31.

Delgado, R.
1989   Storytelling for Oppositionalists and Others: A Plea for Narrative. *Michigan Law Review* 87(8):2411–2441.

1997   Rodrigo's Eleventh Chronicle: Empathy and False Empathy. In *Critical White Studies: Looking Behind the Mirror*, edited by R. Delgado and J. Stefancic, pp. 614–618. Temple University Press, Philadelphia.

Delgado, R. and J. Stefancic
  2001 *Critical Race Theory: An Introduction.* New York University Press, New York.
Dixson, A. D. and C. K. Rousseau
  2005 And We Are Still Not Saved: Critical Race Theory in Education Ten Years Later. *Race, Ethnicity and Education* 8(1), 7–27.
Eichstedt, J. L.
  2001 Problematic White Identities and a Search for Racial Justice. *Sociological Forum* 16(3):445–470.
Epperson, T. W.
  1999 The Global Importance of African Diaspora Archaeology in the Analysis and Abolition of Whiteness. Paper presented at the World Archaeological Congress 4, Cape Town, SA.
  2004 Critical Race Theory and the Archaeology of the African Diaspora. *Historical Archaeology* 38(1):101–108.
Ervin, A. M.
  2000 *Applied Anthropology: Tools and Perspectives for Contemporary Practice.* Allyn & Bacon, Needham Heights, MA.
Falk, J. H. and L. D. Dierking
  1992 *The Museum Experience.* Whaleback Books, Washington, D.C.
Gorski, P.
  2000 Narrative of Whiteness and Multicultural Education. Electronic document, http://www.eastern.edu:93/publications/emme/2000spring/gorski.html. *Electronic Magazine of Multicultural Education* 2(1), accessed January 2007.
Hanel, Shawna
  2001 As Long As You Think You're White. Electronic document, In *Lightwriting: Photography by Shawna Hanel,* http://www.lightwriting.net/_white/hanel_whiteness.pdf, accessed January 2007.
Hooper-Greenhill, E.
  1994 *Museums and Their Visitors.* Routledge, London.
House, G.
  1999 A Brief History of Freedmen's Town. Electronic document, http://www.houstonprogressive.org/FTAbrief.html,. accessed January 2007.
Jensen, R.
  2002a More Thoughts on Why the System of White Privilege Is Wrong. In *STAR: Students and Teachers Against Racism,* edited by C. Rose. Electronic document, http://www.racismagainstindians.org/WhitePrivilege/WhitePrivilegeResponse.htm, accessed January 2007.

2002b White Privilege Shapes the U.S. In *STAR: Students and Teachers Against Racism,* edited by C. Rose. Electronic document, http://www.racismagainstindians.org/WhitePrivilege/WhitePrivilege.htm, accessed January 2007.

Ladson-Billings, G. and I. William F. Tate
1995 Toward a Critical Race Theory of Education. *Teaching College Record* 97(1):47–68.

Little, B.
2005 An Introduction to Archaeology as Civic Engagement. In *Annual Meetings of the Society for Historical Archaeology,* York, England.

Lloyd, K. S.
2004 Teaching the Elusive White Student: Encouraging White Students to Think Multi-Culturally While Challenging the Myth of Whiteness. *AURCO Journal* 10 (Spring):77–92.

Marx, S.
2003 Reflections on the State of Critical White Studies. *International Journal of Qualitative Studies in Education* 16(1):3–5.

Matsuda, M.
1995 Looking to the Bottom: Critical Legal Studies and Reparations. In *Critical Race Theory: The Key Writings that Formed the Movement,* edited by K. Crenshaw, N. Gotanda, G. Peller, and K. Thomas, pp. 63–79. New Press, New York.

McDavid, C.
1997 Descendants, Decisions, and Power: The Public Interpretation of the Archaeology of the Levi Jordan Plantation. *Historical Archaeology,* special issue, In the Realm of Politics: Prospects for Public Participation in African-American Archaeology. 31(3):114–131.

1999 From Real Space to Cyberspace: Contemporary Conversations about the Archaeology of Slavery and Tenancy. *Internet Archaeology,* Special Theme: Digital Publication(6).

2000 Archaeology as Cultural Critique: Pragmatism and the Archaeology of a Southern United States Plantation. In *Philosophy and Archaeological Practice: Perspectives for the 21st Century,* edited by C. Holtorf and H. Karlsson, pp. 221–240. Bricoleur Press, Lindome, Sweden.

2002a Archaeologies that Hurt; Descendents that Matter: A Pragmatic Approach to Collaboration in the Public Interpretation of African-American Archaeology. *World Archaeology,* special issue "Community Archaeology" 34(2):303–314.

2002b   *From Real Space to Cyberspace: The Internet and Public Archaeological Practice.* Unpublished Ph.D. dissertation, University of Cambridge.

2003a   Context, Collaboration and Power: The Public Archaeology of the Levi Jordan Plantation. In *SAA Community Partnership Handbook,* edited by L. Derry and M. Malloy. Society for American Archaeology, Washington, D.C.

2003b   The Death of a *Community* Archaeology Project? Ensuring "Consultation" in a Non-Mandated Bureaucratic Environment. Paper presented at the World Archaeology Congress, Washington, D.C.

2003c   The Internet and Public Archaeological Practice: A Critical look at the Hype of Hypertext. Paper presented at the World Archaeology Congress, Washington, D.C.

2003d   Public Archaeology and the Internet: One Case Study in African Diaspora Archaeology. Paper presented at the Tenth Annual Deerfield-Wellesley Symposium in American Culture, African Cultures in the North American Diaspora: An Interdisciplinary Symposium, Deerfield, Massachusetts.

2004a   From "Traditional" Archaeology to Public Archaeology to Community Action: The Levi Jordan Plantation Project. In *Places in Mind: Archaeology as Applied Anthropology,* edited by P. Shackel and E. Chambers. Routledge, New York.

2004b   A Pragmatic Archaeology for Collaboration and Reform: The Yates Community Archaeology Project. Paper presented at the Society for Historical Archaeology, St. Louis, MO.

2004c   Public Archaeology as a Pathway to Understanding: Rethinking the Heritage "Product." Paper presented at the Making the Means Transparent: Research methodologies in heritage studies conference, University of Cambridge, England.

2004d   Towards a More Democratic Archaeology? The Internet and Public Archaeological Practice. In *Public Archaeology,* edited by N. Merriman, pp. 159–187. Routledge, London.

2005   Activist Archaeology? A Critical Look at an Emerging Disciplinary Interest. Paper presented at the Society for Applied Anthropology, Santa Fe, New Mexico.

(2007)   Public Archaeology as a Pathway to Understanding: Rethinking the Heritage Product. In *Changing the World with Archaeology: Archaeology Activism,* edited by J. Stottman. University Press of Florida, Gainesville, forthcoming.

McDavid, C. and D. Babson (editors)
  1997 *In the Realm of Politics: Prospects for Public Participation in African-American Archaeology,* special issue of *Historical Archaeology* 31:3.
McGuire, R. H. and M. Walker
  1999 Class Confrontations in Archaeology. *Historical Archaeology* 33(1):159–183.
McIntosh, P.
  1988 *White Privilege and Male Privilege: A Personal Account of Coming to See Correspondences through Work in Women's Studies.* Center for Research on Women, Wellesley College, Wellesley, MA.
Merriman, N.
  1991 *Beyond the Glass Case: The Past, the Heritage, and the Public in Britain.* Leicester University Press, Leicester.
Sleeter, C.
  2000/2001 Diversity vs. White Privilege: An Interview with Christine Sleeter. In *Rethinking Schools Online.* Electronic document, http://www.rethinkingschools.org/archive/15_02/Int152.shtml, accessed January 2007.
Solorzano, D. G.
  1988 Critical Race Theory, Race and Gender Microaggressions, and the Experience of Chicana and Chicano scholars. *Qualitative Studies in Education* 11(1):121–136.
Tanarka, K.
  2005 Comments during Martin Luther King Day Celebration at the Gregory-Lincoln Learning Center, Freedmen's Town, Houston (Tanarka is the chair of the Houston Chapter of the Black United Front).
Thandeka
  1999 *Learning to Be White: Money, Race and God in America.* Continuum, New York.
Wallace, M.
  1996 *Mickey Mouse History and Other Essays on American Memory.* Temple University Press, Philadelphia, PA.
Wise, T.
  2002 Honky Wanna Cracker? In *STAR: Students and Teachers Against Racism,* edited by C. Rose. Electronic document, http://www.racismagainstindians.org/WhitePrivilege/HonkyWannaCracker.htm, accessed January 2007.

Chapter 5

Politics, Inequality, and Engaged Archaeology: Community Archaeology Along the Color Line

Paul R. Mullins

Over the last decade a flood of scholars has concluded that society stands at a critical juncture, a moment when we are compelled to confront an alarming decline in community social networks (e.g., Colby et al. 2003; Putnam 1995). The general conclusion that emerges from the civic engagement literature is that Americans have become increasingly disinvested in broadly defined political processes and uninterested in confronting shared civic challenges. In various minds this social alienation is a result of, among other things, women's entry into the workforce, increased residential mobility and suburbanization, post-Vietnam apathy, generational sentiments, and our mass media immersion. Robert Putnam's (1995, 1996, 2000) influential call to civic engagement revolves around his strongly documented evidence that Americans' participation in a variety of voluntary social activities ranging from the PTO (Parent-Teacher Organization) to bowling leagues has decreased significantly in the past quarter century. Scholars interested in reversing this apparently troubling trend have championed a host of strategies that will improve the "density of associational life" and engage us in confronting common civic challenges (Putnam 1995, 76).

Archaeologists have been among the thinkers answering the call for an engaged scholarship. There is exciting potential for an engaged archaeology that shares power, develops knowledge across lines of difference, confronts profound structural inequalities, and even has activist intentions to change those inequalities (examples of such archaeology include Franklin 2001; Leone et al. 1987; McGuire 1992; Orser 2004; Paynter 2001; Wood 2002). However, some of the fundamental tenets of civic engagement scholarship provide a problematic foundation for an engaged archaeology, posing definitions of politicization, empowerment, and collaboration that deserve systematic self-reflection in relation to the community constituencies with whom archaeologists partner (cf. Hyatt 2001).

I am most interested in how an engaged archaeology can embrace various forms of community politicization and grassroots organization, especially across class and color lines. For instance, Putnam's most evocative example of declining engagement is his analysis of rapid drops in bowling league participation (Putnam 2000:112–113). Bowling leagues provide a telling support for his thesis that everyday social collectives like those at the local alley foster important community participation. Yet along the color line even groups as apparently innocuous as bowling leagues are politicized collectives not easily distanced from racial ideology. In Indianapolis, Indiana, for instance, the National Bowling Association today has a local chapter of the organization once known as the National Negro Bowling Association. The National Negro Bowling Association formed in 1939 in direct response to segregated alleys and White-only national organizations, and the African American bowlers included an Indianapolis contingent at their first convention. At that time the American Bowling Congress sanctioned many leagues and the most important national tournaments, but the Congress barred its sizable membership to all who were not "of the Caucasian race" (*New York Times* 1949b).

Despite the boundaries placed before Black bowlers, in 1947 *Ebony* called bowling African America's most popular sport (TNBA from the Beginning 2005). Various sorts of community relationships certainly were forged in Indianapolis's Black bowling alleys, but African Americans could not have ignored how racism shaped even something as prosaic as bowling. Not surprisingly, segregated bowling alleys were among the public consumer spaces targeted by civil rights protests (e.g., *New York Times* 1955, 1962). In the 1940s resistance was already directed at the American Bowling Congress's racial exclusivity codes (*New York Times* 1949b). In 1948, the Congress awarded the 1950 championship tournament to Indianapolis, but at the same conference it refused to change the rule restricting membership to "white persons of the male sex" (*New York Times* 1948). A year later, New Jersey and New York barred the Congress from holding its segregated tournaments in either state, and the Congress of Industrial Organizations lobbied to revoke the Congress's Illinois charter (*New York Times* 1949c, 1949d, 1970). In 1950, the organization grudgingly rescinded its segregation clause (*New York Times* 1949a).

When African American bowlers protested the American Bowling Congress's segregation codes, they also boycotted alleys holding Congress-sponsored competitions (Eisen 1949). Segregated bowling alleys subsequently became targets for civil rights appeals, casting them as appropriately public spaces in the same way as lunch counters, buses, and schools were. The most unfortunate bowling alley protest came in 1968 in Orangeburg, South Carolina, where African American students from South Carolina State College protested at the city's last segregated alley for several days in February (Bass and Nelson 2003). State troopers were called to the school's campus to extinguish a bonfire, and they surrounded a group of students and fired into the crowd, killing three young men in what became known as the Orangeburg Massacre. Today about 90 percent of the National Bowling Association's thirty thousand members are African American, suggesting that at least along the color line alleys and bowling leagues have never become the ideal engaged space Putnam envisions. This does not necessarily undermine Putnam's argument that such informal collectives are the scenes for a variety of forms of civic engagement. However, it does reflect that racial ideology has a significant impact on African American collectivism and community politics. Any engaged scholars who partner with African Americans must acknowledge this and examine how their work can be incorporated within existing antiracist sentiments and initiatives.

Archaeology's mission probably is not most profitably framed as "community empowerment." This smacks of a power inequality from the outset, defines community in a form that may be quite distinct from its definition in everyday experience, and implies that we are working toward a specific sort of politicization that has been defined by academics and not constituents. In most cases local collectives are in fact very much politicized, but that politicization can take a very wide range of locally distinct forms (cf. Gregory 1994). These local politics may not always have the specific community form and goals that academics stereotypically associate with political collectives. In the same way that a rather monolithic vision of politics has been crafted, the notion of "community" often has been defined in a rather mechanical form that has served state interests, such as urban renewal programs that aimed to fabricate particular forms of community. Rather than aspire to a very specific form of political engagement or community, engaged scholarship might most profitably probe how social groups were marginalized and how specific contemporary discourses reproduce and justify their marginalization (cf. Lyon-Callo 2004:11). It seems problematic to define civic engagement in a way that stresses voluntary community service as the heart of "good citizenship" while it at least implicitly ignores the systemic and historical processes that produced and reproduce inequality. Ultimately the goal of an engaged archaeology should be a critical analysis of inequality and not a flood of volunteers who troop off to the PTO to potentially craft collective political interests.

Archaeological Engagement and Urban Renewal

Some of the richest contexts for archaeological civic engagement may be in urban universities where marginalized communities often ring campuses and in many cases were displaced by those very universities. On the many campuses that have faced competing "town/gown" interests, archaeologists have powerful opportunities to examine social and material transformations linked to the state in general and the academy in particular.

Campuses that have expanded into surrounding communities can use archaeology to probe concrete processes of inequality, privilege, and power in ways that productively complicate the boundaries between the academy and the community.

Indiana University–Purdue University, Indianapolis (IU-PUI), is relatively typical of the many universities that rose from postwar inner cities with the backing of federal slum clearance funding and urban renewal ideology. Just after the turn of the twentieth century the Indiana University Medical Center settled beside Indianapolis's City Hospital in the midst of a neighborhood on the city's near-Westside. City Hospital was built in 1857 in an unsettled, poorly drained space outside the city limits that lay along the White River drainage. By the 1870s, though, the city had grown westward, and much of the low-lying surrounding area was filled in, divided into lots, and rapidly settled (Holloway 1870:104). By the time Indiana University began teaching medical school classes at the hospital at the turn of the century, the neighborhood immediately around it was a predominately African American community. The population in the neighborhood around the hospital tripled between 1870 and 1920, when successive migration waves delivered increasingly more African American migrants and a smaller but still significant number of European immigrants. During that period the area became strictly segregated, and by the 1920s the community closest to the medical center was predominately African American.

By the mid-1950s, the only remaining space for medical center expansion was into these surrounding neighborhoods. The neighborhood the medical center looked into after World War II had declined significantly since the 1920s. In the interim, once-spacious homes had been subdivided into modest apartments, and greedy landlords added insubstantial alley housing that left a densely settled working-class community. This rapidly expanding and increasingly impoverished community inspired some uneasiness at the medical school, which had ambitions to add sparkling new facilities and was apparently not keen to be surrounded by a declining neighborhood. In 1947, medical school faculty member Thurman Rice (1947:64) contemptuously described the surrounding neighborhood as "an extremely ugly slum that needs to be eradicated inasmuch as it is directly in front of the Medical Center." Similar thoughts were uttered in many other communities as university and city officials joined a nationwide urban renewal movement that aimed to clear "slum" neighborhoods and focused on displacing Black communities.

Between the late 1950s and 1970s the state gradually emptied out the near-Westside, providing expansion space first for the medical center and then making room for Indiana University's proposed undergraduate campus. In 1969 that campus became known as IUPUI when the state legislature brought together the state's two major universities, Indiana and Purdue, in a single capital city institution. Long before the deal was sealed in the legislature, though, Indiana University was already securing land for the future university, and by the time the legislature made it official in 1969 a campus space was already in the hands of the university. In the 1970s IUPUI rapidly expanded beyond these initial landholdings into what is now roughly 510 acres. The most pressing challenge for the new commuter school was parking, so the campus became an ever-expanding patchwork of hastily laid parking lots dotted by perfunctory institutional architecture. The university gradually moved neighbors off campus and built new structures and paved more former house lots, but that dispossession of the campus's former residents is today largely invisible to the campus community, if not the city at large (Mullins 2003). Many American universities that expanded into surrounding neighborhoods and displaced communities could tell very similar stories today.

In many ways the IUPUI campus provides an ideal context to examine the archaeological evidence of the neighborhood's communities and probe how the contemporary campus landscape was created to serve some groups while it dispossessed others. Many of the people who were displaced by the university are still Indianapolis residents; university administrators are eager to address this experience and their institutional role in it; and many community groups feel some vested interest in both university and community heritage. This provides very valuable building blocks for a constituent-driven archaeology that is based in community interests and uses concrete archaeological data to examine the processes that produced the contemporary community. Such an archaeological project is one of many mechanisms that could encourage various forms of civic engagement among a wide variety of constituents, so we need to examine the underlying premises and goals of such engagement (cf. Solari 2001).

The civic engagement literature champions a wide range of approaches designed to produce a newly engaged citizen. In some eyes, this citizen will be voluntarily invested in common community concerns, which may eventually address more weighty political goals, but such community volunteerism precedes politicization directed toward concrete social change (e.g., Putnam 1995). For virtually any archaeologist working with marginalized communities, though, the question is not whether communities are politicized but instead how they are politicized, toward what ends, and what types of concrete issues archaeology can hope to address.

One of the central challenges of an engaged archaeology is to define constituencies whose own political interests can be served by scholarship conducted in collaboration with archaeologists. This seems somewhat analogous to what Putnam (1995:66) describes as building "social capital," which he considers to be cooperative networks that provide mutual benefits driving democracy and economic growth. Putnam champions building these networks among private voluntary collectives, assuming that such groups are united by social trust and values more than by self-interested political claims (in contrast, such claims would govern a partisan party or a group of marketers). This illuminates the enigma of precisely what we consider "political," and at the grassroots level at which most community archaeology is conducted the line is especially complicated. My own primary community relationship is with the Ransom Place Neighborhood Association, which represents a historically African American neighborhood that escaped the wrecking ball and now sits just north of campus. The Neighborhood Association in many ways is exactly the sort of community group civic engagement theorists consider most productive. The Neighborhood Association represents all of the neighborhood's roughly 150 households, but older residents who voluntarily devote significant amounts of time and energy to neighborhood governance primarily have driven the group. That governance focuses on local issues ranging from refuse pickup to street maintenance to vandalism, so while the neighborhood is very much committed to its heritage it is still a living community with relatively prosaic community problems.

The partnership of the Neighborhood Association with academics introduces a politicized dimension to the archaeology project that is viewed warily by some engagement theorists. However, it seems difficult to see how an archaeology project working with marginalized constituencies and focused on race and inequality could avoid politicization or would even wish to do so. Much of the civic engagement literature borrows from a distinction between political society and civil society that makes the division between political and public life in various ways (Foley and Edwards 1996). Civil society is typically taken as the domain for civic engagement and is defined in Putnam's hands as a sphere dominated by volunteerism that promotes a social civility essential to political citizenship. This is a somewhat difficult entry point for many archaeologists, especially those working with African Americans, who very often place a critical consciousness of the color line at the heart of all community organization. For instance, it would be difficult to find an African American church that does not consider color line inequality a dimension of its mission, though churches' specific responses are distinct to their communities' needs and their denominational perspective and they may advocate a wide range of political tactics.

I assume from the outset that an engaged archaeology should have some activist intentions to share insight into inequality and raise consciousness about specific inequalities. However, this does not assume the actual ways in which such consciousness will play out in engaged relationships or even that it will have a clear political impact. The process of articulating political claims and working toward them is certainly challenging and is a sustained and continually unfolding process. Yet it does not seem sufficient to simply stir up community interest in archaeology and then wait to see if the resulting knowledge finds some concrete activist target, even though it is reasonable for us to be unable to predict how archaeological insight will be used. An engaged archaeology should articulate repressed or ignored political demands, or it risks simply painting evocative emotional pictures of the past with no clear connection to contemporary inequality. In the near-Westside, an archaeology could not be engaged if it did not confront issues of race and class inequality, examine how they were fanned and exploited by the state, and press to see how they have descended to us today. An archaeology that unites all of these things can make a very powerful claim to activist intentions without determining the forms that activism takes.

The initial archaeological step toward concrete archaeological activism in the near-Westside is to actually raise consciousness of the landscape's history. On campus archaeological sites, this is very straightforward, because visitors are confronted by deeply stratified columns of prehistoric wetlands, early historic remains, twentieth-century discards, and dense layers of gravel and soil on which parking lots, campus spaces, and buildings were constructed. In a typical six-week field season we see a stream of school groups, curious passers-by, and campus folks, and they receive tours that examine how archaeology can examine race and materialism on this landscape. Even reaching many visitors in a summer, though, these tours may not really qualify as an especially profound shift in how the landscape is defined by broader campus and city communities, and it is difficult to assess how site presentations change visitors' consciousness. The tours are still important, though, because they literally publicize a heritage that many elders believe will die with their generation. For many of our community partners the archaeology project's most important role is to simply make people conscious of African American heritage on campus and in the broader community. The archaeology project receives a fair amount of local press and regular invitations to various city government and community meetings, and elder partners are able to use these opportunities to discuss community history and focus on whatever issues they choose to highlight.

The issues for many elders revolve around how their memories and archaeological material culture refute stereotypes of the Black community. One of the common assumptions about many impoverished neighborhoods is that high residential mobility and poverty create communities that lack the "stability" of ideologically model neighborhoods (cf. Temkin and Rohe 1998). These model neighborhoods implicitly seem to be White suburban communities, and the assumption has often been that home ownership and economic stability produce a more cohesive community that is more likely to be engaged around shared civic concerns. There may well be some truth to this idea, but it assumes too much about the character and "instability" of life outside home ownership (Portney and Berry 1997).

Transiency and racism have been linked together in discussions of community cohesiveness since the nineteenth century. For instance, when Nelda Weathers (1924:17–18) conducted thesis research in the near-Westside in 1924, she concluded, "The stability of the Negro home is not so firmly rooted as it is with the white man. . . . He does not become a part of any community and so feels no regret at leaving." This conclusion that poor, mobile renters were not closely linked to each other does not seem to be well supported in the near-Westside. Rental tenants did indeed dominate the near-Westside by the 1920s, and skyrocketing post–World War I rents apparently increased tenant mobility, but it is not self-evident that this inevitably had a negative effect on community consciousness. We conducted a study of residential transience in one of the campus's most impoverished neighborhoods, on Beauty Street, to identify the frequency with which people moved and to examine how residents may have defined community. Between 1925 and 1929, three-quarters of the households on Beauty Street moved at least once. This seems to confirm Weathers's own statistical conclusions from her 1924 thesis. However, one-quarter of the 1925 residents stayed in Indianapolis, and another quarter stayed at the same address for this four-year sample. What is perhaps most interesting is that those who changed addresses within the city only moved within a block or two of their earlier homes. For instance, Walter Boone and his family lived at three addresses on Beauty Street between

1925 and 1929, but all were within a roughly ten-house block. His neighbor in 1925 also moved a block away in 1927 and then onto neighboring New York Street in 1929.

This brings into question whether "stability" is defined by connection to neighbors, community institutions, social organizations, or home ownership, all of which might produce a somewhat different vision of community cohesion. In 1924 Nelda Weathers also complicated this idea of community "stability." Weathers (1924:19) noted that "most of those interviewed, when asked if they moved often, answered 'no,' but upon being questioned it was found that if they had lived in a place three years they felt they had been there a long time." Weathers considered this "instability," yet community residents clearly did not. Thirty-one churches dotted the near-Westside in 1930, and several public schools were within walking distance, so residents may have been more tied to these institutions and their neighbors than to specific houses. Weathers found that landlords were exceptionally firm about posting delinquency notices and evicting tenants who did not pay on time, so many tenants were not especially tied to houses and dominating landlords as much as they felt rooted in neighborhoods. The suggestive picture painted in at least this corner of the near-Westside is of a highly mobile community, but that community apparently was committed to the neighborhood and probably shared church ties, school relationships, consumer spaces, and myriad other everyday collective organizations.

There is something unsettling about the assumption that working-class or impoverished folks are not "engaged" in a particular form of civic organization, such as voluntary community service organizations that typically have rejected African Americans as partners but paternalistically served them as subjects. There is a persistent and powerful assumption that urban Black communities lack the values, trust, and relationships that make citizens "engaged," though there is an expansive ethnographic literature documenting the profoundly significant social networks nurtured in even the most difficult conditions (Portney and Berry 1997). The real problem is not the absence of social networks supporting community members in places like the near-Westside as much as it is the absence of capital itself (De-Filippis 2001:797). Our research has examined how communities organize in a vast range of forms that would affect how they define engagement. For example, much of our oral history has illuminated how many African Americans placed retail venues such as corner stores at the heart of their vision of neighborhood space and identity. Marginalized by anti-Black racism and excluded from partisan politics, many African Americans invested their ambitions in marketing and entrepreneurial activity, and aspiring African American entrepreneurs shared knowledge and resources in organizations like churches, fraternal societies, and social clubs. This could be seen in some ways as a mechanism with which a marginalized Black community attempted to take its strong existing social capital and place it on a foundation of literal material capital that was normally hostile to African American ambition. Stores, churches, and similar institutions were also socially important, though, so they cannot simply be reduced to mechanisms to accumulate material resources. Black schools, for instance, are at the heart of community identity in the near-Westside. The segregated Crispus Attucks High School may have been the most significant institution in African American Indianapolis for the half century it was the city's sole Black high school. In these organizations, African Americans have had powerful and profoundly significant grassroots networks that took aim at a very wide range of racist challenges. For instance, Attucks held night classes to educate community members with an eye on improving their laboring lots. In a similar vein, from the 1930s onward, ministers and their congregants picketed chain stores that refused to hire African Americans (Thornbrough 2000:76–77). Residents understood the link between consumer venues and community identity and aspired to ensure that racism did not determine the form taken by either.

The Politics of Urban Renewal Landscapes

The lofty ambition of politicizing the campus landscape may have come long ago, but it was not a politicization of the campus as a product of racism and class inequality. Instead, most faculty, staff, students, and visitors constantly bemoan the landscape's inability to accommodate their cars in spaces that are sufficiently numerous, adequately convenient, or appropriately inexpensive. In 1967 an *Indianapolis News* columnist (Roberts 1967:38) visited the rapidly expanding medical center, and he wondered if neighborhood displacement was meant only to create parking lots: "Seeing all of the parking areas crowded with cars, you realize there can never be such a thing as too much parking." On a commuter campus in a city that has always been exceptionally warm to car culture, complaints about parking are perhaps predictable, but they reveal how the campus community often does not see itself as privileged at all. In the very first issue of the IUPUI newspaper in April 1970, one student already was irate about the number of "unimproved, unlit parking spaces" (*Onomatopoeia* 27 April 1970:4). However, he also revealed that the parking lots, campus, and his very car were mechanisms that were meant to distance him from a neighborhood with which he did not wish to engage at all. He complained that IUPUI had settled in "one of the highest crime-rate districts," so it "should accept the responsibility of the safety of its students. . . . One murder, rape or molesting will make the beautiful campus a cancerous breeding ground for fear and panic."

Similar sentiments have been voiced many times afterwards, and they may support Putnam's picture of individuals alienated from common community interests. However, the real challenge this presents is how we can make the landscape something other than a flat expanse of asphalt provided for commuters' appropriate privilege. Certainly one mechanism has been archaeological excavations in the heart of campus, which bring together former residents and the contemporary campus community to illuminate the campus's past. These archaeological tours may not radically change how the city's broader community sees the campus's past, but the tours do reach critical university administrators who have supported the project in substantial ways that allow us to extend the project beyond excavation alone. Perhaps the most important of these initiatives has been a joint campus-community effort to introduce historical place names to the campus.

During campus expansion many streets were entirely removed for parking lots or grass expanses, and at least one street's name was changed. Consequently, the campus today looks nothing like a grid-based neighborhood, which it did in the 1970s. In an effort to reverse this dehistoricization roughly half of thirty-five new campus dormitories constructed in 2003 were named after figures from the near-Westside. The people who lent their names to these dormitories included professional and working-class people alike, and some were well-known (e.g., Madam C. J. Walker) and others anonymous. The biographical proposals for most of the historic figures were prepared by an archaeology student and then reviewed by a joint community/campus committee. At the dormitories' May 2004 dedication ceremony many descendants and community members accepted the university's invitation to commemorate these community ancestors. Spurred on by this success, an informal campus history group is working to install historic signs on campus documenting communities that once lived on the present-day landscape.

An engaged archaeology in the near-Westside is compelled to involve displaced peoples, but it also must include others who feel a claim on this community's heritage, which includes many African Americans and university students, faculty, and staff. All of these groups have a range of articulate and inchoate sentiments about neighborhood history, so none speak with one "voice" (cf. Zimmerman 2001). This expands narrow definitions of "community archaeology" that revolve around the documentation of a distinctive experience among a particular conscious and articulate group in a certain time and space. For instance, many people in the university community have come to see themselves and the institution as having a tangible if somewhat complex claim on the neighborhood's heritage. This raises the sticky issue of how voices with a claim on neighborhood heritage should be privileged in interpretation: Should we favor the voices of former residents over university community members? If so, then we are compelled to ask exactly which residents' experiences will be favored and what form those voices should take in archaeological interpretation; for instance, community heritage could be represented by first-person oral testimony, standard archaeological analysis, or primary documentary research in forms ranging from technical reports to popular histories to web pages. We also need to examine why groups might make a claim on certain histories. In this case, what does the university have to gain by sharing stewardship for the near-Westside's heritage? I do not question my colleagues' interest in working with the contemporary community, and I am convinced that IUPUI administrators are committed to ethical, reflective scholarship with many of our Indianapolis neighbors. Nevertheless, community-based scholarship and teaching demands an appreciation that marginalized collectives are already historically conscious, politically organized, and very much engaged in everyday community life, and in fact the near-Westside community was quite politicized while it was being targeted by urban renewal.

Our project works most closely with elders whose commitment to near-Westside heritage often reflects their concern that this everyday history will disappear with their generation. For instance, the Lockefield Civic Organization is a collective of former residents of Lockefield Gardens, a 1938 New Deal public housing project that was among the first Public Works Administration projects targeting "slum clearance." The segregated Lockefield complex originally was home to 748 African American households and was a centerpiece of the near-Westside: Carefully manicured lawns lay along the center of twenty-four European-style buildings, a public school sat at one end, and families from throughout the community commonly gathered at the complex. Most of the apartments, though, were torn down to accommodate medical center and campus expansion in 1983, and the remaining units are today marketed as stylish condominiums especially well located for medical students. The Civic Organization's basic goal is simply to ensure that the community remembers the many people who lived in Lockefield over nearly a half century, and its primary interest is in developing a systematic oral history of Lockefield and the surrounding community.

Many former near-Westside residents are especially interested in seeing the project record oral histories of African American elders. Many elders seem to see oral history as a research product that can be used in a very wide range of forms, and the concrete words of community members have somewhat more power in their hands than more narrowly defined archaeological scholarship. The oral histories also cannot be collected without intensive work with the community, and our elder partners almost wholly control the job of identifying appropriate memoirists. Most of our partners visit the archaeological sites and are gratified to see our materials featured in local museums or the city media, but oral histories provide unvarnished personal experiences that appeal very much to many of our community partners. In cooperation with the Indiana African-American Genealogy Group, we developed a plan to interview twenty elders, and we have done about half of those interviews, which now include former Lockefield residents. In 2004 we conducted a project with Bethel African Methodist Episcopal Church, a congregation that formed in 1836 and continues to worship in an 1869 church directly opposite the IUPUI campus. A student interviewed three elders chosen by the pastor on church history and the relationship of the church to the surrounding neighborhoods and the university. The transcripts will find an archival home in IUPUI's University Archives, and representatives of the city's Cultural Trail are examining ways to integrate these oral histories into a proposed bike and pedestrian loop that will run through Indianapolis neighborhoods, including the near-Westside.

Engagement and the Color Line

Many of the IUPUI campus's former residents today live in a neighborhood known as Haughville, which is directly across the White River from campus. Once a predominately European immigrant community attracted to work in foundries and railroad yards, Haughville became predominately African American after World War II. Some of the new residents came from the postwar South, but many were migrants from urban renewal projects that transformed the city's landscape in places like the near-Westside. Haughville today faces many of the same social and material problems that urban planners aspired to eliminate a half century ago through slum clearance programs, public housing projects, and suburbanization. Yet the structural inequalities of a state framed by race and class inequalities simply followed displaced residents to new neighborhoods.

That inequality remains largely invisible to many Americans for whom poverty and racism appear to have lost much of their meaning. In today's civically engaged society, much of the responsibility for addressing impoverishment and inequality has been turned over to volunteerism, but there seems to be a fair amount of indifference about inequalities. There may be many different ways engaged scholars can convince Americans to care about and contribute to a struggle against racism, poverty, and systemic inequalities. Those appeals stand a better chance of success if modest interventions like urban archaeology projects can show the concrete material evidence of impoverishment over time and link that back to long-standing structural inequalities that are not simply the deficiencies of individual communities. The distinction between serving the interests of the state and conducting an engaged archaeology is more complicated than it might initially appear, but archaeology can emphasize that poverty and racist stereotypes simply rationalize continuing government, institutional, and ideological interests. The question for many archaeologists examining inequality is not really how we can make constituent communities civically engaged; instead, the issue is how we can work alongside existing community politics and address long-standing social justice issues like color-line inequalities.

Acknowledgments

Research on the near-Westside has been supported by a Center for Service and Learning Interdisciplinary Community Partnership grant and an Indiana University Arts and Humanities Research initiative grant. Jody Hester conducted exhaustive census research, Brook Wyant conducted transience research, and Genesis Snyder and Aaron Method conducted essential supporting research. My IUPUI colleagues have always been helpful, particularly Karen Whitney, the IUPUI University Archives staff, and the Anthropology Department. Sue Hyatt, Larry Zimmerman, and Liz Kryder-Reid planted many of these ideas. This project would not be possible without the support of the Ransom Place Neighborhood Association, especially Daisy Borel and Thomas Ridley, and that of the Lockefield Civic Organization, particularly Kenneth Adams. Pastor John Lambert of Bethel AME Church graciously coordinated our oral histories with church members. Thanks to Paul Shackel and Barbara Little for inviting me into the volume. None of these people bear any blame for this paper.

References Cited

Bass, Jack, and Jack Nelson.
  2003 *The Orangeburg Massacre.* 2nd ed. Mercer University Press, Macon, Georgia.
Colby, Anne, Thomas Ehrlich, Elizabeth Beaumont, and Jason Stephens
  2003 *Educating Citizens: Preparing America's Undergraduates for Lives of Moral and Civic Responsibility.* Jossey-Bass, San Francisco.
DeFilippis, James
  2001 The Myth of Social Capital in Community Development. *Housing Policy Debate* 12(4):781–806.
Eisen, Arnold
  1949 Not Sporting. *New York Times* 17 April:SM2. New York.
Foley, Michael W., and Bob Edwards
  1996 The Paradox of Civil Society. *Journal of Democracy* 7(3):38–52.
Franklin, Maria
  2001 The Archaeological Dimensions of Soul Food: Interpreting Race, Culture, and Afro-Virginian Identity. In *Race and the Archaeology of Identity,* edited by Charles E. Orser, Jr., pp. 88–107. University of Utah Press, Salt Lake City.
Gregory, Steven
  1994 Race, Rubbish, and Resistance: Empowering Difference in Community Politics. In *Race,* edited by Steven Gregory and Roger Sanjek, pp. 366–391. Rutger University Press, Brunswick, New Jersey.
Holloway, W.R.
  1870 *Indianapolis: A Historical and Statistical Sketch of the Railroad City.* Published by the author, Indianapolis.

Hyatt, Susan Brin
  2001 "Service Learning," Applied Anthropology, and the Production of Neo-Liberal Citizens. *Anthropology in Action* 8(1):6–13.
Leone, Mark P., Parker B. Potter, Jr., and Paul A. Shackel
  1987 Toward a Critical Archaeology. *Current Anthropology* 28:283–302.
Lyon-Callo, Vincent
  2004 *Inequality, Poverty, and Neoliberal Governance: Activist Ethnography in the Homeless Sheltering Industry.* Broadview Press, Peterborough, Ontario.
McGuire, Randall
  1992 *A Marxist Archaeology.* Academic Press, New York.
Mullins, Paul R.
  2003 Engagement and the Color Line: Race, Renewal, and Public Archaeology in the Urban Midwest. *Urban Anthropology* 32(2):205–230.
New York Times
  1948 Racial Ban Is Kept by A.B.C. Tourney. 17 April:18.
  1949a A.B.C. Will Meet on Negro Question. 20 February:S5.
  1949b Segregation Data Are Sent to Mayor. 26 February:3.
  1949c Bowlers' Bias Scored. 12 July:29.
  1949d Seeks Revocation of A.B.C. Charter. 17 October:28.
  1955 Bowling Race Bar Hit. 6 December:31.
  1962 Segregation Test Brings 8 Arrests. 15 August:34.
  1970 Charles T. Carow, Priest on L.I., 62. 22 September:48.
Onomatopoeia
  1970 Letter to the Editor: Parking to be adequate on new campus? 27 April:4.
Orser, Charles E., Jr.
  2004 *Race and Practice in Archaeological Interpretation.* University of Pennsylvania Press, Philadelphia.
Paynter, Robert
  2001 The Cult of Whiteness in Western New England. In *Race and the Archaeology of Identity,* edited by Charles E. Orser, Jr., pp. 125–142. University of Utah Press, Salt Lake City.
Portney, Kent E., and Jeffrey M. Berry
  1997 Mobilizing Minority Communities: Social Capital and Participation in Urban Neighborhoods. *American Behavioral Scientist* 40(5):632–645.
Putnam, Robert D.
  1995 Bowling Alone: America's Declining Social Capital. *Journal of Democracy* 6(1):65–78.

1996   The Strange Disappearance of Civic America. *The American Prospect* 7(24):34–38.

2000   *Bowling Alone: The Collapse and Revival of American Community.* Simon and Schuster, New York.

Rice, Thurman B.

1947   One Hundred Years of Medicine: Indianapolis, 1820–1920, Chapters 1–12. *Monthly Bulletin of the Indiana State Board of Health.*

Roberts, B.

1967   Neighborhood to Vanish Soon. *Indianapolis News* July 11:38.

Solari, Elaine-Maryse

2001   The Making of an Archaeological Site and the Unmaking of a Community in West Oakland, California. In *The Archaeology of Urban Landscapes: Explorations in Slumland,* edited by Alan Mayne and Tim Murray, pp. 22–38. Cambridge University Press, Cambridge, United Kingdom.

Temkin, Kenneth, and William M. Rohe

1998   Social Capital and Neighborhood Stability: An Empirical Investigation. *Housing Policy Debate* 9(1):61–88.

Thornbrough, Emma Lou

2000   *Indiana Blacks in the Twentieth Century.* Indiana University Press, Bloomington.

TNBA From the Beginning

2005   Electronic document, http://www.tnbainc.org/history/nba-glory.html, accessed August 30, 2005.

Weathers, Nelda Adaline

1924   How the Negro Lives in Indianapolis. Thesis submitted to Social Service Department, Indiana University, Bloomington, Indiana.

Wood, Margaret C.

2002   Moving Toward Transformative Democratic Action Through Archaeology. *International Journal of Historical Archaeology* 6(3):187–198.

Zimmerman, Larry J.

2001   Usurping Native American Voices. In *The Future of the Past: Archaeologists, Native Americans, and Repatriation,* edited by Tamara L. Bray, pp. 169–184. Garland Publishing, New York.

Chapter 6

Remaking Connections: Archaeology and Community after the Loma Prieta Earthquake

Mary Praetzellis, Adrian Praetzellis, and
Thad Van Bueren

Before it happened, San Francisco Giants fans had consoled each other that even an earthquake could not save their team from losing the 1989 World Series to their neighboring rivals the Oakland As. Today, no one in the region will forget where they were when the earth rumbled just as the two teams prepared to take the field for the third game at Candlestick Park on October 17, 1989.

As television coverage returned, the Cypress Freeway in West Oakland provided some of the first and most shocking images: the double-decker freeway had collapsed, sandwiching vehicles and their passengers within the tangled ruins of the concrete structure. The residents of this predominately African American neighborhood were the first on the scene. With ropes and ladders, they searched the debris and lowered survivors to safety, ignoring the very real possibility that they might be trapped themselves by an aftershock. Forty-two died on that 1.25-mile section of road, and the toll would have been much worse had not people hurried home from work to catch the ball game on TV. When the California Department of Transportation (Caltrans) announced that it would rebuild the freeway, the neighborhood voiced its opposition and proposed an alternative (Hausler 1990). This resistance and the ability to successfully carry it forward are best understood in the context of West Oakland history.

Background

West Oakland already had a fledgling African American community when it became the western terminus of the Central Pacific Railroad in 1869 (figure 6.1). Along with the railroad came the Pullman Palace Car Company, whose sumptuous sleeping and dining cars catered to the well-heeled traveler. A Victorian home on wheels, the Pullman car was the context for genteel social relations. Attended by porters, passengers had access to a series of increasingly intimate spaces from parlor to dining car to sleeping cubicle. By company policy, only blacks were hired as Pullman porters. These jobs were highly sought after and highly regarded—they paid relatively well, and involved travel and the opportunity to wear the symbols of white-color jobs and to interact with the sophisticated (Crouchett, Bunch, and Winnacker 1989:10; Spires 1994:205–207). The West Oakland rail yards were a hub in the Pullman system, and many porters and their families settled nearby.

Figure 6.1. The Cypress Freeway and Downtown Oakland. From the Seventh Street Post Office complex, we look southeast down Fifth Street to downtown Oakland. The abrupt end of the freeway, just east of Peralta Villa, shows the site of the demolished Cypress structure. Anthropological Studies Center, Sonoma State.

By 1900 over one thousand African Americans lived in Oakland. The great earthquake of 1906 accelerated growth as many businesses moved to Oakland from San Francisco. And as mobilization for World War I took men out of civilian life, industries began to offer employment to African Americans. Civil liberties did not keep step with these economic advances, as the City of Oakland passed a series of ordinances prohibiting blacks from buying property in certain neighborhoods. West Oakland—one of the neighborhoods that allowed African American homeownership—did not develop into a ghetto, however, but continued to be the home of a multiethnic mix of middle- and working-class families (Crouchett, Bunch, and Winnacker 1989:15–22).

Black-owned businesses flourished in the 1920s, as Seventh Street developed as a social center for jazz lovers and a regional hub of African American culture. Porters were instrumental in politicizing the community, where a full one-third of the population worked for the railroad. In 1925 the Brotherhood of Sleeping Car Porters was formed as a militant labor union with C. L. Dellums as the local leader and an office on Seventh Street. During World War II, recruiters for Oakland shipyards traveled throughout the South encouraging African Americans to come work in California. Between 1940 and 1950, Oakland's black population grew from 8,400 to nearly 50,000 (Crouchett, Bunch, and Winnacker 1989:45–46; Spires 1994). But with prohibitive ordinances still in place, the housing market for the new arrivals was extremely tight. Individual residences sheltered as many as fifty men, who would sleep in shifts in so-called "hot beds" (Crouchett, Bunch, and Winnacker 1989:49). Predictably, black workers were the first laid off at the shipyards at the end of the war.

Although West Oakland was designated a "blighted" district in 1949, New Deal progressives had been busy in the neighborhood since the late 1930s, when several blocks of Victorian residences were declared a slum, condemned, and replaced with rows of austere, concrete international-style apartment blocks. Peralta Villa was completed in 1942. It was one of the first public housing projects in California. One hundred and fifty wood-framed nineteenth-century homes on regular-sized city blocks were replaced with thirty-five residential behemoths on so-called "super blocks," designed to change the character of the entire neighborhood. In accord with the social ideas and planning concepts of the era, there were no private outer spaces; and the uniformity and openness of the concrete block rows provided a clear line for surveillance. Privacy was a thing of the past.

The double-decker Cypress Freeway was built in the 1950s, bisecting West Oakland with a massive physical and visual barrier. Again, despite neighborhood opposition, homes were destroyed and families relocated (Solari 2001:29). In 1958 the Oakland Redevelopment Agency made the judgment that over half of West Oakland was blighted and should be cleared. The upshot was that most government projects that would benefit the public generally at the expense of a local neighborhood were now sited in West Oakland. Seventh Street was chosen as the site of a massive new postal facility grandiosely called Project Gateway. "We're doing this area a favor," insisted the postmaster general (*San Francisco Chronicle*, 19 July 1960). Local residents disagreed. Nevertheless, in 1960 three hundred families lost their homes as twelve city blocks were leveled. Giving a new slant on the slogan "war on poverty," an enterprising former race car driver made quick work of the demolition by using a Sherman tank, which could level a residence in ten minutes flat (*Oakland Tribune*, 16 August 1960). The government had no relocation plan for the long-time residents displaced for the project, and few could afford to buy homes elsewhere in Oakland with their meager settlement payment. Despite the haste with which the old houses were leveled, construction of the postal facility did not even begin for another six years. What had been the center of West Oakland was now deserted and desolate, and became a dumping ground (Hope 1963).

Increasingly marginalized, the residents of West Oakland began to protest the devastation and neglect of their neighborhood. In 1965 the Housing Authority began to tear down backyard fences built by tenants of Peralta Villa in their attempt to create a more personal and human-scale landscape. Outraged, the tenants formed the Peralta Improvement League and staged a protest that forced the Housing Authority to abandon the plan (Solari 2001:33).

The following year, the Black Panther Party for Self-Defense was born in West Oakland. Cofounder Huey Newton had moved to the neighborhood as a child and remained connected for his lifetime. "The first house that I remember was on the corner of Fifth and Brush streets," he wrote (Newton 1995:16); this house was torn down for the Cypress Freeway in the 1950s. The Black Panther Party fought for self-determination for the black community and preached the politics of revolution within the community and to radical whites. They armed themselves and their followers and shadowed the police on their West Oakland beats. The Panthers also provided free breakfasts for schoolchildren, and free shoes, clothing, and medical care; and they engendered a sense of pride in the community and an awakening to the idea that, in the slogan of the era, "Black is beautiful!" The fourth plank of the Black Panther Party Program was "decent housing, fit for shelter of human beings." The Black Power movement as a whole can be said to have originated, in part, from the powerlessness of the West Oakland community to save their homes, businesses, and vibrant culture from the ravages of urban renewal.

The leveling of West Oakland clearly contributed to rampant paranoia within the party in the late 1960s. Many black nationalists preached that the U.S. government had genocidal intentions, and a belief in the so-called "King Alfred Plan" was widespread. According to some, this strategy involved the government secretly renovating and expanding Japanese American internment camps, wherein rebellious blacks were to be confined. That formerly independent black homeowners had been forced onto public assistance in the prisonlike confines of the housing projects provided convincing evidence of such a plan for the Panther revolutionaries. Others found proof of this Machiavellian scheme in the use of their neighborhood for freeways, mass-transit projects, and urban renewal (Heath 1976:71).

On the eve of the 1989 earthquake, West Oakland had suffered through years of economic decline. Unemployment averaged 21.5 percent and, with a median income of $13,123, more than 35 percent of the area's residents lived below the poverty level. It was a community of renters: only 15 percent of the district's 8,735 housing units were owner occupied. The ethnic mix had come to include a majority of African Americans (77.3%), with Euro-americans (11%), Hispanics (5.7%), Asians and Pacific Islanders (3.5%), and Native Americans (0.3%) making up most of the rest (Caltrans n.d.:3–4). Although the Port of Oakland continued to play a vital role in America's economy and required a large workforce, relatively few West Oakland residents worked there then or now.

The Black Power movement of the 1960s and 1970s had transformed Oakland politics, and African Americans were better represented in city government and on powerful planning agencies (Rhomberg 2004; Self 2000, 2003). Within days of the Loma Prieta earthquake, community leaders formed the Citizens' Emergency Response Team (CERT) and demanded that the Cypress Freeway not be rebuilt along its original alignment. CERT membership included a Bay Area Rapid Transit (BART) director, a former Port of Oakland chief executive officer, and an Alameda County supervisor and former mayor of Berkeley—this time the community had the clout and expertise to protect itself and to retake some of what had been lost.

Civic Engagement as Dialogue

While the collapse of the Cypress Freeway was a tragedy of significant proportions, it also presented an unprecedented opportunity. Out of the rubble of the structure that had physically divided the community since 1957 came a chance to influence not just where the freeway would be rebuilt, but how the public understood and redressed impacts of the original freeway. Taking advantage of the limelight, the people of West Oakland placed *history* at the center of their dialogues with transportation officials, the City of Oakland, and the world. Historical impacts of the Cypress Freeway provided a nexus for civic engagement over issues that ranged from relocating the transportation route to revitalizing the community. And historical archaeology played an important role in reclaiming the past and engaging the community in a meaningful dialogue.

A sea change in how public projects were planned and approved had, since the late 1960s, structured discussions between the local community and transportation officials. Passage of the Department of Transportation Act of 1966 initiated special consideration of parks, playgrounds, cultural resources, and other public assets. The National Historic Preservation Act of 1966 required that agency officials consider the effects of their actions on important cultural resources. Most importantly, the National Environmental Policy Act of 1969 mandated public involvement in decisions about federal projects. These and other laws sought to provide greater transparency and accountability in government. It was in that spirit that Caltrans actively sought input from local stakeholders as it planned the reconstruction of the vital transportation link between the heavily urbanized southern portion of Alameda County, the Oakland harbor , and San Francisco.

Community activists organized several groups, including CERT and Oakland Citizens Committee for Urban Renewal, to promote their agendas. They also sought strategic support from national organizations such as the Red Cross, the National Association for the Advancement of Colored People (NAACP), and the Sierra Club, as well as local city and county officials, churches, business organizations, including the West Oakland Commerce Association (WOCA), and others. United in its opposition to rebuilding the freeway along its original route, community action effectively coalesced around the theme of environmental justice. Activists agreed that moving the freeway out of the neighborhood was the most important step in redressing past injustices, although they did not always agree on the importance of other related issues.

Some groups, like CERT, WOCA, and the City of Oakland, sought economic revitalization for West Oakland. Just six months after the disaster a black women's lifestyle magazine noted those groups

> are pressuring civic leaders and charitable organizations to provide funds and build shops, parks and housing to revitalize the devastated area near the collapsed Cypress Freeway—and

it's paying off: The Red Cross will provide $52 million for the restoration. . . . Citing the pollution and isolation the Cypress Freeway brought, CERT is also lobbying to ensure that no new freeways are built in residential West Oakland. (Malveaux and White 1990:2)

While CERT focused on the negative consequences of the freeway on West Oakland's economic vitality, others emphasized the adverse health and environmental impacts as key reasons for moving the freeway. Residents claimed car exhaust fumes contributed to higher incidences of underweight babies, infant deaths, and acute and chronic diseases in West Oakland than elsewhere in Alameda County, a claim supported by health officials (California Department of Health Services 1993; Children's Hospital of Oakland 1994). Noise pollution was also cited as an issue. Residents and their allies argued convincingly that those negative health and economic effects were visited disproportionately on poor minority communities like West Oakland.

Faced with widespread community opposition and the resonance of the environmental justice issue, Caltrans shifted its focus to selecting a new freeway alignment that would meet the needs of the traveling public *and* the community of West Oakland. After two years of dialogue, Caltrans selected an alignment that largely circumvented residential areas of West Oakland. It included a ramp to service the Port of Oakland, lessening truck traffic through neighborhood streets. Some local groups like CERT and WOCA supported the proposal. But others felt it did not adequately address local concerns and brought suit for discrimination under Title VI of the Civil Rights Act of 1964 with the help of the Sierra Club and the NAACP (*Clean Air Alternative Coalition v. United States Department of Transportation*, Case No. C93–0721VRW in Fisher 1994). Eventually settled out of court, the case broadened the scope of the mitigation measures included in the 1993 Cypress Freeway Replacement Project Performance Agreement between Caltrans and the City of Oakland.

Measures taken to mitigate the adverse effects of the freeway reconstruction eventually included

- programs to employ and train local residents for work on the project,
- temporary relocation of residents, and compensation for those whose property was needed for the new alignment,
- noise and pollution abatement measures,
- toxic waste cleanup,
- transformation of the former freeway alignment into a landscaped boulevard,
- creation of a sculpture garden using recycled construction materials and native plants,
- construction of a memorial park, and
- an ambitious historical archaeology program that raised awareness and pride in the rich and diverse history of the community.

A key lesson that came out of the dialogue between the community and transportation officials was the need to engage a broad cross section of the community, rather than assuming certain groups represented the common interests of the neighborhood (Caltrans n.d.).

Cypress Freeway Replacement Project Cultural Resources Study

A construction project of huge proportions, the Cypress Freeway Replacement Project presented Caltrans with a mammoth challenge and an equally great opportunity: to replace the demolished Cypress structure without inadvertently destroying an irreplaceable source of West Oakland's history. And thus began the Cypress Project cultural resources study, spanning over thirteen years from the beginning of pre-field research in 1992 to the completion of a popular monograph in 2005. Directed by the Anthropological Studies Center (ASC) at Sonoma State University, this project was intensively collaborative, involving professionals in archaeology, history, museology, oral history, ethnomusicology, historical geography, and vernacular architecture. Neighborhood residents contributed their perspectives through oral history interviews, through opening their homes to architectural historians, and through sharing of their family pictures and memorabilia.

The study's goal was to link past with present by constructing and reconstructing how life was lived in historic West Oakland. The archaeological research design looked at how forces such as social class, ethnicity, and consumerism were expressed in the evidence from individual households and populations. The focus was not to be, for example, consumerism per se, but rather its effects on matters of everyday life from health to ethnic identity. In examining the history of Oakland, historian Robert Self points out that we cannot separate change, and the people who carried it out, from this location that was the focus of their lives. The civil rights and Black Power movements, he wrote, "did not call for rights in abstract terms and ill-defined places. They called for very specific things in relation to very specific places" (Self 2003:17).

Discoveries from Below Ground: Archaeology

Between 1994 and 1996, ASC archaeologists worked on twenty-two archaeologically sensitive city blocks that would be affected by construction. Of the nearly 2,600 archaeological features discovered, 121 were deemed legally important and were fully analyzed. These features contained more than 400,000 artifacts and ecofacts dating between the 1850s and around 1910. Focused historical research linked most features with families of known occupation and background; their origins included the United States, Ireland, Scotland, Germany, Italy, Canada, China, Prussia, and Portugal. The reports on this work were numerous and widely distributed; most were still available at the time of writing in print, on compact disc, or on the World Wide Web (http://www.sonoma.edu/asc/cypress/finalreport/index.htm; A. Praetzellis 2005; M. Praetzellis 1994, 2001; Praetzellis and Praetzellis 2004).

Of particular interest here are four collections of archaeological artifacts associated with West Oakland's pioneer black families. With members working as porters, barbers, and hairdressers, these families took leadership roles in the local African American community. The families' material goods, as reflected in the archaeological assemblages, have in common a sense of style and sophistication. Dining was formal, as represented in the tea and liquor services. Meals featured high-priced beef loin steaks and roasts, ham, and leg of mutton, as well as cheaper cuts representing soups and stews. Many personal items also found their way into the refuse, including elegant toiletry sets, jewelry, and other items of adornment, which speak to the refinement of the households. Unique teawares, dolls, figurines, and other memorabilia decorated their parlors. Seeds show that the porters grew Scarlet Pimpernels and geraniums in their gardens, and flowers graced the households in matching vases; a caged bird was well cared for and fed a mix including marijuana seeds to encourage it to sing.

Generalizing from these assemblages we venture to say that, in keeping with their relatively high social and economic status within the community, African American porter households replicated in their homes the Victorian formality and opulence found in the Pullman cars where they worked. Fresh flowers and knickknacks graced the parlors, and they ate a varied diet of fresh foods in formal, fashionable settings. The aesthetic of Pullman's cars influenced the taste of those who worked in this sumptuous environment, if not their social values. Purchasing goods above their ascribed status can be thought of as a form of resistance among African Americans at this time, since dressing well and furnishing one's home with genteel artifacts contradicted contemporary racist assumptions. It may be that the meaning of these artifacts lies not in their conventional connotations in white society but rather as symbols of civility and personal dignity, qualities for which these families were striving against the odds.

Discoveries from Above the Ground: Architecture, Oral History, Local History

To connect the archaeology with place, people, and present, Caltrans approved a program focusing on oral history, local history, and the built environment that coincided with the end of the fieldwork and the early stages of analysis. Karana Hattersley-Drayton conducted eighteen interviews with former West Oakland residents and transcribed seven earlier interviews held by the Oakland History Room. These interviews went beyond the groups and occupations represented in the archaeological assemblages to include the histories of the various ethnic groups residing in the neighborhood during what has been identified as the "Golden Age of West Oakland"—from 1911 through the 1920s. These interviews covered Italian, German, Greek, Chinese, Irish, Croatian, Portuguese, Mexican, Austrian, and Japanese immigrants, as well as native-born Oaklanders of various ethnicities and origins. Willie Collins conducted thirty interviews on occupational lore with African American porters, car cleaners, barbers, hairdressers, manicurists, railroad workers, musicians, dancers, and others who formerly lived and worked in West Oakland. Transcriptions of all interviews are on file at the Oakland History Room and at ASC.

Meanwhile, architectural historians Paul Groth and Marta Gutman and their team recorded the built environment of the project corridor and beyond. Beginning with detailed studies of three houses in the construction path, they moved into the wider neighborhood, recorded other residences, and developed a classificatory system for the plain wooden workers' houses found in West Oakland, as well as in industrial cities throughout North America. Groth and Gutman examined their properties through time, connecting changes in use and design of interior and exterior spaces with changing ownership and household composition. They examined how people used and revised the interiors, how their rooms connected, how they increased their space, how they used their yards. In according the same status to these residences as is generally reserved for high-style architecture, this study recognized the rationality of these houses and interpreted their meaning to those who lived there once and those who continue to do so. Moving beyond definitions of "blight," it is important to understand how such houses functioned and continue to function in urban North America.

Video footage played a part in the site recording system, with the added plus that it could also become part of an interpretive video. After Caltrans authorized the production of a video, footage also became part of the oral history program. The oral history video footage focused on two realms: women's history and the reenactment of work duties within Pullman sleeping and dining cars. Three women who grew up in the project area—of African American, Greek, and Chinese origin—talked separately about their family histories and then held a discussion on life in West Oakland: how people got along, class differences, local institutions, women's roles, and the importance to them of West Oakland. A walking tour followed and included other local residents and their dwellings.

The railroad retirees had been away from their work environment for many years when interviewed for the Cypress Project. The interviews afforded them a vital, cherished opportunity to recall anecdotes, bits of philosophy, and other work-related memories. Realizing that recreating the long-lost work environment would further stimulate the retirees' recollections, interviewer Willie Collins arranged for these men to be feted and interviewed amid the vintage railroad cars at the California State Railroad Museum in Sacramento. Using the museum's Canadian National Railway standard sleeping car "St. Hyacinthe," the former Pullman sleeping car porters demonstrated their role aboard the open-section sleeping car. On camera, they acted out the process of making down a berth from storage/day use to night use and vice versa, described typical working conditions faced by a typical porter while onboard the car, and talked about a porter's interactions with fellow Pullman and railroad employees and with the traveling public. They also were filmed on the museum's Atchison, Topeka and Santa Fe Railway streamlined dining car "Cochiti." The Railroad Museum provided a luncheon and awards ceremony followed the video filming.

Giving Back: Completing the Circle

The interviews, video, and architectural studies touched dozens of families; they dignified and recorded lives of labor that to many may have seemed mundane. But as long as the interviews and notes lay in files and on tape their impact was small. So in

1997, while the archaeologists were still in the midst of their analysis, *Sights and Sounds: Essays in Celebration of West Oakland* (Stewart and Praetzellis 1997) was born. Prior to *Sights and Sounds,* the study had created several thick technical volumes to guide research. This was the first report targeted at a general audience. Recognizing that the archaeological results were years off, Caltrans sponsored this interpretive report as an interim contribution to the neighborhood's history and culture. *Sights and Sounds* focused on six research topics that had aroused local interest and that were also relevant to the archaeological remains that drove the process: Pullman porters, oral histories of various ethnic groups, Sunshine Corner (a nineteenth-century social reform institution), lodging houses and hotels, occupational lore, and the built environment. *Sights and Sounds* was designed to fill the middle ground between the kind of technical reporting required by the historic preservation regulations that mandated the work in the first place and conventional public outreach products designed for the mythical "general" reader. The articles are substantive, yet written in an accessible style. For visual interest, almost every page has an illustration. Caltrans distributed hundreds of copies of *Sights and Sounds,* which has achieved "coffee-table book" status in Oakland. Families are very proud of the pictures of their relatives and homes, and of the status accorded by the printed words recording their family and neighborhood histories (figure 6.2).

Caltrans held a successful public screening of the project video, *Privy to the Past: Historical Archaeology of West Oakland, California,* in July 1999. Many of those interviewed for the project attended the large event and the catered lunch that followed. The short documentary provides an introduction to the field of historical archaeology—the study of the recent past using the familiar artifacts that people left behind. Caltrans distributed the video to the local community and further afield; it has become a favorite in introductory college archaeology courses.

The Cypress Project created four public exhibits, including *Barber Poles and Mugs: Black Barbering and Barbers in West Oakland* that greeted visitors to the Oakland History Room at the main library for two months in 1997. The most ambitious of the

Figure 6.2. Cover of Sights and Sounds: Essays in Celebration of West Oakland. The first interpretive report for the Cypress Project has achieved "coffee-table book" status in Oakland for its documentation of the city's rich historic and cultural heritage. Anthropological Studies Center, Sonoma State.

public exhibits was *Holding the Fort: African American Historical Archaeology and Labor History in West Oakland.* Cypress Project staff and Robert Hayes, then curator of the African American Museum and Library at Oakland (AAMLO), jointly conceived this display. It sought to combine archaeology and the black railroad labor movement, one of the most important themes in West Oakland history. As the archaeological excavations had uncovered many artifacts from Pullman porter households, this was a natural and effective combination. This traveling exhibit was installed at fourteen public venues from Oakland City Hall to the State Railroad Museum in Sacramento to the National Civil Rights Conference in Arizona. Cultural resource project personnel spoke at most of the exhibit openings.

Connectivity: Linking Past and Present

Rerouting the Cypress Freeway physically reconnected the neighborhood. The cultural resource study also reconnected the neighborhood to its past through artifacts, buildings, documents, and individual histories. These objects and forgotten histories would come to be woven into stories about the families who once lived there, highlighting the struggles, successes, and failures of these people; the study stands as a memorial of sorts to their lives. In some ways, the quest to resurrect the story of Morris "Dad" Moore exemplifies this process.

Dad was born somewhere in Virginia in 1854. A Pullman car porter, he moved to West Oakland in 1919 to take charge of the porters' quarters—two converted sleeping cars in the West Oakland rail yards. After he retired, Dad became a tireless worker for the Brotherhood of Sleeping Car Porters, the black porters' union, mentoring C. L. Dellums, who would come to be a national leader in black unionism. Although he was lauded by Brotherhood President A. Philip Randolph for his "splendid work, noble character, fine spirit, indomitable courage," Dad Moore's grave lay unmarked in an Oakland cemetery for sixty-five years until Cypress Project historian Will Spires (1997) relocated the plot. On August 25, 1995—the seventieth anniversary of the founding of the Brotherhood—a headstone was dedicated at Dad Moore's grave. Those present represented the Retired Railroad Men's Club, AAMLO, and one of Moore's descendants; standing with them were members of the Cypress Project who had come to know and respect this important figure through their research (figure 6.3).

Figure 6.3. Morris "Dad" Moore, September 1929. Dad Moore attended the first Brotherhood of Sleeping Car Porters convention, in Chicago, Illinois, and sat in a position of honor for the delegates' portrait. This drawing made from that portrait captures Moore's simplicity and strength. Drawing by Olaf Palm for the Anthropological Studies Center, Sonoma State.

In the Cypress studies we have tried to demonstrate a principle we call "connectivity." It means simply the connections between past and present as played out on a given geographically defined space. Historical archaeologists are in an excellent position to make these connections given their access to numerous sources, including stratigraphy, material culture, oral history, and archives. It is through these connections that the public can be given most ready access to and clear understanding of the uniqueness and complexity of their pasts and an empathic realization of the pasts of others. The 2004 Section 106 guidelines put out by the Advisory Council on Historic Preservation (36 CFR 800) would seem almost to require such connections be made in order to address "interested parties" and to realize the "public values" of our work. It is in the "small things forgotten" that our humanity lies and that is where the important questions can be asked and answered.

Cypress Archaeology as Civic Engagement and Social Justice

Archaeologists can participate in environmental justice reconciliations through civic engagement and making social justice a theme of their research. The Cypress Project made some contributions to both although, in retrospect, we could have done more. Through the research design, we required ourselves to involve local organizations in the project's development and its conduct, both to inform local people about what we were doing and to get their ideas about what issues we should be examining. We don't claim the Cypress Project as a community archaeological endeavor in the civic engagement sense. Caltrans' public relations professionals managed contacts with the news media and other official outreach efforts, which were considerable. To get local input into the project, ASC worked with AAMLO. Together with their curator (an historian), we identified a series of interconnected themes of place, labor, and ethnicity that ASC incorporated into our research, creating the outcomes described in this chapter.

While this aspect of the project was very successful, it did not achieve its full potential. For purely practical reasons, our relationships with official citywide and large-scale organizations were developed at the expense of contacts with truly local organizations such as neighborhood schools, neighborhood social organizations, and local elected officials. Keeping fieldwork ahead of construction on this emergency project was our highest priority and, in retrospect, overshadowed other important aspects of the cultural resources study. While we held some site tours, safety and insurance concerns mainly limited physical access to just ASC personnel. This problem may have been resolved by having advance input into the general contractor for construction's health and safety plan that determined who could set foot on the site. Next time we'll try harder.

The project's achievements in the realm of social justice are more impressive. The contextual presentation of West Oakland's history that resulted from these studies is inclusive and multivocal. It makes clear and explicit connections between the neighborhood's past and its present, creating a pathway toward restorative justice.

Caltrans' initial proposal to reconstruct the Cypress Freeway was met with rumblings of legal action by city officials and beyond. By the 1999 screening of *Privy to Past*, Caltrans' district director could (and did) say that the cultural resources component was the one aspect of this massive undertaking that West Oaklanders liked. In 2004 the city council issued a proclamation commending Caltrans and ASC for their "outstanding achievements in the preservation of West Oakland archaeology and the dissemination of its history."

References Cited

California Department of Health Services
1993   Alameda County Census Tracts 4018, 4019, 4020, 4021, 4022, 4025 combined. The Incidence of Invasive Cancer, Selected Anatomic Sites, 1987–1993. Sacramento.

California Department of Transportation (Caltrans)
  n.d.   Cypress Freeway Replacement Project. Part of a series of Environmental Justice Case Studies by the United States Department of Transportation, Federal Highway Administration. Electronic document, http://www.fhwa.dot.gov/environment/ejustice/case/case5.htm, accessed April 8, 2006.
Children's Hospital of Oakland
  1994   Discharges by Zip by Age Group (Asthma). Datis Database, Oakland.
Crouchett, Lawrence P., Lonnie G. Bunch III, and Martha Kendall Winnacker
  1989   *Visions Toward Tomorrow: The History of the East Bay Afro-American Community, 1852–1977.* Northern California Center for Afro-American History and Life, Oakland, California.
Fisher, Marièa R.
  1994   On the Road from Environmental Racism to Environmental Justice. *Villanova Environmental Law Journal* 5(2). Electronic document, http://www.ejrc.cau.edu/artonroadertoej.htm, accessed April 7, 2006.
Hausler, Donald
  1990   The Cypress Structure and the West Oakland Black Community. *From the Archives* 1:1. Newsletter of the Northern California Center for Afro-American History and Life, Oakland.
Heath, G. Louis (editor)
  1976   *Off the Pigs: The History and Literature of the Black Panther Party.* Scarecrow Press, Metuchen, New Jersey.
Hope, Dave
  1963   Post Office Site Now a "Dump." *Oakland Tribune,* 15 July:1,4. Oakland, California.
Malveaux, Julianne, and Evelyn C. White
  1990   Oakland: Symbol of the Struggle. *Essence* (May 1990). Electronic document, http://www.findarticles.com/p/articles/mi_m1264/is_n1_v21/ai_9005557, accessed April 7, 2006.
Newton, Huey P.
  1995   *To Die for the People: The Writings of Huey P. Newton.* Edited by Toni Morrison. Writers and Readers Publishing, New York. Originally published by Random House, New York, 1972.
Oakland Tribune
  1960   Tank Clears Path for Mail Center. 16 August:1. Oakland, California.

Praetzellis, Adrian
  2005   *Digging West Oakland: What Archaeologists Found Under the Cypress Freeway.* Prepared by Anthropological Studies Center, Sonoma State University, Rohnert Park, California. Prepared for Caltrans District 4, Oakland.

Praetzellis, Mary (editor)
  1994   *West Oakland: "A Place to Start From." Research Design and Treatment Plan, Cypress I-880 Replacement Project.* Prepared by Anthropological Studies Center, Sonoma State University, Rohnert Park, California. Prepared for Caltrans District 4, Oakland.

  2001   *Block Technical Report: Historical Archaeology, I-880 Cypress Freeway Replacement Project.* 7 vols. Prepared by Anthropological Studies Center, Sonoma State University, Rohnert Park, California. Prepared for Caltrans District 4, Oakland.

Praetzellis, Mary, and Adrian Praetzellis
  2004   *Putting the "There" There: Historical Archaeologies of West Oakland.* Prepared by Anthropological Studies Center, Sonoma State University, Rohnert Park, California. Prepared for Caltrans District 4, Oakland.

Rhomberg, Chris
  2004   *No There There: Race, Class, and Political Community in Oakland.* University of California Press, Berkeley.

San Francisco Chronicle
  1960   Summerfield at Mail Site: "Favor for West Oakland." 19 July:1. San Francisco, California.

Self, Robert O.
  2000   "To Plan Our Liberation": Black Power and the Politics of Place in Oakland, California, 1965–1977. *Journal of Urban History* 25(6):759–792.

  2003   *American Babylon: Race and the Struggle for Postwar Oakland.* Princeton University Press, Princeton and Oxford.

Solari, Elaine-Maryse
  2001   The Making of an Archaeological Site and the Unmaking of a Community in West Oakland, California. In *The Archaeology of Urban Landscapes: Explorations in Slumland,* edited by Alan Mayne and Tim Murray, pp. 22–39. Cambridge University Press, Cambridge.

Spires, William A.
  1994   West Oakland and the Brotherhood of Sleeping Car Porters. In *West Oakland "A Place to Start From": Research Design & Treat-*

ment Plan: Cypress I-880 Replacement Project, edited by Mary Praetzellis, pp. 205–220. Prepared by Anthropological Studies Center, Sonoma State University, Rohnert Park, California. Prepared for Caltrans District 4, Oakland.

1997   The Quest for "Dad" Moore: Theme, Place, and the Individual in Historical Archaeology. In *Sights and Sounds: Essays in Celebration of West Oakland,* edited by Suzanne Stewart and Mary Praetzellis, pp. 223–232. Prepared by Anthropological Studies Center, Sonoma State University, Rohnert Park, California. Prepared for Caltrans District 4, Oakland.

Stewart, Suzanne, and Mary Praetzellis (editors)

1997   *Sights and Sounds: Essays in Celebration of West Oakland.* Prepared by Anthropological Studies Center, Sonoma State University, Rohnert Park, California. Prepared for Caltrans District 4, Oakland.

Chapter 7

Voices from the Past: Changing the Culture of Historic House Museums with Archaeology

Lori C. Stahlgren and M. Jay Stottman

House Museums and Revealing the Silenced Past

Scholars have long understood that history is created by the powerful in the present (Wolf 1982). The production of historical narratives includes the uneven contributions by competing groups. These groups, those wielding power and those at the mercy of the powerful, have unequal access to the creation of history (Trouillot 1995:xix). This uneven contribution creates places where the traditional histories do not tell the entire story. The untold stories are effectively silenced by those with more power. These histories include those of African Americans, women, immigrants, the poor, children, those in ill health, and many others. The production of history, what is emphasized, what is deemed important, is created at the time of the event, the recording of the event, and probably most importantly, in the present. Silences enter the historical record at all these levels of historical production (Trouillot 1995:26). In reality, the moments where history is "made" and where silences enter the historical record occur seamlessly. The power to control the production of history is not necessarily a visible form of power, yet it is no less powerful than a political crusade, a riot, a strike. Quite possibly the most important mark of power is its invisibility and the challenge we face is its exposure (Trouillot 1995:xix).

The historic house museum is one place where history is created, mainly for public consumption. Traditionally, house museums tend to present a snapshot of the past—what was important to the place, when so-and-so slept here, the wealth of the first owner—in essence freezing history at one particular time and ignoring the dialectic of that time. When this past is presented to the public, it is often presented from one perspective, leaving little room for alternative interpretations. Invariably many voices from the past are omitted from these presentations of history. The lives of enslaved African Americans, women, the poor, immigrants, and others are often omitted or marginalized in favor of the histories of those more powerful.

House museums have long been creating and relating history for public consumption. The American house museum movement began with sites related to George Washington during the mid-nineteenth century. In 1850, the Hasbrouck House, which housed Washington's military headquarters in New York State, opened as a museum. By 1853, Ann Pamela Cunningham, the daughter of a South Carolina planter, began the effort to save Washington's plantation, Mount Vernon. Both of these ventures were developed against the backdrop of increasing tensions between the North and South. Both sites created a mission of fostering cultural pride in the Union (West 1999). Like house museums today, the first house museums were employing the past for use in the present.

Throughout the twentieth century house museums have continued to reflect current issues. After World War I, Henry Ford's Greenfield Village celebrated the common man and nostalgia for the utopian "good ole days" (Wallace 1996:12). John D. Rockefeller funded the restoration of Colonial Williamsburg, the recreated town of eighteenth-century Virginia planters. Mike Wallace argues that both Greenfield and Colonial Williamsburg presented visions of the past that had much more to do with their present than the actual past. Greenfield was a static interpretation of the western movement and early industrialization of the United States, focusing on presenting the pioneer virtues of hard work, discipline, and self-reliance. Ford celebrated the so-called common man, banning the elite and their influence and control of economics from being represented at Greenfield. Thus, Ford effectively silenced the economic depression, strikes and labor movements, and radical political parties that actually helped to form the Ford empire and life in early twentieth-century America. At Colonial Williamsburg, Rockefeller created an inaccurate picture of the past. Colonial Williamsburg was planned, orderly, and tidy with no visible signs of exploitation (Wallace 1996:15). In the recreated Williamsburg Rockefeller declined to show that more than half of the town's population were enslaved African Americans, effectively silencing the entire history of slavery (Wallace 1996:15).

While these museums have made great inroads toward including the portions of the past that were previously silenced, many house museums have been slower to include alternative visions of the past. Sherry Butcher-Younghans argues that interpretative programs at museum houses should begin with a mission statement created by the director, board of regents, or curator and that an accurate account of the history of a house or its residents is a necessity for sound interpretation (Butcher-Younghans 1993:186–191). While she provides sensible instructions for conducting historical research and even advocates the use of historical archaeology for finding outbuildings and to "fill [the] many gaps in the historical record" (Butcher-Younghans 1993:196), there are no recommendations that the interpreter delve any deeper than traditional histories. More recently, Patricia West has recognized the nuanced past of house museums by analyzing the politics and power behind the individual inceptions of Mount Vernon, Orchard House (the home of Louisa May Alcott), Monticello, and the Booker T. Washington birthplace (West 1999). West relates the inception of each house museum to the politics of the day, particularly the disintegration of the Union, women's suffrage, and the creation of popular and "official" histories (West 1999:xii). West argues that house museums are both products and the disseminators of histories, not politically aloof, neutral undertakings (see also Summar-Smith 2003).

Jennifer Donnelly believes a "primary goal of historic house interpretation should be creating experiences and telling stories within the context of the lives represented by the house and its collection and about things that mean something to visitors—things they care about and that bear some relation to their interests and lives" (Donnelly 2002:9). Even with this goal in mind, many house museums struggle to maintain relevance to their community. Spurred on by more available research and the progress of well-known historic sites like Williamsburg, Mount Vernon, and Monticello, the public now challenges such museums to portray the entirety of their history in context.

Changing House Museum Culture with Archaeology

Archaeologists have had a long and often contentious relationship with historic house museums and historic sites, dating back to the 1930s. The field of historical archaeology was born from the historian's need for archaeological methods, at a time when historical reconstructions were popular. When a building needed to be found or a fort discovered, archaeologists were called in to find it. Archaeologists were often at the mercy of traditional visions of the past and were rarely engaged in historical interpretation for the public, instead being relegated to being a "handmaiden" to history (Fish 1910; Harrington 1955; Noël Hume 1964). That debate has long since passed; historical archaeology is solidly part of the field of anthropology and research has become focused on those who have been silenced in traditional histories. However, this research has been slow to become integrated into historic house museum interpretations and presentations. While archaeologists have been successful at interpreting the culture of those who lived long ago, they have had a much more difficult time dealing with the culture within historic house museums today.

Although a more critical public is challenging traditional historic house museum interpretations and presentations, archaeologists and archaeological data have also taken them to task. The focus on topics such as slavery, ethnicity, gender, and socioeconomic status has led to the questioning of traditional historic house museum interpretations, forcing the reexamination of histories that have been silenced or sanitized. While new information generated from archaeology can be ignored or manipulated to fit traditional interpretations, the increased exposure of this information through public and educational archaeology programming at house museums and historic sites has led to the occasional clash of interpretative focus.

As archaeologists have become more self-reflexive through the proliferation of critical approaches in archaeology, they have begun to examine the role of the products and process of archaeology in shaping public perceptions of history (Leone et al. 1987; Pinsky and Wylie 1989; Potter 1994). The continued development of public and educational archaeology has exposed many archaeologists to the public and forced them to become more actively engaged with that public, as well as with historic house museums and historic sites (Derry and Malloy 2003; Little 2002; Shackel and Chambers 2004). Archaeologists now find themselves as partners in research, interpretation, fundraising, programming, and presentation rather than just collectors of information about specific questions. Some archaeologists have become more civically engaged, employing archaeology as a mechanism of change within the historic house museum context as well as a way for the community to become involved in investigating history. By giving those previously silenced in the past a voice and creating a forum for people to learn about and reinterpret the past, archaeologists can effect a kind of social justice, a revisionist history that includes and examines a multivocal world. This chapter presents two brief examples of how archaeologists have become civically engaged with historic house museums fostering just such social justice.

"Looahvull": Capturing Louisville's Identity

Just like pronouncing the city's name as the natives would say it, Louisville, Kentucky, is difficult to characterize. Not fully southern or northern, the city is home to large numbers of immigrants, has many racial and class issues, and is an industrial city in a primarily agricultural state. These characteristics shaped Louisville's history and its continued racial difficulties (Cummings and Price 1990). Located in Jefferson County, at the falls of the Ohio River, the only natural impediment in the river between Pittsburgh and New Orleans, Louisville is part of the Bluegrass Region. This region is well known for its agricultural production, bourbon, and racehorses; it was also the area of Kentucky that had the highest population of enslaved African Americans in the antebellum nineteenth century. By the late eighteenth century Louisville and Jefferson County were filled with thriving farms and plantations (Jones 1981; Neary 2000; Yater 1987).

The arrival of the steamboat in Louisville in 1810 and the construction of a canal around the Falls, which opened in 1830, as well as a large number of German and Irish immigrants, arriving in the 1840s, had a huge effect on Louisville's population and economy. The Portland Canal allowed unfettered steamboat travel around the falls of the Ohio, and by 1850 Louisville was the tenth largest city in the United States (Yater 1987:61). As Louisville was quickly becoming industrialized, the Civil War broke out and challenged the city's emerging identity. Although officially siding with the Union, Louisville had many southern sympathies, which led to its lack of strong support for either side and fostered contentious racial relationships that have underlain the city's identity to this day. As an industrialized city in a slave state, its official support of the Union allowed it to survive the war relatively unscathed, and it even profited handsomely from the conflict. Kentucky historiographies on the era produced in the mid-twentieth century promoted the idea that slavery there was of a much different and milder sort than that found in the Deep South (Clark 1929; Coleman 1940; McDougle 1918). While clearly propagandized and ideologically informed, this view permeated Kentucky history and presentations of slavery in Kentucky house museums.

After the war, Louisville settled into a seemingly comfortable situation as one of America's many medium-sized cities. While most Louisvillians will rarely fail to point out to nonnatives the history of famous people from Louisville, the famous horse races and baseball bats, or even the fact that chewing gum was invented there (Yater 1987), they generally fail to acknowledge the contentious racial and economic tensions that permeate Louisville's history and present.

Through archaeology, two historic museum houses in Louisville, Kentucky, have gone beyond the role of a traditional purveyor of history to one of social and community activism. Farmington, an antebellum hemp plantation, is using its own history of slavery to open up channels for discussion of racial inequities still experienced by Louisvillians. Riverside, the Farnsley-Moremen Landing, has developed a unique relationship with archaeology to not only tell the story of the past, but also engage the present in the discovery of the past to help repair a community's identity.

Farmington

In the early nineteenth century, Farmington was a sprawling, self-sufficient 554-acre hemp plantation owned by John and Lucy Speed. The property was owned by the Speeds until 1865 when the property was divided. The main house and some of the land around the nucleus of the plantation remained intact; this land was farmed until 1958 (figure 7.1). At that time, Farmington was purchased by the Historic Homes Foundation and opened to the public in 1959 as a historic house museum. Farmington was typical of historic house museums during the height of the historic house museum movement of the mid-twentieth century, focusing on the illustrious Speed family and their national connections. The Speeds were hugely influential in Louisville and Kentucky politics and even on the national political scene through connections to both Thomas Jefferson and Abraham Lincoln. It is through Lucy Speed that Farmington claims a connection with President Thomas Jefferson. Lucy's maternal grandfather, Dr. Thomas Walker, was one of Thomas Jefferson's guardians after the death of his father. It is believed that Farmington's main house is based loosely on one of Thomas Jefferson's architectural plans.

Figure 7.1. The main house at Farmington, built ca. 1815. Photograph by Lori Stahlgren.

The connection with Lincoln comes first from Joshua Speed. Joshua, the younger son, moved to Springfield, Illinois, to begin a mercantile business and befriended Abraham Lincoln. Lincoln visited Farmington for a number of weeks during the summer of 1841. During his visit, Lincoln also became acquainted with James Speed, older brother of Joshua. James, an attorney, eventually became part of Lincoln's cabinet in 1864 as attorney general.

At patriarch John Speed's death in 1840, an inventory recorded fifty-seven slaves, a rather large slave population for Kentucky. While there is no known written record of how the enslaved at Farmington felt about their lives, there are indications that many were unsatisfied with their position in life. One of the enslaved individuals, Bartlett, burned down the hemp factory and was sold down the river as punishment, while others attempted to flee to freedom in the North, as attested to by ads for their return posted by John Speed. The attitudes toward slavery among the Speed family were varied. All of the Speed children inherited slaves at their father's death in 1840. Some eventually freed their slaves, but others held them until 1865.

Archaeology and Race Relations at Farmington

Until recently, Farmington, like most small house museums, focused on the Speeds and their illustrious connections to interpret the museum's history. Little mention of the numerous slaves who actually performed the work on the plantation was ever made. Actual research into and interpretation of the lives of those slaves was virtually nonexistent, which indirectly served to perpetuate the belief in the "mildness" of Kentucky slavery. As with many historic sites and museums developed during the height of the historic house museum movement of the mid-twentieth century, Farmington has a long history of result-oriented archaeology. Although archaeological research was recognized as important to Farmington, the focus was on the results of archaeological investigation, generally the location of nineteenth-century buildings, and there was no involvement of the public in interpretation.

In 1997 and 1998 a University of Louisville archaeological field school discovered and excavated an undocumented outbuilding at Farmington. The foundation of the structure was made of dry-laid stone and measured sixteen by sixteen feet. Given the recovery of high amounts of ceramics and general items of daily living, such as faunal remains, buttons, wine bottles, and container glass, the building is thought to represent a dwelling rather than a locus of work on the plantation. The ceramics recovered generally date to the first half of the nineteenth century, placing the occupation of the building within the Speeds' tenure at Farmington. Artifacts that may be associated with enslaved African American contexts, such as a blue glass bead and a pierced coin with Xs scratched on it, were found at the site. Given the antebellum domestic function of the building and some possible association with African Americans, the archaeologists hypothesized that the structure most likely housed some of the fifty-seven enslaved African Americans who lived and worked at Farmington.

The excavations generated news coverage in local television and newspapers and sparked interest in slavery at Farmington and in Louisville generally. While the excavations were being conducted, a new exhibit, which included information about enslaved African Americans, was being installed within the visitors' center. This installation took place without the input from the site director or the archaeologists involved with the excavations. The exhibit was to illustrate, through pictures, text, documents, and some artifacts, the history of Farmington, providing a short synopsis of what one might hear about in greater detail during a tour. While many of the panels within the exhibit were benign, those dealing with slavery portrayed a kind of "magnolias and moonlight" picture of antebellum life in Kentucky, not something the archaeologists would have espoused. An example illustrates the general tone of the exhibit. Within the panel titled "African Americans and Farmington," one paragraph stated that "the slaves remained with the Speeds throughout their lives, with each family group experiencing the highs and lows of one another's lives and that by the time John Speed died neither family could imagine life without the other." The runaway ads placed by John Speed are just one example that the enslaved African American population could very well imagine life without the Speeds. The same panel went on to state, "Slavery for the Speeds must have been a paradox; it was an economic necessity that went against their fundamental beliefs," which is contradicted by the slave ownership by some Speed family members until passage of the Thirteenth Amendment to the U.S. Constitution in 1865 (Kentucky only ratified the amendment in 1979). Although the inclusion of a discussion of African Americans in the exhibit represented a departure from the focus on the white owners, the content of the exhibit reflected the typical Kentucky history of a mild and benevolent form of slavery, which served to continue to silence and distort the African American past at Farmington.

Because of the interest generated by the archaeological investigations, local African American leaders, historians, and the archaeologists critiqued the exhibit. At the same time, Farmington experienced significant leadership changes. The critiques and the leadership changes led to the editing of the exhibit, creating a more nuanced depiction of slave life at Farmington; the creation of an Interpretation Committee, which includes members of the local community, including African Americans and archaeologists; and a general refocus of interpretation on the entire plantation, including those enslaved.

The Farmington Interpretation Committee has been quite active in refocusing the way the museum is presented to the public. The Interpretation Committee successfully published a brochure about slavery at Farmington, created a walking tour of the grounds around the main house that focuses on slavery, and erected a memorial to the enslaved people who resided at Farmington (figure 7.2). The brochure discusses slavery in much more realistic terms than previously presented, giving specific information about those enslaved and what their lives at Farmington may have been like. In an effort to refocus interpretations on the economic production within the plantation, the committee has

Figure 7.2. The slave memorial located on the grounds of Farmington. Photograph by Lori Stahlgren.

developed a walking tour of the grounds. Because the enslaved at Farmington primarily lived and worked outside the main house, the grounds tour focuses on their lives rather than the Speeds'. While not directly involved with the production of the memorial to those enslaved at Farmington, the descendant community has participated through informal yet invaluable consultation. The memorial has become a place of pilgrimage for the descendant community, which has begun to hold family reunions on the museum grounds. All of these forms of communication have begun a dialogue with the local community, creating more interest in slavery and African American life at Farmington.

Farmington has fostered that dialogue through new programming and new projects. Members of the descendant community are currently participating in interpretations and informally researching the oral history of the plantation. It is hoped that more information on those enslaved at Farmington will be forthcoming as a result of their involvement. Another important reoccurring special event at Farmington is a fictional reenactment of an exchange between an enslaved woman, Dinah, and John Speed. The reenactment occurs at the end of a typical house tour and lasts only about five minutes. Within five minutes one gets just a taste of the frustration of the enslaved, the dehumanizing aspect of slave ownership, and the paternalistic view of slavery by whites. Immediately following this "play" the visitors are invited back to a meeting room to discuss their thoughts and feelings. Many times, these discussions are led by members of the descendant community. Also, Farmington continues to develop public archaeology programs to introduce the public to the process of archaeology and archaeological interpretation, continuing to focus on slavery at Farmington.

With this new perspective of historical research and public archaeology, Farmington is making inroads in recognizing and interpreting slavery in the past, in turn helping to deal with present racial tensions by providing a place for dialogue. It has begun to reconnect Farmington with its neighbors and with the African American community of descendants of those enslaved at Farmington. The picture of the past presented by any museum is powerful, and Farmington's presentation of an alternative to traditional histories, along with the involvement of the public, is helping to effect real change. While Louisville's racial rela-tions have been and are still an ongoing struggle, archaeology at Farmington has gone beyond simply interpreting those past relations and is working toward changing the present ones.

Riverside, the Farnsley-Moremen Landing

Riverside, the Farnsley-Moremen Landing, is a product of more recent philosophies of historical interpretation. Founded in 1992 as a historic house museum, Riverside was not the site of a fa-mous historical event or the home of a famous person, nor was it connected with anyone famous. It was a typical nineteenth-cen-tury plantation and farm that happens to be located in a forgot-ten and ignored area of present-day Louisville.

Riverside is a 300-acre site situated along the banks of the Ohio River. The centerpiece of the property is an 1830s Kentucky "I" house, known as the Farnsley-Moremen House. The house had seen much over the last 160 years, being the home to Gabriel Farnsley and the Alanason Moremen family (Linn and Neary 1998). It survived the great flood of 1937 and years of neglect, much like the southwest Louisville community around it. South-west Jefferson County (as it has been known since before the city-county merger in 2003) has always had the stigma of being rural, backwards, and working class. In contrast to the affluent eastern part of the county and the urban central part of the county, the people of Southwest Jefferson County have always felt ignored. By the 1980s, like the image and identity of Southwest Jefferson County, the Farnsley-Moremen house was in an awful state of disrepair and was on the verge of collapse. However, through the hard work of the local community and political interest from county leaders, the Farnsley-Moremen house was purchased by the county and restored. The house has become a symbol of re-birth and community pride in Southwest Jefferson County.

Community-Based Archaeology at Riverside

The reality of Riverside as a house museum was born from dedicated local residents and from politics. Seeing this project as a way to appeal to disenfranchised voters, county leaders made a commitment to purchase and develop Riverside as a museum. Through private donations, the house was restored and Southwest Jefferson County had its only historic house museum. Although developed in the 1990s at a time when scholars were critical of traditional interpretations of the past, Riverside was well on the way to becoming a museum formed around the traditional philosophies of historic site interpretation. This philosophy included the traditional role of archaeology as only a method to find buildings.

Because Riverside had no connection to the famous, its mission became the "restoration of a way of life" along the Ohio River during the nineteenth century (Linn and Neary 1998). One of the main goals of Riverside in accomplishing this mission was the location, reconstruction, and interpretation of former outbuildings (figure 7.3). Archaeology was seen as an important tool for locating these buildings. Through civically engaged archaeology, Riverside got more than just the location of an outbuilding; it got a unique community-based archaeology program and a relationship with archaeologists that became the

Figure 7.3. The detached kitchen under construction at Riverside, with students excavating the washhouse site. Photograph by Jay Stottman.

nucleus around which Riverside quickly became one of the most visited house museums in the region.

During the excavation of the detached kitchen, the first out-building to be researched at Riverside, a number of important factors came together to create a relationship that changed the traditional philosophies of historic house museum interpretation in Louisville (Stottman and Watts-Roy 1995). First, civically engaged archaeologists from the Kentucky Archaeological Survey conducted the excavations and stressed the potential of public and educational archaeology to benefit the historic site. Second, Riverside's site director and the director of the Jefferson County Office of Historic Preservation and Archives had previous experience with archaeology and understood its potential for the historic site. As a new museum, Riverside was free from the dogmatic cultural and historical baggage that accompanies much older museums. Finally, and luckily, Riverside's board of directors was open-minded. From this philosophy, a multidisciplinary field trip for schools that incorporated archaeology, architecture, and history, called the Building Blocks of History, was created. This program allows students to participate in a tour of the house, a brick-making activity, and an archaeological excavation. All of these activities were tied together as the process of discovering history. The idea was to not relegate archaeology to a behind-the-scenes method of research, but to make the process of research a focus and attraction for the museum. The purpose of the program was not just to have children come and see a bunch of old stuff, but to have them touch, feel, and discover history. In essence, the program did not want to just give a community its history; it encouraged the community to participate and discover that history for itself.

Over the last ten years the program has been a great success and exceeded all expectations. Nearly five thousand students participate in the program annually, and the philosophy and relationships developed from it have permeated all aspects of research, interpretation, and reconstruction at Riverside. The process of discovering history was emphasized not only during the archaeological excavations, but also during the architectural design and reconstruction of the detached kitchen. The philosophy of interpreting history as a public process has become the basis of this house museum, which in turn has provided many benefits to the site and the community (figure 7.4). The programs developed from this philosophy bring large numbers of people to the site, generate extensive press coverage of the site, and expose the general public to the real Southwest Jefferson County, not the stigmatized one.

While Riverside has been a symbol of the community since it opened, public archaeology and a philosophy that emphasizes the process of history helped give the people of Southwest Jefferson County ownership of the site. The community has a vested interest in the site through its participation in the discovery of its history. Schoolchildren come back on the weekends to share with their parents their experiences, most specifically the unit they helped to excavate. People return to Riverside periodically to check on the progress, and they tell their families and friends that they helped build the kitchen or that they found the kitchen. The archaeology projects at Riverside have had a positive influ-

Figure 7.4. The public participates in an excavation during a public archaeology event at Riverside. Photograph by Jay Stottman.

ence on the community around it—not because it has become a tourist attraction for outsiders, but because it is a part of the local identity. Riverside and the archaeology programs became a source of pride for the local community; Riverside is its front door. It is not only that it has a historic house museum like more elite communities; it is that it has a unique and dynamic museum. The archaeology projects at Riverside have drawn thousands of schoolchildren from all over the county who had never once been to Southwest Jefferson County. When they arrive, they see a thriving community, not the stigma. Thus, archaeology at Riverside helped establish a dialogue between residents and the museum that fostered participation in the discovery, interpretation, and creation of history. More importantly, the public programming at Riverside has helped create a dialogue between a disenfranchised Southwest Jefferson County community and the larger Metro Louisville community that has tended to ignore it.

Conclusion

Archaeologists have been calling for a practice that recognizes the potential of archaeology to effect change, however subtle. This entails involving the public in archaeological research, recognizing and giving voice to silenced pasts, and illuminating the inherent biases within our society. In his postscript to his work *Public Archaeology in Annapolis,* Parker Potter reflects on an editorial in the Annapolis newspaper titled "Historic Annapolis needs Direction from Annapolitians" (Potter 1994). Even though the editorial was bemoaning that fact that the majority of the members of the Historic Annapolis Board of Directors lived outside the city, it shows that local participation in the historical process is crucial for true success. Tilley (1998) argues for the use of archaeological knowledge as sociopolitical action in the present. He suggests elements for a program of action, calling for archaeologists to abandon objectivism as an impossibility; to continue employing a critical approach, involving the public and public institutions which deal with history, and illuminating multiple pasts (silenced histories);

and to foster an understanding of power and ideology (Tilley 1998:318–325). Likewise, Terrence Epperson argues for the recognition and illumination, through archaeological inquiry, of structural inequalities within and codified by our society (Epperson 2004:104).

Following these ideas, the Farmington and Riverside projects featured civically engaged archaeologists who employed archaeology in a different way to develop productive relationships with historic house museums, giving voice to the silenced past in order to help change the present. These archaeologists did not view archaeology just as a means to locate or interpret the past, but also as a process and a tool for communities to access and help control the production of their history. Civically engaged archaeologists can help change the culture within historic house museums by developing relationships with directors, boards, volunteers, and governments to develop a philosophy of historical interpretation and presentation that gives a voice to those silenced in the past and opportunity to those silenced in the present. Whether directly or indirectly, archaeologists working in the context of historic house museums have a role in the creation of dialogue between and among stakeholders in the past and present. Archaeologists can foster this dialogue through public and educational archaeology, participation on boards and committees, or serving as advisors to museum leadership. In essence, archaeologists can be participants in dialogues with stakeholders, but they also can help create the conditions and an environment that fosters dialogue, which can reveal hidden history and change communities. Whether it is helping a historic house museum come to grips with slavery and race or helping a community to redefine its image and identity, civically engaged archaeologists can have a role in the creation of social justice.

References Cited

Butcher Younghans, Sherry
   1993   *Historic House Museums: A Practical Handbook for Their Care, Preservation and Management.* Oxford University Press, New York.

Clark, Thomas D.
   1929   *The Trade between Kentucky and the Cotton Kingdom in Livestock,*
          Hemp and Slaves from 1840–1860. Unpublished Master's thesis,
          University of Kentucky, Lexington, Kentucky.
Coleman, J. Winston, Jr.
   1940   *Slavery Times in Kentucky.* The University of North Carolina
          Press, Chapel Hill, North Carolina.
Cummings, Scott, and Michael Price
   1990   *Race Relations in Louisville: Southern Racial Traditions and North-*
          ern Class Dynamics. The Kentucky Population Research Proj-
          ect, University of Louisville, Louisville, Kentucky.
Derry, Linda, and Maureen Malloy (editors)
   2003   *Archaeologists and Local Communities: Partners in Exploring the*
          Past. Society for American Archaeology, Washington, D.C.
Donnelly, Jennifer
   2002   Introduction. In *Interpreting Historic House Museums,* edited by Jes-
          sica F. Donnelly, 1–17. AltaMira Press, Walnut Creek, California.
Epperson, Terrence
   2004   Critical Race Theory and the Archaeology of the African Dias-
          pora, *Historical Archaeology* 38(1):101–108.
Fish, Carl Russell
   1910   "Relation of Archaeology and History," *Proceedings of the Wis-*
          consin State Historical Society 57:146–152.
Harrington, J. C.
   1955   Archaeology as an Auxiliary Science to American History,
          American Anthropologist 57(6):1121–1130.
Jones, Elizabeth
   1981   *Jefferson County: Survey of Historic Sites in Kentucky.* Jefferson
          County Office of Historic Preservation and Archives, and the
          Kentucky Heritage Division, Louisville, Kentucky.
Leone, Mark P., Parker Potter, and Paul A. Shackel
   1987   Toward a Critical Archaeology. *Current Anthropology* 28:283–302.
Linn, Patti, and Donna Neary
   1998   *Riverside, the Farnsely-Moremen Landing: The Restoration of a Way*
          of Life, Exploring the History of a Nineteenth-Century Farm on the
          Ohio River. Jefferson County Fiscal Court, Louisville, Kentucky.
Little, Barbara J. (editor)
   2002   *Public Benefits of Archaeology.* University Press of Florida,
          Gainesville, Florida.
McDougle, Ivan E.
   1918   *Slavery in Kentucky, 1792–1865.* Dissertation reprinted in *The*
          Journal of Negro History 3(3):1–125.

Neary, Donna M. (editor)
  2000   *Historic Jefferson County.* Jefferson County Fiscal Court, Louis-
         ville, Kentucky.
Noël Hume, Ivor
  1964   Archaeology: Handmaiden to History. *North Carolina Histori-
         cal Review* 41(2):214–225.
Pinsky, Valerie, and Alison Wylie
  1989   *Critical Traditions in Contemporary Archaeology: Essays in the
         Philosophy, History, and Socio-Politics of Archaeology.* University
         of New Mexico Press, Albuquerque, New Mexico.
Potter, Parker B.
  1994   *Public Archaeology in Annapolis.* Smithsonian Institution Press,
         Washington, D.C.
Shackel, Paul A., and Erve J. Chambers (editors)
  2004   *Places in Mind: Public Archaeology as Applied Archaeology.* Rout-
         ledge, New York.
Stottman, M. Jay, and Jeffrey L. Watts-Roy
  1995   Archaeological Research of the Riverside Detached Kitchen.
         Kentucky Archaeological Survey, Lexington, Kentucky.
Summar-Smith, Joy T.
  2003   *Interpretation of Slavery in Southern Historic House Museums.*
         Unpublished Master's thesis, Baylor University, Texas.
Tilley, Christopher
  1998   Archaeology as Socio-Political Action in the Present. In *Reader
         in Archaeological Theory: Post-Processual and Cognitive Ap-
         proaches,* edited by David S. Whitley, pp. 215–330. Routledge,
         New York.
Trouillot, Michel-Rolf
  1995   *Silencing the Past: Power and the Production of History.* Beacon
         Press, Boston.
Wallace, Mike
  1996   *Mickey Mouse History and Other Essays on American Memory.*
         Temple University Press, Philadelphia.
West, Patricia
  1999   *Domesticating History: The Political Origins of American's House
         Museums.* Smithsonian Institution Press, Washington, D.C..
Wolf, Eric
  1982   *Europe and the People Without History.* University of California
         Press, Berkeley, California.
Yater, George
  1987   *Two Hundred Years at the Falls of the Ohio: A History of Louisville and
         Jefferson County.* The Filson Club Historical Society, Louisville, KY.

Chapter 8

Archaeology—the "Missing Link" to Civic Engagement? An Introspective Look at the Tools of Reinvention and Reengagement in Lancaster, Pennsylvania

Kelly M. Britt

From the beginning of the twentieth century to the present, many political and social scientists, urbanists, and economists have discussed the inherent meaning and use of social capital, tying the rise of social productivity to the increase of social capital (Putnam 2000:19). With Robert Putnam's (2000) publication *Bowling Alone: The Collapse and Revival of American Community*, attention shifted from the rise of social capital, seen as the willingness of citizens to perform acts of engagement in the United States, to its relatively recent demise, seen as brought about by changing lifestyles. Suburban living, more women in the work force, faster forms of transportation, advanced technology, and the growing sense of individualism are cited as the main reasons for the declining participation of citizens in civic organizations (Putnam 2000). Putnam argues that (1) with a decrease of civic engagement social capital weakens, and (2) social capital is needed to maintain all aspects of society from individual health and happiness to the economy and democracy (Putnam 2000:28). Some critiques of Putnam's suggestions (i.e., Armony 2004; Rich 1999) propose he mistook change for decline (Rich 1999), while recent studies have shifted focus from large national organizations to small-scale local voluntary ones (Rich 1999).

This shift in focus reflects the recent community-building and civic-minded initiatives that extend into local spheres through new approaches of engagement such as heritage tourism. Tourism has become one of the fastest-growing industries in the world, with heritage tourism as one of its most popular forms (see Ford 2003; McKercher and duCros 2002; World Tourism Organization 2003). Heritage is a mode of cultural production in the present that relies on the past for authentication (Kirshenblatt-Gimblett 1998, 149). Historical validation provides a use value and an intrinsic value, both being consumed while one experiences a heritage tourist destination (McKercher and duCros 2002). This validation is essential as visitors and residents search for a sense of place, while these destinations produce the locality needed to provide the sense of belonging for which people are searching (Hobsbawm 1983), and which residents and visitors experience through heritage narratives. Historical sites, museums, and archaeological sites may be the new town halls of the community, providing a physical environment for voicing concerns and desires about a sense of place. The production of heritage sites, at times, relies on volunteers and civic-minded citizens creating a direct link between heritage and social capital. However, the audience or visitors, many of whom are citizens themselves, also become involved in the creation of social capital as patrons of the site, creating a link not only between past and present (at a historic site) but also between producer and consumer and building social capital among all participants. This process creates the community as stakeholder, and with such a large and diverse group, contestation over heritage narratives is inevitable. The current popularity of heritage tourism, and its use in an urban culturalization project, affects the local community politically, economically, and socially. These influences can either foster or discourage civic engagement within the community. With the rise of the use of archaeological sites in heritage tourism projects, archaeologists now find themselves in the role of heritage tourism professionals. This new role can require archaeologists not to rely as much on the traditional academic training they have received but to decipher political and economic demands for which many have no formal training. As historical sites provide the backdrop and context for discussions, what roles do the archaeologist or heritage professional play in these discussions? In addition, what are the reasons that a heritage outreach project could succeed or fail? (Britt and Chen 2005a; Britt and Chen 2005b).

Lancaster, Pennsylvania, is an ideal setting in which to discuss the use of heritage, historical sites, and archaeology in civic action. From smart growth programs, cultural heritage planning initiatives, and community action groups such as the newly formed Civic Action Network for the Built Environment (CANBE) to the salvage archaeological excavations and outreach project for the Thaddeus Stevens and Lydia Hamilton Smith Historical Site, heritage and historical sites illustrate how heritage can be used as a tool to reengage the public with other civic organizations to promote democratic values and social justice. However, enforcement of preservation ordinances in Lancaster has been or continues to be oligarchic in nature, which constricts dialogue between groups and takes the democratic aspect out of the process. This paper will look at why heritage and archaeology are being used as tools of civic engagement in Lancaster, Pennsylvania, and what my role as an archaeologist was in this endeavor, with the Thaddeus Stevens and Lydia Hamilton Smith Historic Site as a case study to explore past and present approaches to civic engagement in Lancaster. It also seeks to assess whether these methods work adequately to connect the public with significant social issues and promote the democratic process or whether inherent conflicts constrict the process. Does archaeology used as a tool of engagement change the nature of the current top-down structures of many active civic organizations? If not, what needs to be done for change to occur?

Where Does an Archaeologist Fit In?

Archaeologists are increasingly being called on to act as mediators for heritage projects, especially within urban revitalization projects where historical sites act as catalysts to stimulate the economy and establish a renewed sense of civic pride (see Little 2002; Shackel 2004; Shackel and Chambers 2004). Yet there are few models or strategies available for use by archaeologists in this new role as heritage mediators. While archaeology conducted at historical sites provides several avenues of civic engagement through service learning projects, lectures, volunteer opportunities, and archaeological outreach programs, there is no specific role for the archaeologist in these endeavors. However, a case-by-case approach for the role of archaeology and the archaeologist should be advocated in order to investigate and define this role. Rather than archaeology adhering to a specific theory and putting it into practice, the practice itself will give rise to innovative theory (Britt and Chen 2005c). The Thaddeus Stevens and Lydia Hamilton Smith Historic Site case study will explore past and present civic organizations that have focused on heritage, historic sites, and archaeology. In addition, the case study will assess an archaeologist's specific techniques for public outreach to determine which methods worked and which ones fell short, and to suggest possible new methods for future use.

Case Study: The Thaddeus Stevens and Lydia Hamilton Smith Historical Site

Lancaster City is located in the center of Lancaster County in the southeastern section of Pennsylvania, eighty miles west of Philadelphia. By the mid-twentieth century, Lancaster had developed a thriving industrial and retail economy. After the city's social and economic peak in the 1950s, the city went through deindustrialization and "white flight" to the suburbs, changing the economic and social structure of the city (Schuyler 2002). Several urban renewal programs in the 1960s and '70s attempted to mitigate these consequences but only further increased blight and continued segregation (Schuyler 2002).

In the late 1990s, a new urban revitalization project was introduced—the transformation of the landmark Watt and Shand department store building into a hotel and convention center (figure 8.1). The hope of this new project was to capitalize on the already successful agricultural and Amish tourism market that exists within the county, and reinvent the city through its historical sites as a new tourist destination. The construction of the ho-

Figure 8.1. Watt and Shand Department Store. Photograph by Kelly M. Britt.

tel and convention center provided an unexpected opportunity for archaeology to enter into the revitalization process. Because a portion of the proposed convention center is located on a site that had historical easements held by the local historical preservation group, the Historical Preservation Trust of Lancaster County, the homes and offices of the nineteenth-century Radical Republican Thaddeus Stevens and his housekeeper Lydia Hamilton Smith, both known for their antislavery viewpoints, would be researched (figures 8.2 and 8.3) (Delle and Levine 2004; Levine et al. 2005).

City-Sponsored Civic Organizations in Lancaster

Despite the fact that the Stevens and Smith Historic Site is situated within a historic district that is listed in the National Register of Historic Places as well as within the local Heritage Conservation District, the site review process for this site was not required. As a result, I was led to research the review process for clarifica-

Figure 8.2. Thaddeus Stevens House and the Kleiss Saloon. Photograph by Kelly M. Britt.

Figure 8.3. Lydia Hamilton Smith Houses. Photograph by Kelly M. Britt.

tion. I conducted formal and informal interviews with community members, and discovered that the politics surrounding the present state of historic preservation has deep roots in the past. These interviews and ethnographic research provided information needed to better understand the past, present, and future aspects of this project. A brief discussion of the history of historic preservation ordinances and laws in Lancaster will help to clarify the current issues that affect the Stevens and Smith Historic Site.

Ordinances and organizations have been in place in Lancaster since the early twentieth century, intended to provide an organized and objective review of the city's planning process. One of the purposes of the first Comprehensive City Plan of Lancaster, produced in 1929 by John Nolen, the city planning consultant, was to protect and preserve the built environment while creating modern developments that had the same high standards of the past, embodying the "Spirit of Lancaster" (Stallings 2005). However, it took almost forty years, until 1967 (a year after the passage of the National Historic Preservation Act), for Lancaster's city council to respond to a local citizen advocacy group for the preservation of architecture and pass an ordinance creating the first historic district in the city. With this ordinance in place, proposed alterations to the built environment or streetscape would be reviewed by a Historical Architectural Review Board (HARB) before being allowed to proceed. Currently nine hundred properties are located in areas within the city that are protected under HARB, but the Stevens and Smith buildings are not (Stallings 2005). Instead, the site is located within the Historic Conservation District or the Historic Overlay District, which was implemented through the Municipalities Planning Code (MPC) Act of 1968, P.L. 805, No 247. This code enables municipalities to delineate areas where they may regulate, restrict, or prohibit the alteration, removal, or construction of structures (Wilson 2005). These regulations are administered by a city-appointed zoning officer of the Department of Housing and Neighborhood Development, whose decisions are informed by an appointed Historical Commission made up of city residents and the city-appointed historic preservation specialist (Bennett-Gaieski 2004).

The Historical Commission is composed of citizens of the city with appropriate interests and skills for the preservation tasks at hand. Its mission is to provide guidance and expertise for the zoning officer and to help guide historic preservation decisions within the city. This is where the disjuncture in the process occurs. Discussions with informants indicate that there are two main obstacles prohibiting a democratic process of review from taking place. Projects should be guided through the historical preservation review process by the municipality, with the appointed Historical Commission reviewing projects first to offer advice *before* a decision is made by the municipality regarding the preservation of the site. However, all projects appear to be reviewed by the municipality first. Only *after* review and preliminary determinations are made by the municipality are the projects then brought to the Historical Commission for review, and then only at the discretion of the municipality. In short, projects reaching the Historical Commission have already been reviewed and decisions have made about them by the municipality. Thus, the Historical Commission, unlike the HARB, holds no overarching power over the municipality's decisions, making open discussion and disagreement with the municipality almost impossible. In addition, I have also been informed that a city employee must serve on the Historical Commission, negating or severely limiting an open flow and civic engagement of thoughts and ideas. Such a situation creates a "Big Brother" approach to conducting community discussions. This is what appeared to have happened with the Stevens and Smith Historic Site.

The Convention Center project received federal funds for planning, not for demolition, which both the state and local municipalities asserted did not require a Section 106 review. The municipalities claimed that because the federal funding was not used for demolition purposes, a Section 106 review was not needed. In addition, the municipality of Lancaster City does not have its own local review process in place akin to a Section 106 review (Lancaster City has a Historical Commission that is supposed to provide guidance, and the HARB reviews projects as stated above; neither is equal to a Section 106 review). However, representatives of the PHMC did tour the site and were of the opinion that no demolition should occur anywhere on the site. The oversight of the Stevens and Smith Historic Site during the review process is one illustration of a problem in many city-sponsored civic organizations—that is, a top-down, politically influenced approach to civic-based groups.

The proposed convention center and hotel is a joint public/private venture, with the public portion comprising the Lancaster County Convention Center Authority, another community-based city-sponsored group, while the private portion is composed of several key community investors (Penn Square General Corp, a High Associates affiliate, Fulton Bank, and Lancaster Newspapers), or as one informant called them, the "Bishops of Lancaster." This public/private sponsorship may be the key as to why this project "fell through the cracks." The political pressure to quickly pass the project through the municipal historical review phase may have hindered an objective review of the project. Furthermore, there had been no archaeological project in Lancaster City prior to the Stevens and Smith excavations to use as a model upon which to base the review process, creating a difficult situation for the decision-making groups.

Since no mitigation work was performed nor planned for this site, the threat of destruction of the Stevens and Smith structures was imminent. Thankfully, a local nonprofit preservation group, the Historical Preservation Trust of Lancaster County, hereafter called the Trust, decided to try to save the houses. The Trust had previously acquired a historic preservation easement on the property through a donation, which prevented the buildings from losing their architectural integrity. This only bought the properties time, but in hindsight, some very valuable time. The Trust contacted James Delle of Kutztown University, who solicited the participation of Mary Ann Levine of Franklin and Marshall College to conduct a small salvage excavation project behind the Stevens and Smith structures in the hopes of unearthing some small pieces of the past that could be put on display in the future. Students from Franklin and Marshall College, Kutztown University, the University of Pennsylvania, and Columbia University, along with other volunteers, conducted salvage archaeological excavations that began in the fall of 2002.

Numerous artifacts and several features from various time periods in Lancaster's urban history were uncovered. In particular, a modified cistern with possible implications of Underground Railroad activity was discovered (Delle and Levine 2004). This modified cistern suggests that the noted antislavery proponents Stevens and Smith were not just speaking against slavery but also acting against it by possibly participating in the Underground Railroad. The cistern appears to have been modified in the 1850s when it was no longer in use so that an individual could enter the cistern through an opening in the wall in the basement of the adjacent Kleiss Saloon (Delle 2002a; Delle 2002b; Delle and Levine 2004). Thanks to this find and its possible implications, and the efforts of many persistent preservationists, the Lancaster County Convention Center Authority allowed excavations to continue through July 2003.

Findings—Tying Past to Present

Stevens was known as the "Great Leveler" and this attribute can be seen in many of his accomplishments throughout his career. Of most note, Stevens has been credited with saving public education in the state of Pennsylvania, and his antislavery stance led to his role in the drafting of the Thirteenth and Fourteenth Amendments, outlawing slavery and granting due process to persons born or naturalized in the United States (Trefousse 1997; Woodley 1934).

Lydia Hamilton Smith, although not as well known as Stevens, was an important figure in nineteenth-century Lancaster. Born in Gettysburg, Pennsylvania, to a mother of African descent and a father of Irish background, she moved to Lancaster with her two sons to attend to Stevens's household affairs. She was a prominent businessperson in her own right and owned properties in Lancaster and Washington, D.C. Although the exact nature of the relationship between Stevens and Smith is unclear, it was obvious he held her in high respect, by commissioning a portrait of her by a leading artist of the day and leaving her five thousand dollars in his will at the time of his death.

The project planners of the hotel and convention center saw

the economic and social benefits of historical and archaeological inquiry for the creation of a tourist destination with a sense of place for both residents and tourists and sought to incorporate the Stevens and Smith narrative into the revitalization project. As a result, the historical houses will be partially restored and the Thaddeus Stevens and Lydia Hamilton Smith Historic Site Museum will be created. Artifacts that were recovered will be interpreted and displayed in the proposed Thaddeus Stevens and Lydia Hamilton Smith Historical Site Museum. This museum and educational center dedicated to Stevens and Smith, the Underground Railroad, and the themes of equality, justice, and freedom will be created in the original portions of all four of the Stevens and Smith buildings that will be preserved as part of the new Hotel and Convention Center complex (for a more detailed overview of the Stevens and Smith excavations and findings, see Delle and Levine 2004). However, the community contention over historical narratives and funding for the revitalization project and its resulting impact on the creation of the site and community identity were not foreseen.

Community Contentions

Media attention on Stevens and Smith and the history of the Underground Railroad in Lancaster County have prompted interesting debates and discussions within the community over the hotel and convention center issues, Thaddeus Stevens, Underground Railroad activity, slavery, and racism. One issue raised during the excavations and development of the museum project was the use of the Underground Railroad narrative. The historic Bethel AME church in Lancaster, located south of the proposed Hotel and Convention Center, has since 1998 incorporated the Underground Railroad narrative into its reenactment titled *Living the Experience*, an audience-inclusive theatrical interpretation of slavery and the Underground Railroad. At the same time that discussions regarding the Stevens and Smith Historic Site Museum were first being held, the church had applied for city and state funds to redevelop the historic neighborhood. This led to competition over funds (tourist revenue) and a debate over who should tell the interpretation of the Underground Railroad narrative. Discussion ensued and was seen in letters to the editor in the local newspapers (the *Intelligencer Journal,* the *Lancaster New Era,* and the *Lancaster Sunday News*) and discussion at public meetings such as Lancaster City Council meetings, as well as correspondence to the Trust. Although this contention is no longer in the public eye, what still remains is how to reconcile the participation of the disparate stakeholders in the interpretation of this archaeological site.

Further discussions and debates over slavery, abolitionism, and their effects on the present have also started to play out in the print media. The *Lancaster Sunday News* in August 2005 featured two front-page articles and one smaller article on slavery and abolition in Lancaster and "the wounds that remain open" (Huynh 2005; Huynh and Schwartz 2005; Schwartz 2005). Also published was a full list of Lancaster County slaveholders according to the 1800 census, including slaveholders' names and the names of the enslaved (when information was available). One article discussed the socioeconomics of slaveholding and the gradual abolishment of slavery in Pennsylvania. The name of one local slaveholder family and its relations were also provided, seemingly to build upon the past by linking slavery to this specific family and tapping into the effects of slavery on contemporary society. Also highlighted was an ordinance that was recently passed in Philadelphia in February of 2004, independent of the circumstances in Lancaster, "requiring that any company doing business in or with the city search its records and publicly disclose any ties to slavery" (Huynh and Schwartz 2005). This ordinance required Wachovia Bank to disclose its acquisition of two companies that directly profited from slavery and issue a public apology, which has produced mixed responses from the public and raised questions regarding the politics of power and the power of politics at hand at both local and national levels. While this ordinance affects the city of Philadelphia, and not Lancaster City, it serves as an example of how retribution for past actions is playing out presently in the state of Pennsylvania.

While many community members express themselves in the print media and are vocal in public meetings, there are only a few who are active in voicing their opinions and ideas to the community as a whole and actually participate in community organizations such as the Lancaster Peace Coalition, CANBE, the Shriners, and so on, to change the situation at hand. Others remain private with their thoughts and actions. Given the anticipation of civic engagement by myself and based on responses by the public, the behavior I encountered might be described as a form of community "apathy." I first noticed this indifference toward engagement during excavations at the Stevens and Smith Site in the spring of 2003, when residents would walk by the site and inquire about the project. Many residents seemed interested and excited, and said they would come back to inquire about the site. However, very few of the interested residents actually came back to the site to inquire further (note: active participants and volunteers were recorded in the fall of 2002 prior to my work on the site and various inquiries about the site have been made directly to Delle and Levine, but not to myself).

This "apathy" was also seen with a separate project sponsored by the Community Media Lab of Lancaster at Franklin and Marshall College. The project went door to door within the Churchtowne neighborhood giving free passes to the next day's performance of *Living the Experience,* the Underground Railroad interpretation at Bethel AME Church. While many people who were given these passes expressed excitement and desire to attend the performance, which was not related to a religious service, no one given the free passes actually participated. This indifference in civic organizations seems to be a growing phenomenon within the city, as seen in a recent newspaper article in the August 27, 2006, *Lancaster Sunday News* (Eby 2006). This article states that the national trend in the decrease of community membership in local civic organizations can also be seen in Lancaster in organizations such as the Pioneers, League of Women Voters, and so on. Although there is no specific explanation of this lack of civic involvement in community affairs, one possible explanation can be traced back to the location of the leading organizations of these two projects—The Stevens and Smith Site, and the media center project—both of which do not have direct ties to the communities they are trying to mobilize. This can be explained further to state that these two organizations, the Media Lab of Lancaster and the Trust, both have various projects in various communities throughout the area and cannot physically be located in all the communities they wish to mobilize. In addition, my outreach efforts were limited to the locality of my home, which could not be located in all the communitites I wished to be involved with.

Postexcavation Initiatives

After the excavations took place and archaeology was no longer in the public view, an outreach component was established to bring the archaeological findings from the site to the local community. A service-learning project in Mary Ann Levine's classes at Franklin and Marshall College visited neighboring schools, and I set up an outreach program that serviced the rest of the city and county with assistance from the Trust and a Woodrow Wilson Practicum Grant given in 2003 (Levine et al. 2005). As many papers presented at the 2003 ICOMOS conference in Annapolis, Maryland, showed, projects with a public outreach component for school-aged children are an important step in creating a working relationship with the community. Children tend to discuss the information from the outreach projects with their families at home, and in turn the family may be more motivated to participate in the project on a community level.

Since the project has an Underground Railroad component, it was anticipated that it would be more appealing to the local African American community, with hopes that it would want to be more involved in the process of creating this heritage tourist destination and revitalization project. My immediate goal for the outreach portion I was developing was to bring a discussion to students on local heritage that would extend beyond the classrooms into homes, with hopes of reaching the greater community whose voice has not always been present in previous urban renewal projects in Lancaster. The ultimate goal was to diversify the input regarding the project and raise historical and contemporary issues of race and class by discussing the archaeology of the Stevens and Smith Historic Site with school-aged children of the county.

The modified cistern and Underground Railroad component to this historic site provided the catalyst for public outreach. Information about Stevens and Smith as well as nineteenth-century Lancaster was illustrated through the built environment, material culture, and historical documents, providing wonderful tools to conduct outreach workshops. Outreach efforts by the Trust such as sponsored talks and lectures and articles in the local papers to reach the general public prior and during the excavations were fruitful. My goal was to continue these outreach efforts by concentrating on school-aged children. The intended audiences were students and teachers from public and private schools in grades K–12 throughout Lancaster County. Since Pennsylvania history is taught in grade four, a more intensive concentration was placed on conducting outreach workshops for this grade to highlight the local subject matter of Thaddeus Stevens, the Civil War, and the Underground Railroad within the Pennsylvania History curriculum. Bringing information about Thaddeus Stevens, Lydia Hamilton Smith, and the Underground Railroad to the community provided a supplement to educational curriculums and the stimulus for future discussions surrounding current local issues about racism, revitalization, and preservation. With an awareness of some of the previous problems encountered, the intent was not to have a top-down approach to the outreach workshops, but rather to provide a base of information so that a dialogue about Lancaster's past and its future could take place.

From 2003 to 2005, local students from the fourth and fifth grades from two private schools and two public schools attended in-class presentations and workshops held at the laboratory at Franklin and Marshall College. Most classes had fifteen to twenty-five students, and were held either as a supplement to the Pennsylvania history section of the curriculum taught in fourth grade or as part of a Pennsylvania Pride Day celebrating Pennsylvania's history. In addition, local teacher workshops were held on the Underground Railroad through an NEH grant from Millersville University's Teaching and New Media Program, and an online KEEP Toolkit was produced on the Stevens and Smith Site and its outreach efforts. Both student and teacher workshops provided opportunities to discuss pertinent issues of inequality in both past and present contexts.

Despite letters being sent to all public and private schools within the community about my outreach project, only four schools, two of which were private, responded to my outreach efforts. However small the number of respondents, all gave positive feedback and one asked for a return visit the following year, which was a great response considering the outreach project was not directly affiliated with an academic learning institution, but rather with a nonprofit preservation organization that is not widely known and not located in the schools' neighborhoods. In addition was the fact I asked for a small fee ($0–$25.00 per class or hour) to cover transportation and all classroom supplies, such as worksheets, crayons, and modern ceramics, that I used in the mending stations that I set up.

Impacts from Engagement

The archaeological project and its findings, and the media coverage of them, have prompted many discussions in the community. Some general topics include slavery, the Underground Railroad, abolitionism, and racial inequality, as well as more local aspects of these topics. It has also prompted a newfound interest in Thaddeus Stevens himself, with a *Lancaster Sunday News* Perspective column on August 14, 2005, titled "Rediscovering Thaddeus Stevens," dedicated to this recent rediscovery and the importance of Stevens's legacy in the civil rights movement (Butcher 2005). This resurgence of dialogue surrounding issues of democracy and social justice can only grow larger with the proposed Thaddeus Stevens and Lydia Hamilton Smith Historic Site Museum, providing another town hall for community interaction and environment for outreach initiatives.

While it is too early to gauge the long-term effects of the outreach program on the community and whether my personal objectives of the project will meet its goals, I feel there have been both successes and areas where improvement is needed. The feedback received thus far has been positive and has forged the beginnings of working relationships. Although this outreach program is separate from Franklin and Marshall College's student service learning program, both have had a very positive feedback in the college and community. Mary Ann Levine's program at Franklin and Marshall targets schools within its proximity, reaches many classes and students, and involves a large group of the college community members. Service learning also plants seeds of civic engagement in the minds of young adults, enabling a new, younger group to participate in community action. My outreach program, while larger in scope (available to all countywide schools), did not reach as many classrooms as Levine's service learning program. However, both the public outreach program with which I have been involved and Mary Ann Levine's service learning project have provided a base on which to build community relationships. These relationships may develop over time with the construction of the proposed museum and educational center and create a "town hall" for the community. At present the museum has proposed to incorporate classes and school group tours of its collections, making the current outreach workshops an important first step to these educational programs. Insights gained and relationships forged from the current outreach workshops will aid future working relationships with educators and community leaders once the museum and educational center is built.

Although the response from the outreach programs was positive, my idealistic desire to help transform a community through widespread participation was shattered. Where I feel the most work needs to occur is difficult to address. Mobilization of communities is a long and hard process, and patience and determination are key to success. It is necessary to be an active member within the community and be associated with a community organization or create a community organization entrenched in the neighborhood you wish to mobilize. As my research has begun to show, Lancaster has a dynamic insider/outsider mentality to its community and in turn, to its community action networks. Although I moved to the city of Lancaster, and became active in community meetings and organizations, I was seen as an outsider and not as a "cultural investor," someone who is putting money into the city as a place to live. In addition, I was not entrenched through an organization in the community in which I wanted to work, the African American community. Similar responses in participation in outsider projects affecting the African American community can be seen in Lancaster. Franklin and Marshall's Media Lab project for the Bethel AME interactive theater had similar results. Neither project has local ties (whether ethnically, economically, or physically) in the neighborhoods in which they were working, and therefore their projects had little to no participation response. The organizations that are successful recruiting residents as participants, such as *Dig IT*, a community garden program, are located in the heart of the community they are mobilizing.

Support for this analysis can be seen in Kent Portney and Jeffrey Berry's chapter, "Mobilizing Minority Communities," in their edited book *Beyond Tocqueville: Civil Society and the Social Capital Debate in Comparative Perspective* (2001). The authors discuss the issue of outreach to minority communities through research in five U.S. cities with active citizen participation systems. Their research showed that local neighborhood associations deeply imbedded in the community were more effective with their outreach efforts, especially in predominately black neighborhoods (2001:77). In this case study, there was difficulty in affiliating the outreach program with neighborhood groups or schools since the outreach program was working through the auspices of the Trust, a county-wide preservation organization and not a local educational institution or educational organization. As a result, it did not get the desired amount of feedback and participation. This is not the case with the service-learning component of the project, where the students focused on schools within their community and through an established institution, Franklin and Marshall College, and therefore had more success in obtaining its goals, which were focused on the surrounding community. A link was needed between the outreach program and local groups to establish permanent ties to the community and neighborhoods to build the outreach efforts, a lesson now learned for future endeavors.

In addition to these valuable lessons some larger questions and thoughts are raised. How does one effectively become a cultural investor in a community so that projects can succeed in making a difference? This case study showed that in order for the outreach project I envisioned to succeed, the role of archaeologist needs to be that of activist. Yet activism and mobilization are not in the archaeologist's proverbial "training manual"; rather they are hands-on and case specific. Moreover, being an activist can be both an asset and a disadvantage to a project, especially when politics is involved. Actions such as critiquing aspects of a heritage project at a city council meeting or a Lancaster County Convention Center meeting may be seen by some as disruptive, negative, and damaging to the project, for the critique goes against the thoughts or actions of the political leaders in a organization or community, while others find it ethically necessary and a positive action. Additionally, how do you balance ideology and business in an organization or project without one overwhelming the other? Perhaps the outreach program's goals were idealistic and mobilization efforts too weak in the outreach agenda, and therefore these goals were unattainable, but how will these lessons learned play out with future endeavors? Only time will tell.

Note

I thank the Historic Preservation Trust of Lancaster and the Woodrow Wilson Practicum Grant Program, as well as James A. Delle and Mary Ann Levine, for their support.

References Cited

Armony, Ariel C.
  2004   *The Dubious Link: Civic Engagement and Democratization.* Stanford University Press, Stanford, California.
Bennett-Gaieski, Jill
  2004   The Death of a Nation: Lessons on the Decline of CRM Law in Pennsylvania. Paper presented at the 37th Annual Conference of the Society for Historical Archaeology, St. Louis, MO.

Britt, Kelly M., and Christine I. Chen

2005a The (Re-)Birth of a Nation: Urban Archaeology, Ethics, and the Heritage Tourism Industry. *Archaeological Record* 5(3):26–28.

2005b When to Hold'em and When to Fold'em: Lessons Learned from the Heritage Profession. *Anthropology News* 46(4):14.

2005c Calling All Heritologists? An Introduction to Becoming the Heritage Professional. Paper presented at the 104th Annual Meeting of the American Anthropological Association, Washington, D.C.

Butcher, Louis., Jr.

2005 Rediscovering Thaddeus Stevens. *Lancaster Sunday News* 14 August:P1, P4.

Delle, James A.

2002a Report and Recommendations, Stevens and Smith Archaeology Project. Manuscript on file at Historic Preservation Trust of Lancaster County, October 14, 2002.

2002b Thaddeus Stevens/Lydia Hamilton Smith Site Archaeological Resource Recovery: Second Report. Manuscript on file at Historic Preservation Trust of Lancaster County, December 2002.

Delle, James A., and Mary Ann Levine

2004 Excavations at the Thaddeus Stevens/Lydia Hamilton Smith Site, Lancaster, PA: Archaeological Evidence for the Underground Railroad? *Northeast Historical Archaeology* 33:131–152.

Eby, Melissa

2006 Looking for New Members? Join the Club. *Lancaster Sunday News* 27 August:B1, B9.

Ford, Larry R.

2003 *America's New Downtowns: Revitalization or Reinvention?* The Johns Hopkins University Press, Baltimore.

Hobsbawm, Eric

1983 Introduction: Inventing Tradition. In *The Invention of Tradition,* edited by Eric Hobsbawm and Terrence Ranger, pp. 1–14. Cambridge University Press, Cambridge.

Huynh, Diana

2005 The Demise of a Peculiar Institution: Even Freed, Blacks Were Tracked by Law. *Lancaster Sunday News* 7 August:A1, A6

Huynh, Diana, and Michael Swartz

2005 The Demise of a Peculiar Institution: By 1800, "Only" 544 Countians, Most of Them Wealthy, Still Owned Slaves. A

Look at Gradual Abolition and Wounds that Remain Open. *Lancaster Sunday News* 7 August:A1, A5

Kirshenblatt-Gimblett, Barbara
  1998 *Destination Culture: Tourism, Museums, and Heritage.* University of California Press, Berkeley.

Levine, Mary Ann, Kelly M. Britt, and James A. Delle
  2005 Heritage Tourism and Community Outreach: Public Archaeology at the Thaddeus Stevens and Lydia Hamilton Smith Site in Lancaster, Pennsylvania, USA. *International Journal of Heritage Studies* 2(5):399–414.

Little, Barbara J. (editor)
  2002 *Public Benefits of Archaeology.* University Press of Florida, Gainesville.

McKercher, Bob, and Hilary duCros
  2002 *Cultural Tourism: The Partnership Between Tourism and Cultural Heritage Management.* Haworth Hospitality Press, New York.

Portney, Kent E., and Jeffrey M. Berry
  2001 Mobilizing Minority Communities: Social Capital and Participation in Urban Neighborhoods. In *Beyond Tocqueville: Civil Society and Social Capital Debate in Comparative Perspective,* edited by Bob Edwards, Michael W. Foley, and Mario Diani, pp. 70–82. University Press of New England, Hanover, Massachusetts.

Putnam, Robert D.
  2000 *Bowling Alone: The Collapse and Revival of American Community.* Simon and Schuster, New York, NY.

Rich, Paul
  1999 American Voluntarism, Social Capital, and Political Culture. *Annals of the American Academy of Political and Social Science, Civil Society and Democratization,* edited by Isidro Morales, Guillermo de Los Reyes, and Paul Rich, 565:15–34.

Schuyler, David
  2002 *A City Transformed: Redevelopment, Race, and Suburbanization in Lancaster, Pennsylvania, 1940–1980.* Pennsylvania State University Press, State College.

Schwartz, Michael
  2005 Religion and Slavery Had Complicated Relationship. *Lancaster Sunday News,* 7 August:A5.

Shackel, Paul A.
  2004 Working with Communities. In *Places in Mind: Public Archaeology as Applied Anthropology,* edited by Paul A. Shackel and Erve J. Chambers, pp. 1–16. Routledge Press, New York.

Shackel, Paul A., and Erve Chambers (editors)
  2004   *Places in Mind: Public Archaeology as Applied Anthropology.* Routledge, New York.
Stallings, Suzanne
  2005   Lancaster's Historic Districts. *Lancaster Heritage Outlook* 4(2):1–2.
Trefousse, Hans L.
  1997   *Thaddeus Stevens: Nineteenth-Century Egalitarian.* University of North Carolina Press, Chapel Hill.
Wilson, Carole E.
  2005   Historic Districts: Dispelling an Urban Legend. *Lancaster Heritage Outlook* 4(2):4.
Woodley, Thomas Frederick
  1934   *The Great Leveler: The Life of Thaddeus Stevens.* Stackpole Sons, New York, NY.
World Tourism Organization
  2003   Tourism and the World Economy. Electronic document, http://www.world-tourism.org/facts/eng/economy.htm, accessed January 21, 2007.

Chapter 9

Civil Religion and Civically Engaged Archaeology: Researching Benjamin Franklin and the Pragmatic Spirit

Patrice L. Jeppson

Civic engagement involves undertaking public activities for the purposes of empowering people to build communities and participate effectively in democracy (Jeppson 2000; Little 2002; Shackel and Chambers 2004). For archaeologists, this can mean helping traditional and nontraditional communities to make connections between heritage and contemporary social, cultural, or political issues (Little and Shackel 2005). We do this by broadening our interpretations so as to make archaeology stories inclusive and accessible to the community and by examining the networks of interaction between past and present that a particular site represents. In this latter, we utilize the difference between the study of the past and its uses: "*History* explores and explains pasts grown ever more opaque over time; *heritage* clarifies pasts so as to infuse them with present purposes" (Lowenthal 1998:xv).

The example of civic archaeology that follows here deals with new public history interpretations for an archaeological site that has a *civil religion* dimension. By this I refer to the role of a state in the constant regeneration of a social order (Moodie as noted by Jeppson 2003:225; see also Jeppson 1997; Moodie 1975:296). In this case, I speak of the symbols of the civil faith of American democracy reenacted by civil ritual at a historical site in a national park. The park in question is Independence National Historical Park, which is a National Park Service unit created to commemorate the birthplace of American democracy. The specific archaeological site in question is Franklin Court (in what is now Independence Park), which is the location of the home of Benjamin Franklin, who personified the spirit, ideals, curiosities, and ingenuity of a developing America (Greiff 1985; National Park Service INHP 1969, 1997; Philadelphia National Shrines Park Commission 1947). The discovery of the Franklin house ruins and the associated creation of a Franklin memorial are central to the thematic framework established for Independence Park.[1]

This civic engagement case study investigates the most recent stratigraphic layer at the Franklin Court site, which dates to the making of the monument. The data under consideration relate to the original archaeological research undertaken to locate the ruins of the Franklin home and its associated cultural landscape. In other words, the archaeological historiography of the site itself is excavated. As with the assemblages recovered earlier from the deeper site layers, the material culture evidence of this more recent past helps to inform about the everyday life of a particular time and place. More importantly, these recent artifacts of archaeological practice are found to lend themselves well to new interpretations that can speak to society's needs in the present.

The following discussion briefly summarizes this *archaeology of archaeology* research at Franklin Court and highlights some of the resulting newly identified material culture evidence. I contextualize this archaeological site as a national shrine and then consider the civic engagement potential of the new findings in terms of *how* and *whether* (i.e., *by whom* and *to whom*) these new interpretations will be told.

The Archaeology of a Shrine for the Nation

Fifty years ago, archaeological investigations were conducted in the city of Philadelphia to locate existing remains of Benjamin Franklin's Philadelphia home. This investigation identified the location of a mansion built at Franklin's direction in 1765, where his wife and daughter lived while he served in England as an agent representing several colonies. Franklin resided at the house during the period 1775–1776—the critical time of the American nation's birth in which he played an important role—but then he left again to serve as a diplomat in France. Franklin lived at the house during the final years of his life, from 1785 until his death in 1790. Twenty-two years later (in 1812), Franklin's son-in-law demolished the house so that the property's assets could be equally divided among heirs.

In 1953, 141 years later, in advance of the approaching 250th anniversary of Franklin's birth (January 17, 1706–1956), an archaeological reconnaissance study was undertaken on the sidewalk of a small Philadelphia side street to try to determine the exact location of Franklin's extinct house and to identify whether any ruins of the house survived below ground (Schumacher 1953a, 1953b, 1956). This exploration was mounted by the American Philosophical Society (the APS is one of Franklin's many creations) and the National Park Service (NPS). The NPS provided the archaeologist and the APS provided monies for hiring a field crew (Greiff 1985:374). Confirmation came on the first day of excavation with the discovery of appropriate dating artifacts associated with stone wall foundations. Through the rest of this field season, and another one, in 1955, the buried foundation walls were followed out under the sidewalk and into a nearby vacant lot, with the NPS picking up the tab for the field crew when the original APS contract ran out. The NPS then bought the adjoining property lots, demolished the extant structures, and began extensively excavating the house site, first in the early 1960s and then again in the 1970s, as part of the Master Plan for establishing a sacred shrine to American democracy (known today as Independence National Historical Park).[2]

Building a shrine to democracy was a response to the 1947 report of the Philadelphia National Shrines Park Commission (which was a response to Public Law 711) that called for "investigating the establishment of a National Park in the old part of the city of Philadelphia for the purposes of conserving the historical objects and buildings therein" (Philadelphia National Shrines Park Commission 1947:3; for Franklin's house ruins specifically see pages 283–295). The broader context of this shrine's development also included the 1935 Historic Sites Act (which charged NPS with the acquisition and management of historic properties), local Philadelphia efforts to encourage revitalization of the neighborhood (which had become a tenderloin), and the aftermath of World War II (which fueled interest in protecting important buildings from a feared firebombing, coupled with an upsurge of patriotism). The congressional act enabling the new park set as an agenda preserving Independence Hall and other historic structures in Philadelphia significantly associated with the American Revolution and the establishment of the United States, to help visitors understand the men, the events, and the ideas of which these buildings are living memorials. Public Law 195 of the 80th Congress established Franklin's home as Area C of the federal project, there being no other existing national monument to Franklin (NPS INHP 1969, Appendix). Once underway, this federal commemorative project was seen to reflect the tensions of the Cold War: Acting Secretary of the Interior Oscar L. Chapman supported the park as "particularly appropriate for the Nation . . . at the present time when the ideals of our democratic government and way of life are being tested in a world theater" (as quoted in Mires 2002:217).

The Franklin Court Memorial Site

The purview of Franklin Court as part of Independence National Historical Park is all encompassing. The park's mission is teaching and/or reminding the public about Franklin and his connection to our lives today. In doing so, the whole scope of the man is interpreted—philosopher, scientist, printer, postmaster, writer, statesman, and founding father. The house ruins and the surrounding area once forming Franklin's property (the urban landscape that Franklin created at this location and the adjacent, extant, architecturally innovative tenant houses he constructed) have been made into a memorial and educational museum complex. The Franklin house archaeological ruins are interpreted in a unique melding of present and past: an architectural sculpture made of one-foot-diameter steel tubing is erected over the foundations.[3] This *ghost* house isometrically outlines the location and volume of the long-absent brick building. Colored paving interprets the interior wall divisions and floor plan. Glass-covered observation portals allow visitors to view the original house, providing the public a touchstone with the man and his times.

This *tangible* evidence of the past provides the visitor to the site an immediate, personal connection to localized Franklin experience and thereby also helps to contextualize the other interpretive exhibits presented as part of the Franklin Court educational complex: a functioning reconstructed colonial-era post office with a small philately exhibit (the B. Free Franklin Post Office in honor of the first postmaster general), a reconstructed printing office and bindery with demonstrations done by costumed interpreters, an architectural history and archaeological display in one of Franklin's rental properties, and the Underground Museum, which presents decorative art and scientific Frankliniana, an interpretive diorama, interactive exhibits, and an orientation film (see the 360-degree interactive panorama images at The Electric Franklin web page (Independence Hall Association 1995) and the 2002 University of Delaware Museum Technology Course Franklin Court web pages [National Park Service 2002]). Indeed, the archaeological concept of peeking into the ground is carried into the design of the modern subterranean construction for the Underground Museum "whereby the visitor descends under the ground, moving away from the sights and sounds of the twentieth century" (Philadelphia Museum of Art 1976:640). In its "pragmatic functionalism, paralleling both *form* and *insight*," the archaeologically derived and constituted memorial site and education complex of Franklin Court is Franklinesque in its very nature (Philadelphia Museum of Art 1976:640).

Since it opened in 1976, during the year of the American Bicentennial, more than six million visitors have toured Franklin Court and learned about Franklin and his times as a direct result of archaeological site interpretations. Franklin Court is the second most visited site at Independence National Historical Park after the Liberty Bell. More than 150,000 students visit Franklin Court annually to learn about Franklin as part of formal, curriculum-based educational enrichment (INHP Educator Sue Glennon, personal communication, February 24, 2004). More than 100,000 have visited via the Internet.[4] Franklin Court is unquestionably one of the most significant sites that the public accesses for learning about Franklin and his times.

The Archaeology of Archaeology at Franklin Court

In 2002, fifty years after the first exploratory excavations at Franklin Court and more than a quarter century since the last excavations, legislation by the 107th Congress established the Benjamin Franklin Tercentenary Commission (H.R. 2362) to study and recommend activities to honor Franklin on the 300th anniversary of his birth (January 17, 2006). A consortium of five Franklin-related Philadelphia institutions (the American Philosophical Society, the Franklin Institute of Science Museum, the Library Company of Philadelphia, the Philadelphia Museum of Art, and the University of Pennsylvania) commissioned an assessment of Franklin-related historical archaeology research to meet the needs of several commemorative programs (a traveling exhibit, a Frankliniana database, and an educational website) and form a legacy contribution (Benjamin Franklin Tercentenary Consortium 2003; Jeppson 2005). This research involves no formal reanalysis of previously recovered archaeological evidence but rather investigates and evaluates the findings of previous archaeological researchers undertaken at different times by different people for different purposes. In short, it involves the *archaeology of archaeology.*

In using the process of archaeology as an artifact in itself, the previous fieldwork is considered in terms of its broader intellectual context and the implication this setting has for the materiality of archaeological practice. In this case, this archaeology of archaeology strategy employs a theoretical perspective that argues against a progressive (or evolutionary) account of the fieldwork. Instead, it considers the complex historical and sociopolitical interactions that conditioned each fieldwork episode, recognizing that each archaeological phase of study is an artifact of its time. In essence, each phase of excavation is treated as part of the history of the Franklin house site, as an added layer of stratigraphy (i.e., Eighteenth Century, Nineteenth Century, Twentieth Century, Excavation 1950s, Excavation 1960s, Excavation 1970s, NPS Memorial Garden).

This assessment has identified important, unrecognized, and untapped resources useful for new stories of Franklin Court. These include previously identified artifacts postulated for a new interpretive use, previously *un*identified resources, and altogether new artifacts created as part of archaeological practice itself. These last are available only with the passage of time, which has made once irrelevant information relevant and useful for telling the story of Franklin and of Franklin's mansion and its discovery (Jeppson 2004). The particular example of civic engagement discussed here makes use of what the past archaeology research at Franklin Court has left behind (Lucas 2001:202).

As Gavin Lucas points out (2001:202), archaeology not only studies material culture but also produces material culture in the process—the textual and graphic materializations of archaeological practice produced in our field notes and drawings, reports, and photographs. Of course, information recording at an archaeological site is imperative because archaeology is a destructive science. So, in point of fact, our materializing practices are not passive representations but are "an operational strategy enabling the archaeological record to be subject to repeated investigation" (Lucas 2001:202). As Lucas notes, this is "our answer to scientific experiment" (Lucas 2001:211–212). As a result of this strategy, we have available today artifacts of the archaeological process created during previous archaeological research. This is archaeological collections reuse in the broadest sense of the term (Bacharch and Boyd 2003; Ellick 2003).

In this Franklin Court assessment, the primary resources utilized include original archaeological site records, site drawings, field notes, field photographs, preliminary and final reports, and artifact catalogues—as well as the recovered artifact assemblages. Oral history was conducted with some of the archaeological practitioners involved in these archaeology projects. Secondary sources on Philadelphia and colonial-era archaeology and its history were also consulted. Primary NPS research resources (e.g., the INHP Archives Card File, Historic Structure Reports) and primary and secondary NPS administrative history resources (general management plans and studies detailing the construction of Franklin Court as part of Independence National Historical Park) were accessed, cultural resource management documents related to the park's National Register nomination and amendment were considered, and academic studies evaluating Franklin Court's archaeology and its interpretation were utilized. The history of the public interpretation at the site was also examined via popular tourism publications, period newspaper clippings, slide and photograph collections, interpretive training and outreach materials, surviving exhibition materials, and oral history interviews. Informal observation study was done on-site. Information was likewise gathered from NPS personnel who interface regularly with the public at Franklin Court and from the NPS manager of the INHP web pages containing the Franklin archaeology content. Many of these resources had not been accessed for research purposes in thirty or more years.

Lucas generally (2001), and Marley Brown and Andrew Edwards in historical archaeology in particular (Brown and Edwards 2004), advocate the use of such *artifacts of practice* for reexcavation needs. Asa Berggren and Ian Hodder (2003), as well as Nick Sheppard (2003), have used these resources for examining the process of the construction of archaeological knowledge. In specific, they have examined the context of the subaltern field-worker in knowledge production. This Tercentenary project demonstrates the potential value of such materialized products for interpretation needs, specifically civically engaged interpretation.

Materialized Artifacts of Archaeological Practice at Franklin Court

Historical archaeologists study "the small things left behind" (Deetz 1977). The assessment of the Franklin Court archaeology identified as artifacts several things that the previous archaeology research and researchers left behind. Useful discoveries began on the very first day upon opening the very first file—a preliminary report written in 1956 by National Park Service archaeologist Paul Schumacher. Eight black-and-white photographs—archaeological record shots—were glued onto the back pages of the report. The field workers visible in these and other archived photographs are African American (figure 9.1). While African American contributions to 1930s-era Works Progress Administration archaeology projects were known to me (see for example, White et al. 1999), I was unaware of African American participation in the excavation of this seminal urban archaeology site (NPS INHP Archive Photograph and Slide Collection 1950).

Fig. 8b   Trench 4, section b. Wall F facing
Note steps #2 to the left and the brick rubbl
the right.

Figure 9.1. African American crew members searching for Franklin house remains. Site record shot included in a 1956 report (Schumacher 1956, 8; Photograph 6a). It is likely that the field crew members were included for the purposes of providing scale. Caption: "Trench 4, section b, Wall F facing N. E. Note steps #2 to the left and the brick rubble to the right" (NPS INHP Archives).

The field notes indicate that these field crew members helped conduct the excavation and also processed artifacts (Schumacher 1953b): "One very thin man has been digging out the privy pit C" (May 13, 1953); "one man digging in the southwest corner over pit G and two men excavating in wall pit E located in Trench 3, sec. B" (May 22, 1953); "I had the men washing artifacts and set up work tables for displaying the artifacts from the excavation" (May 25, 1953); "4 men working. Two in Pit E in the clay. Reached bottom by noon—15.3'" (May 28, 1953); "Had one man dig under Wall T to locate any walls underneath" (June 8, 1953). These field crew members are not formally documented by name in the field documentation archived for Franklin Court, although this information may exist in other NPS archives. The only identifying designations mentioned are in a fieldnote entry for May 26, 1953 and it isn't clear if these are actual surnames: "It poured . . . Only two men showed up (Ransom and Sample)."

The identities and presence of these field crew are partly explained by the original hand-typed onionskin-paper contract titled "Estimate for Excavation of Benjamin Franklin's Court to locate and record all walls which may give us clues as to the location of Benjamin Franklin's home," which is present in the INHP Archives (Schumacher 1953a). This document provides the pay scale for an archaeologist (GS-9 at $422 per month) and "6 laborers . . . *if at union wages* . . . $1.75 per hour" [emphasis mine]. There is likewise a recommendation for using workers from Local 57, which is the Laborers' International Union—a construction and industry or building trades union (Schumacher 1953a:1). The daily field notes for the first day of excavation, in May of 1953, record that four laborers were hired from the union at that pay to excavate in search of Franklin's house (figure 9.2).

Secondary research provides context for this information, revealing that this 1953 archaeological laborer wage of $1.75 per hour is $1 higher than the then national minimum wage of 75 cents an hour. The field notes include a table calculating labor costs for the 1953 May–June field season (Schumacher 1953b:10):

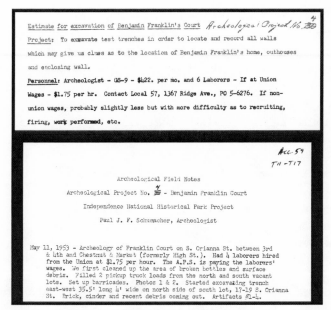

Figure 9.2. NPS archaeologist Schumacher's typed field notes from 1953, indicating the hiring of union workers (NPS INHP Archives).

APS: 612 manhours, 76½ man-days; 4 weeks; $1071.00
NPS: 332 manhours, 41½ man-days; 2 weeks; $581.00
Total: 944 manhours, 118 man-days; 6 weeks; $1652.00
Numbering Artifacts 74 hours

In the context of its time, this wage appears to represent a fair compensation: the National Average Wage Index for 1953 was $3140, while the Median Wage Index for a family was $4100. Wage data for the time also reveal that the average income for Black households in the northern states (e.g., in Philadelphia, Pennsylvania) was twice the average income of Black households in the nation (U.S. Census Bureau 1953, 2004a). Union membership among black residents in Philadelphia and other northern cities is presumably partly responsible for the higher northern state incomes.

The archived archaeological slide collections from the 1960s archaeological research at Franklin Court likewise reveal that African Americans served as field crew during the second phase of study (figures 9.3 and 9.4). Regional NPS archaeologists B. Bruce Powell and Jackson Ward "Smokey" Moore, Jr., who directed a crew of between three and eleven NPS construction workers, undertook this fieldwork. This field crew, averaging six men over the many months of excavation, reexposed the work done a decade earlier and excavated several new features associated with Franklin's mansion (NPS INHP Photograph and Slide Collection 1960, NPS INHP Archive John Cotter Collection 1970; Powell 1961, 1962a).

The field notes for this period of site research mention several names for the field crew: Rocky Harris, Grossman, Smallwood, Crawford, White, and Werner (Powell 1961). Oral History with Jackson Ward "Smokey" Moore, Jr., contributes the information that the field crew were African American and Italian American (e-mail correspondence, May 23, 2005).

Figure 9.3. African American field crew members excavating at Franklin Court in the early 1960s. INHP Working Photograph Collection: Franklin Court, 1960's, #6810. Caption: "Franklin Court Archaeology—Men clearing cellar floor (Feature 42), left; excavating south and 1765 east wall trenches (Features 37 & 65), mildew ground to right; and preparing to patch broken wall of privy (Feature 38), ground. Photo by: B. B. Powell (sic), 9/28/60" (NPS INHP Archives Photograph and Slide Collection, 1960).

Figure 9.4. African American field crew members screening for artifacts at Franklin Court. Multiplex Slide Collection, Franklin Court, FC 1:32. Caption: "Franklin Court Archaeology/Screening Fill from Feat. 38. B. B. P. [B. Bruce Powell] 9-28-60" (NPS INHP Archives Photograph and Slide Collection, 1960).

My immediate assumption upon seeing the photographic documentation from the 1950s and 1960s excavation phases was that construction workers engaged as field crew on an archaeology site would bring invaluable insight to the Franklin archaeological project. They could contribute their experience with building construction and with the city's underbelly (its web of utilities) at a time when urban archaeology was only beginning. Further research on the 1960s phase of work led me to a 1962 *American Antiquity* article by Powell (1962b), who writes about the special artisans, equipment, and skills needed to interpret the concrete bowels of the city. He also mentions that archaeology in the urban context is significantly costly, noting that "$2.20 per hour is paid for common labor" (Powell 1962b:581). He furthermore states, "It might not be entirely out of line to note that laborers [in Philadelphia] make more than archaeologists do in some areas" (Powell 1962b:581).

A 1978 cassette tape in the park archives helps confirm the

contributions of these crews (NPS INHP [Yoelson] 1978). On this tape, NPS staff and ex-staff are gathered together to view silent film footage shot between ten and twenty years earlier. As the film footage unwinds, and as the gathered parties attempt to identify sites, cardinal directions, and the who, what, when, where, and why of what they are seeing, one of the officials centrally involved in making Independence Park says in response to the archaeology then on the screen, "Many of these contract laborers were very very good even though they had never done any archaeological investigation work or been part of a team. They knew what to throw away and what to keep."

A New, Civically Engaged Story from Franklin Court

This history *is* interesting—if overlooked at the time. And it *is* overlooked, both in terms of the archaeological discipline and within the community at large. The formal recognition of the long-forgotten role of the early field-worker has recently emerged as an academic concern. Elsewhere, several researchers are examining subaltern field-workers as replaceable tools in the machinery of excavation (Berggren and Hodder 2003). They discuss a distanced control of the unskilled worker that was possible because there was little interest in detailed contextual relationships in the object-centered approach found in early archaeology. This approach recognizes an important contribution to understanding archaeology's social practice and its developing methods. This approach, however, doesn't apply to Franklin Court, where artifact context was the basis for identifying period structural remains. Moreover, this approach is about making a more democratic archaeology rather than about archaeology helping make a more democratic society (Jeppson 2000). For the needs of a civically engaged interpretation, the passage of time has made this kind of once-irrelevant Franklin Court information relevant and potentially useful for telling the story of Franklin and Franklin's mansion and its discovery by the American people.

Significantly, this *archaeology of archaeology* study comes at a time of renewed interest in Franklin's later life, the last five years of which are spent at Franklin Court and which represent the pinnacle of Franklin's enlightenment thinking put into practice—including that which goes beyond his contributions to the American Revolution and independence.[5] This period of Franklin's life is marked by his participation in the abolitionist movement. Once a slaveowner, Franklin becomes president of the antislavery movement in the New World. He pens and submits antislavery petitions to Congress (which are not accepted).[6] He opens his house to the antislavery society for meetings and lends his name and image to their cause (one of the first, if not the first, uses of celebrity for such a secular cause). In 1788, the first cameos in the New World bearing the inscription *Am I not a man and a brother* are shipped from England by Wedgwood to Franklin.

Among other uses, the materialized archaeology artifacts from Franklin Court demonstrate, in one sense, the story of Franklin the slaveholder and then abolitionist coming "full circle"[7]: Figuratively speaking, the descendants of the community Franklin worked to help free excavated Franklin's history for the needs of the American people (i.e., the creation of a national historical memory).

The new Franklin Court story is also a labor union story. Philadelphia is a union town. The beginning of the sustained trade union organization of U.S. workers began in Philadelphia in 1794, and the key structural elements characterizing U.S. trade unionism found today started in Philadelphia in 1827 (when central labor bodies united craft unions within a single city). Philadelphia's labor history, like all labor history, is the story of the struggle for collective rights of workers, and Philadelphia workers and their organizations were and are important defenders and progenitors of democratic change in society. Union laborers have a long history of embracing the language of the U.S. founding fathers at the site of what is now Independence Park—creating a physical connection between workers' grievances and the nation's founding ideals. In the nineteenth century, strikes over working conditions were staged at the site of

Independence Hall. In 1835, demonstrations grew in size over a one-year period from two thousand to ten thousand members (Mires 2002).

A union worker chapter in the new Franklin Court story may resonate with the union family, especially given that at this time labor unions are under contraction—and also under attack (even called un-American and, in one case, labeled a terrorist organization) by today's political, social, and economic leaders on the conservative Right. Given the erosion of job security and the decline of real wages (and the reality of a transforming economy), work is a highly problematic arena for *all* twenty-first-century American workers. Maybe the story of the monument "brought to you (in part) by the union " will be relevant to this large local community, and maybe the role of the citizen worker building a site of memory about American democracy will resonate with the American worker who is conscious of the shriveling of human and civil rights in the workplace (Green 1997:5–7). Franklin himself of course had much to say on the value of work, on the value of play, and on the importance of social justice. The union angle has been realized as useful for mitigating the new use of the 1950s artifacts in any case.

Qualitative support for the viability of this new interpretation exists in other materialized artifacts generated at Franklin Court. Previous historic preservation scholarship on Franklin Court as a tourist destination (Allen 1998) indicates that even before these artifacts of archaeological practice aged (over time) into important material culture evidence, the history of the rediscovery of Franklin's house in general had been recognized, on a practical level, as an interpretation *opportunity* and *need*. Park ranger Joanne Blancoe, quoted in a master's thesis (Allen 1998:227), states that interpreting the making of Franklin Court would be particularly valuable for Philadelphians: "They remember how the place looked in the 50's and 60's. And it is interesting to see how similar or not, Market Street looked 30 or 40 years ago to today. . . . Some Rangers tell that story in 318 Franklin Street [the Fragments of Franklin Museum at Franklin Court] . . . you need to involve the visitor into this process and let them draw their own conclusions." In the same study, Penelope Batchelor, a retired NPS INHP historical architect who was central to the planning and development of Franklin Court, relates that, in retrospect, this information "should be stated somewhere. . . . I'll also say I don't think that the archaeology is played up enough right at the house. . . . [recovered objects] could be part of an exhibit on the archaeology of Franklin's house there. Possibly a logical explanation, step-by-step, as to what was found and why (Allen 1998:262).

Also on a practical level, previous in-house (NPS) evaluations on interpretation practice at Franklin Court show that the value of interpretation aids for explaining the archaeology to the public, and especially children, was identified long ago (NPS INHP Interpreter Staff 1977, c1980). Such aids are noted as useful for referencing both the archaeological research methods used at the site and the production/creation of the original site features (i.e., privy shafts) as the source of the objects on display.

Presently, there is a binder with a handful of historical images about the history of the site stored as a resource on a shelf under the interpreter's kiosk in the Fragments of Franklin Museum at Franklin Court. These depict the Franklin Court property in the 1950s prior to development of the park. Also included are copies of notices from late-eighteenth- and early-nineteenth-century newspapers advertising Franklin's house for rent after his death. This resource was at one point (decades ago) attached to the wall so as to be available for the public but is now in need of repair. In any case, this brief practical history of the site's creation exists in minor form and could be easily augmented at minimum cost to present the new story from Franklin Court as part of an instructive, civically engaged interpretation.

Reflecting on Civic Engagement

Importantly, Independence National Historical Park is trying hard to work more cooperatively with local ethnic and minority communities to find better ways to interpret diverse cultural heritage within the park's portrayal of the American experience (see Director's Order 75A for NPS generally [NPS 2003a, 2003b] and Low et al. 2002 for INHP).[8] Among other agenda items, there is an acknowledgment that African American cultural representations need to be better addressed and that the local history of the city of Philadelphia—a predominantly black city—needs to be better addressed since the park is currently perceived as only for tourists and for whites (Low et al. 2002).

The park interpreters at Franklin Court whom I have talked about this data with think that this information would be very useful for interpretation with the thousands of schoolchildren who visit Franklin Court, many of whom are African American. This is only anecdotal support for the new story, as is the comment by a black staff member at the park who said that he had been working at the park for decades and only now was "his" history starting to be "part of it." National Park Service Cultural Resources staff have expressed interest in this story, albeit there was an initial reasonable concern that not all of the names for these field-workers are currently known for citation. There was also an initial, again reasonable concern, that a racial disparity could be seen in the data, given that the African Americans held lower-paying fieldwork positions. The new artifacts, perceived this way, would not meet the needs of the Park Service's new initiative. The fact that union workers were involved makes a significant difference in this case.

This new story of the making of a national shrine extends beyond the 1976 Bicentennial-era theme used to plan and interpret Franklin Court. With this new story, the Franklin Court site is assimilated and represented in terms that also speak to society's needs in the present. The process of archaeology artifacts contribute contextual richness for a new understanding of American history and historicity.

After hearing me present this interpretation (along with other findings) in a public forum, the NPS INHP chief curator intends to mount a display of this identified information in an exhibit case at the park's new Public Archaeology laboratory (Karie Diethorn, personal communication, October 15, 2005). I have also committed to sharing these and other findings with front-line interpretation staff during an upcoming in-house training session (Mary Jenkins, personal communication, November 14, 2005). These are positive indications that this new story will be heard.

However, this interpretation also raises issues that are critical for any civically engaged archaeology. Indeed, I have wondered a lot about the following: Is using archaeology to support minority histories that broaden the national metanarrative actually contributing to the co-opting of minority history (essentially reestablishing institutional "power" via a new metanarrative)? In point of fact, the story of Franklin as an abolitionist is not embraced by all constituencies. For example, I was thinking that part of the Tercentenary's contribution might include seeking a formal designation marking Franklin's abolitionist activities. This included researching the possibilities of recognition for the site under the Underground Railroad Archeology Initiative (a National Historical Landmarks Archeology Initiative).[9] I found that the park has already adopted the Franklin site in its Underground Railroad Addendum updating the park's National Register listing:[10]

> As a printer Benjamin Franklin had owned and sold slaves, but through his work in the 1750s with the Bray Associates sponsored by Christ Church, he had grown to appreciate the innate talents of African Americans. At age 81 in 1787 he accepted the office of President of the Pennsylvania Abolition Society. As an old but renowned figure, his leadership gave real import to the regenerated Abolition Society. In poor health, Franklin often ran meetings in his home, where strategies were laid to assist free and enslaved blacks illegally kidnapped and provide other humanitarian assistance. In 1789 he signed a society publication, *Address to the Public*, which appealed for support and funds, and likely wrote the society's petition against the slave trade submitted on February 12, 1790, to the First Federal Congress then seated in New York City.
>
> A month before his death, Franklin as his last public act wrote and published "On the Slave Trade," a satirical letter that compared American slavery with the practice of the much despised Algerine pirates who were taking Christians on the seas captive and making them slaves. This clever polemic may not have won new activists for the cause, but Franklin's international prestige and the philanthropic work done by the

Abolition Society while he served as president likely encouraged more fugitives to pass through Philadelphia on their escape to freedom. (Franklin Court details in the September 2000 National Register Amendment supplement, "INHP Underground Railroad and Anti-Slavery Movement" [prepared by Anna Coxe Toogood].)

However, I also learned that the site had already been nominated—and then unnominated—for recognition as part of the NPS-coordinated Underground Railroad Network to Freedom program. This latter constituency's decision was that it couldn't recognize the site of Franklin Court—the site where the first president of the first American abolitionist society lived and where the society occasionally met—because the activities at the site were aboveground, not underground.[11] No illegal acts took place at Franklin Court (that we know of). Therefore the site doesn't fit its mandate and it is *its* mandate, not mine. Its emphasis on formerly neglected history is both laudable and important.

Then I learned of happenings elsewhere in Independence Park, which rendered other insights into community needs and outlooks. Specifically, ideas advanced for displaying Wedgwood's abolitionist medallion (the first American shipment of which was sent to Franklin) were rescinded when African American park interpreters were advised about community views of the item's supplicant-figure imagery.[12] From this I learned that any new presentation about Franklin's abolitionist activities via the use of this Franklin-related historical and symbolic item might not be a universally acceptable idea. I also learned that one of the new crop of biographers (Waldstreicher 2004) rejects positive interpretations by others of Franklin's antislavery actions, considering them, at best, exaggerated.

I personally feel that it isn't up to *us* to write *another* community's history. As archaeologist Jed Levin explains, "We can only write *about* it" (personal communication, August 2003). Communities should and need to be free to write the history that they want and need. I am now left wondering, vis-à-vis civic engagement, does rejection of or conflict over a new historical interpretation necessarily mean a failure of engagement? Might it instead be a sign that communities have access to new tools for participation with divisive stances anew? Might communities be defining themselves in their *not* using our resources? Considering these kinds of questions and concerns is an especially relevant responsibility in this particular case because Franklin himself is an early, central figure in the philosophical tradition of American pragmatism that holds that inquiries should aim at enlightening the common experience and advancing the common good (Campbell 1999; Rorty 1998; West 1989, 2004).

In any case, I believe that Franklin would have found this peek at twentieth-century Americans at work on America's history to be fascinating. For myself, I continue to reflect on what civic engagement with Franklin Court archaeology means. Given my pragmatist orientation I want to describe the country and its history in terms of what it can become as well as in terms of what it once was and is now. While we need to face existing unpleasant truths about ourselves, we need to understand that these are not the last words about our national character. Maybe this new story at this civil religion site can offer up hope as well as knowledge.

Acknowledgments

The B. Franklin 300 historical archaeology assessment—from which this paper topic was abstracted—was made possible through the invaluable assistance of many others. In relation to this specific topic, this included (at Independence National Historical Park) Karen Stevens, Andrea Ashby Leraris, Bob Giannini, Mary "Missy" Hogan, Thomas Degnan, Anne Coxe Toogood, Karie Diethorn, Jim Mueller, and Renee Albertoi. Tara Morrison, NPS Northeast Regional Coordinator for the Underground Railroad Network to Freedom, took time to discuss the place of the Franklin mansion archaeology site in the memorialization of abolitionist history in the United States. Jackson Ward "Smokey" Moore provided interesting and important details about the Franklin Court archaeology (including the work's context) during oral history sessions via telephone and in e-mail correspondence. Betty Cosans-Zeebooker, William Hershey, and Dave Orr helped me make sense of early Philadelphia historical archaeology research. The development of this particular research topic also benefited from a brief discussion with Nick Sheppard in 2003. In terms of the B. Franklin Tercentenary project more generally, Connie Hershey, Page Talbot, and Conover Hunt provided helpful guidance. Thanks are owed to Robert Schuyler and Benjamin Pyckles, who facilitated my involvement in that project. Jed Levin and Karen Lind Brauer gave me helpful feedback during the writing of this paper. I thank Barbara Little and Paul Shackel for inviting me to give a presentation in their 2005 symposium on this topic.

Notes

1. Cultural resources in U.S. National Parks are organized in terms of *thematic frameworks*. Park *themes* reflect current scholarship and are designed to represent the diversity of the American past. Theme topics are identified as part of park planning and represent the professional judgments of NPS cultural resource specialists, state historic preservation offices, specially convened boards or committees of scholars, other federal agencies, and other sources. For more on NPS thematic frameworks see Little (1997).

2. This is a period usage of the term *shrine*. NPS reserves the use of the term *shrine* for specific attribution and Independence Park is not designated an NPS national shrine.

3. Further discussion of this sculpture can be found in *Philadelphia: Three Centuries of American Art* (Philadelphia Museum of Art, 1976: 639–640).

4. Since 2002, more than seventy informational Franklin Court web pages created by the University of Delaware's 2002 Museum Technology Course (under the direction of INHP curator Robert Giannini) have been posted at the park's web site (NPS INHP, http://www.nps.gov/inde/Franklin_Court/Pages/index.html). These web pages are accessed by thousands of persons each month (making an estimated 36,000 accesses calculated for 2004 [ParkNet/Daily Figures for the Northeast Regional Report, http://www.nps.gov/helpdesk/stats.htm; no IP counts are available]). Based on present usage rates, at least

100,000 accesses will have been made by 2006—an estimate that is conservative at best as it can most reasonably be assumed that usage will increase exponentially as computer technology is made ever more available (especially to schools) and interest in Franklin intensifies due to the tercentenary of his birth in 2006.

5. For example, twelve new books and major History Channel and PBS television specials have recently appeared. See, among others, the books by Campbell (1999), Isaacson (2003, 2005), Morgan (2002), and Wood (2004).

6. In 1789, Franklin wrote *Address to the Public* urging abolition, which was sent to the Congress of the United States (http://www.quotes2u.com/histdocs/franklin.htm or http://www.quotes2u.com/index.htm and search with terms "Franklin Slavery.")

7. I thank Coxe Toogood for this succinct interpretative phrase.

8. The Park Service is actively involved in civic engagement in rethinking the parks for the twenty-first century: *"Civic engagement* is all of the activities that strengthen the public's understanding of the contemporary relevance of our heritage resources, both natural and cultural, and encourage participation in and dialogue about their future. Our philosophy and expectation for civic engagement goes beyond legal requirements for including the public in decision-making" http://www.nps.gov/civic/policy/policy5.html (accessed December 31, 2004). A Rapid Ethnographic Assessment Procedure (REAP) conducted by Low et al. (2002) was commissioned at INHP in 1997 (in preparation for a new General Management Report) to assess ethnic group values and identification with the park.

9. According to Morrison (1998), "Though many underground railroad–related *standing structures* were identified through the federal NPS UGRR program, it was recognized that many related structures are no longer extant but rather exist as archaeological ruins. The UGRR *Archeology* Initiative . . . extension combines the NPS coordinated Special Resource Study to commemorate and interpret the Underground Railroad (UGRR) with the National Historical Landmarks *Archeological* Initiative. In 1997, the Executive Board of the Society for Historical Archaeology passed a resolution that endorses the Underground Railroad Archaeology Initiative and which encourages participation in it by professional archaeologists. The NHL *Archaeological* Initiative has three components: to develop nominations of new archaeological sites; to increase public and professional awareness of archaeological NHLs; and to improve documentation about existing archaeological NHLs. This initiative provides the framework for the Underground Railroad

Archeological Initiative and supports the ultimate goal of improving public understanding and appreciation of the history of the Underground Railroad from the perspective of archaeological resources and cultural landscapes. In addition, the NHL Underground Railroad Archeological Initiative will result in information that can be used by federal, state, and local governments and agencies to protect, preserve, and commemorate archeological properties associated with the Underground Railroad." See also the Underground Railroad Resources in the U.S. Theme Study, http://www.cr.nps.gov/nr/travel/underground/themef.htm (accessed July 2006).

10. The INHP UGRR National Register Supplemental Amendment came in response to legislation (H.R. 1625) whereby each park prepared National Register documentation for resources related to the Underground Railroad. INHP identified several structures with the Underground Railroad theme, including Franklin Court.

11. I thank Jed Levin for this succinct explanation and terminology.

12. The medallion was proposed for use in interpreting the history of slavery at the site of the executive mansion, which once stood at the location of the new Liberty Bell Pavilion—and where the enslaved workers that George Washington brought to Philadelphia lived and worked. NPS Regional archaeologist Jed Levin advised me of this possible community response to the medallion when I spoke to him about the possibilities of using the medallion's history for an updated interpretation of Franklin. Information on the medallion as an abolitionist symbol *for whites* was presented in the Winterthur exhibit "'Am I not a Man and a Brother?' Decorative Arts of the Antislavery Movement," which showed how the decorative arts were used to convey the horrors of slavery and promote the cause of abolition. See Sam Margolin's "And Freedom to the Slave": Anti-Slavery Ceramics, 1787–1865, in (2002) Robert Hunter (ed.) *Ceramics in America* http://www.chipstone.org/publications/CIA/2002/Margolin/2002MargolinText.html (accessed September 2003).

References Cited

Allen, Jeffrey R.
    1998   Learning from Franklin Court. A Cultural Reappraisal of Tourism and Historic Preservation at Independence National Historical Park. Unpublished Master's thesis, Department of Historic Preservation, University of Pennsylvania.

Bacharch, Joan, and Christine Boyd
    2003   Out of the Basement: The Use and Accessibility of Archaeo-logical Collections. Session presented at the 5th World Ar-chaeological Congress, Washington, D.C.
Benjamin Franklin Tercentenary Commission [Consortium]
    2003   About the Consortium. Electronic document, www.benfrank-lin300.org, accessed September 2005.
Berggren, Asa, and Ian Hodder
    2003   Social Practice, Method, and Some Problems of Field Archae-ology. *American Antiquity* 68(3):421–34.
Brown, Marley, R. III, and Andrew C. Edwards
    2004   The Third Time's the Charm at Colonial Williamsburg: Archae-ologies of Archaeology and the Refinement of Site Interpretation in Historical Archaeology. Paper presented at the Society for Underwater and Historical Archaeology annual meeting, St. Louis, MO.
Campbell, James
    1999   *Recovering Benjamin Franklin: An Exploration of a Life of Science and Service.* Open Court, Chicago.
Deetz, James
    1977   *In Small Things Forgotten: The Archeology of Early American Life.* Anchor Press, New York.
Ellick, Carol
    2003   Collections and Education: The Potential of an Under-Used Resource. Paper presented at the 5th World Archaeological Congress, Washington, D.C.
Green, James
    1997   Why Teach Labor History? *OAH Magazine of History,* Special Volume on Labor History, 11(2):5–7.
Greiff, Constance M.
    1985   *Independence: The Creation of a National Park.* Heritage Studies, Inc. MS, INHP Archives, Independence National Historical Park, Philadelphia.
Independence Hall Association
    1995   The Electric Franklin, Franklin Court. Electronic document, http://www.ushistory.org/franklin/info/court.htm, ac-cessed July 2005.
Isaacson, Walter
    2005   *A Benjamin Franklin Reader.* Simon and Schuster, New York.
    2003   *Benjamin Franklin: An American Life.* Simon and Schuster, New York.

Jeppson, Patrice L.
   2005   *Historical Fact, Historical Memory: The Archaeological Evidence Related to Benjamin Franklin and His Life: Historical Archaeology Research Undertaken for the Benjamin Franklin Tercentenary Consortium.* Manuscript on file, INHP Archives, Philadelphia, Pennsylvania.
   2004   "Not a replacement but a valuable successor . . . ": A new story from Franklin's mansion in colonial Philadelphia. Paper presented at the Society for American Archaeology Annual Conference, Montreal, Canada.
   2003   Archaeology in the Public Interest: Applied Historical Archaeology in a South African Museum Educational Exhibit. In *Public or Perish: Archaeology into the New Millennium—Proceedings from the 28th Annual Chacmool Conference, 1995,* edited by Beau Cripps, Ruth Dickau, Latonia J. Hartery, Murray Lobb, Daniel Meyer, Lesley Nichols, and Tamara Varney, pp. 213–31. The Archaeological Association of the University of Calgary, Calgary, Canada.
   2000   An Archaeologist/Educator Collaboration: Lessons learned during a year of archaeology in the Baltimore County Public Schools. Paper presented at the Society for Historical and Underwater Archaeology Annual Conference, Quebec City, Canada, January 2000, http://www.pj.net/pjeppson/AAA2000/Papers/shaJeppson1.htm, accessed July 2006.
   1997   "Leveling the Playing Field" in the Contested Territory of the South African Past: A "Public Versus a "People's" Form of Historical Archaeology Outreach. In *In the Realm of Politics: Prospects for Public Participation in African-American and Plantation Archaeology,* edited by C. McDavid and D. W. Babson, special issue of *Historical Archaeology* 31(3):65–83.
Little, Barbara (editor)
   2002   *The Public Benefits of Archaeology.* University of Florida, Gainesville.
   1997   The New National Park Service Thematic Framework for History and Prehistory. *SAA Bulletin* 15(2), http://www.sandaa.org/publications/saabulletin/15–2/SAA12.html, accessed December 2005.
Little, Barbara, and Paul Shackel
   2005   Session Abstract. Archaeology as a Tool of Civic Engagement. Society for Historical and Underwater Annual Meeting held in concert with the Society for Medieval Archaeology, York, England.

Low, Setha M., Dana Taplin, Suzanne Scheld, and Tracy Fisher
  2002   Recapturing Erased Histories: Ethnicity, Design, and Cultural Representation—A Case Study of Independence National Historical Park. *Journal of Architectural and Planning Research* 19(4):282–99.
Lowenthal, David
  1998   *The Heritage Crusade and the Spoils of History.* Cambridge University Press, New York.
Lucas, Gavin
  2001   *Critical Approaches to Fieldwork: Contemporary and Historical Archaeological Practice.* Routledge, London.
Mires, Charlene
  2002   *Independence Hall in American Memory.* University of Pennsylvania Press, Philadelphia, Pennsylvania.
Moodie, T. Dunbar
  1975   *The Rise of Afrikanerdom: Power, Apartheid, and the Afrikaner Civil Religion.* University of California Press, Berkeley.
Morgan, Edmund S.
  2002   *Benjamin Franklin.* Yale University Press, New Haven, Connecticut.
Morrison, Tara
  1998   The UGRR Archaeology Initiative. *CRM* (4):46–47, http://crm.cr.nps.gov/archive/21–4/21–4–15.pdf, accessed September 2003.
National Park Service (NPS)
  2003a Directors Order #75A: Civic Engagement and Public Involvement. Memorandum issued November 17, 2003, Electronic document, http://www.nps.gov/policy/DOrders/75A.htm, accessed July 2006.
  2003b *Civic Engagement: Working with Communities to Tell the Whole Story through Preservation, Interpretation and Education,* Electronic document, http://www.nps.gov/civic/index.html, accessed December 31, 2004.
National Park Service, Independence National Historical Park [NPS INHP STAFF]
  2000   National Register Amendment, Independence National Historical Park, Underground Railroad and Anti-Slavery Movement [prepared by Anna Coxe Toogood], Electronic document, http://www.nps.gov/inde/archeology/NRamend.htm, accessed July 2006.
  1997   General Management Plan, Abbreviated Final Report. Manu-

script on file, INHP Archives, Independence National Historical Park, Philadelphia.

c1980 A Summary of Problems Identified in Brainstorming Sessions and Their Suggested Actions to Aleve [sic] Them. Manuscript on file, INDE INHP Archives/East Division Library, Library II. File: Interpretation Ideas.

1978 [Yoelson, Marty] Commentary on Silent Films of Archaeology Dig, Independence Square in 1957, Demolition of Franklin Court, 1959; Franklin court Dig, 1970–71. Cassette Tape. INHP Archives, Tape Collection. Independence National Historical Park, Philadelphia.

1977 Year End Wish List. Manuscript on file, INDE INHP Archives/East Division Library, Library II. File: Interpretation Ideas.

1970 Independence National Historical Park Archives Photograph and Slide Collections, John Cotter Slide Collection.

1969 Master Plan, Independence National Historical Park. Manuscript on file, INHP Archives, Independence National Historical Park, Philadelphia.

1960 Independence National Historical Park Archives Photograph and Slide Collections, Franklin Court 1960, Working Photograph Collection.

1950 Independence National Historical Park Archives Photograph and Slide Collections, Franklin Court 1960, Working Photograph Collection.

National Park Service, Independence National Historical Park/University of Delaware Museum Technology Course

2002 Franklin Court web pages. Electronic document, http://www.nps.gov/inde/Franklin_Court/Pages/318.html, accessed July 2005.

Philadelphia Museum of Art

1976 *Philadelphia: Three Centuries of American Art, Bicentennial Exhibition Catalogue.* Philadelphia Museum of Art, Philadelphia.

Philadelphia National Shrines Park Commission

1947 Final Report to the United States Congress. Manuscript on file, INHP Archives, Independence National Historical Park, Philadelphia.

Powell, B. Bruce

1961 Franklin Court Collections: T-31, Orianna Street Trench, July–Dec. 1960. April–Sept. 1961. Manuscripts on file, INHP Archives: Powell Acc. No. 696 (4). Series I: Reports, Box 10, Folders 17–25. Independence National Historical Park, Philadelphia.

1962a The Archeology of Franklin Court. Manuscripts on file, INHP Archives: Powell, Acc. No. 696 (3). Series I: Reports, Box 10, Folders 26–28. Independence National Historical Park, Philadelphia.

1962b Problems of Urban Archaeology. *American Antiquity* 27(4):580–83.

Rorty, Richard

1998 *Achieving Our Country: Leftist Thought in Twentieth Century America.* Harvard Press, Cambridge, Massachusetts.

Shackel, Paul A., and Erve J. Chambers (editors)

2004 *Places in Mind: Public Archaeology as Applied Anthropology.* Routledge, New York.

Schumacher, Paul

1953a Estimate for excavation of Benjamin Franklin's Court [Archaeological Project No. 30, renumbered as "4"]. Manuscript on file, INHP Archives: Schumacher, Acc. No. 59. Series I: Reports, Box 10, Folders 1–3. Independence National Historical Park, Philadelphia.

1953b Archeological Field Notes: Franklin Court Archeology—East Side—Archeological Project No. 4. Manuscript on file, INHP Archives: Schumacher, Acc. No. 59. Series I: Reports, Box 10, Folders 1–3. Independence National Historical Park, Philadelphia.

1956 Preliminary Exploration of Franklin Court Archeological Project No. 4, May–Sept. 1953. 1956. Manuscript on file, INHP Archives: Acc. No. 117. Series I: Reports, Box 10, Folder 12. Independence National Historical Park, Philadelphia.

Sheppard, Nick

2003 "When the Hand That Holds the Trowel Is Black": Disciplinary Practices of Self-Representations in Archaeology and the Question of "Native" Labour. Paper presented at the 5th World Archaeology Congress, Washington, D.C.

U.S. Census Bureau

2004a Historical Income Table P-53, Electronic document, http://www.census.gov/hhes/income/histinc/p53.html, accessed July 2005

1953 U.S. Census Bureau Full Time Employee Annual Wage 1953, Electronic document, http://nces.ed.gov/programs/digest/d00/dt079.asp, accessed July 2005.

U.S. Congress, 107th

2002 H.R. 2362: Benjamin Franklin Tercentenary Act, http://

thomas.loc.gov/cgi-bin/query/z?c107:H.R.2362.ENR, accessed July 2006.

Waldstreicher, David
  2004   *Runaway Franklin: Benjamin Franklin, Slavery and the American Revolution.* Hill and Wang, New York.

West, Cornel
  2004   *Democracy Matters.* Penguin Books, New York.
  1989   *The American Evasion of Philosophy: The Genealogy of Pragmatism.* University of Wisconsin Press, Madison.

White, Nancy Marie, Lynne P. Sullivan, and Rochelle A. Marrinan
  1999   *Grit-Tempered: Early Women Archaeologists in the Southeastern United States.* University Press of Florida, Gainesville.

Wood, Gordon S.
  2004   *The Americanization of Benjamin Franklin.* Penguin Books, New York.

Chapter 10

Reconnecting the Present with Its Past: The Doukhobor Pit House Public Archaeology Project

Meagan Brooks

In 1899, escaping persecution, thousands of Doukhobors made new lives in the province of Saskatchewan, Canada. Like many immigrants to North America, many Doukhobors feel they have become divorced from the history and traditions of their pioneering ancestors and are searching for ways to renew their understanding of their past. The Doukhobor Pit House Public Archaeology Project sought to reestablish this connection by actively involving descendants in the excavation of two early Doukhobor sites. Although this project has yielded a body of quantitative archaeological information, the analysis of qualitative data determined the successes, failures, and benefits of the project. Analysis of the material demonstrated several hallmarks of a successful ethnic community archaeological project. While the processes are focused upon the inclusion and revitalization of the Doukhobor community, they can be applied to other communities searching for ways to maintain and renew a connection with the past, as well as find their place within their country's history.

Doukhobor Religion and History

The Doukhobors originated as a reformation movement against the Russian Orthodox Church in the eighteenth century (Tracie

1996:1). The term *Doukhobor,* meaning spirit wrestler, was originally meant as a derogatory term. However, the group transformed the term to suggest that its members were wrestling *for*
rather than *against* the Holy Spirit (Woodcock and Avakumovic
1968:19). Key to the Doukhobor outlook is a belief in a divine
spark. Every living thing, human and animal, has a spark of God
within it. Violence, eating, and even poor treatment of another
living creature were considered the gravest of sins. As a result of
these beliefs, the Doukhobors supported an egalitarian, peaceful
way of life, opposing many tenets of the Orthodox Church and
Russian state (Woodcock and Avakumovic 1968:19–20).

In response to violent persecution the Doukhobors immi-
grated to Canada in 1899. The Canadian government, desperate
to populate its western lands with European farmers, provided
financial aid, free rail transportation, and special allowance of
communal land tenure (Kozakavich 1998:8). Approximately
7400 Doukhobors made their way across Canada, settling in
Saskatchewan. Those who settled along the North Saskatchewan
River built temporary dugout shelters in the side of ravines and
over time built communal villages (Tracie 1996:3).

Beginning in 1907, in response to political changes in Canadian immigration and homesteading policies, the Doukhobor
group began to disperse. Those who remained in Saskatchewan
did so as independent Doukhobors living on their own homesteads according to the Canadian Homestead Act regulations
(Kozakavich 1998:10–11; Woodcock and Avakumovic 1968:198).
During World Wars I and II, due to their pacifist beliefs many
Doukhobor men were sent to labor camps for alternative service.
This persecution left a legacy of fear within the community, hin-
dering growth and creating large generation gaps. Today many
descendants recognize a need to actively reconnect with their
heritage, their past, and each other (figure 10.1).

Project Background

The project began and was carried forward through the interest
and hard work of a small group of people. Brenda Cheveldayoff,

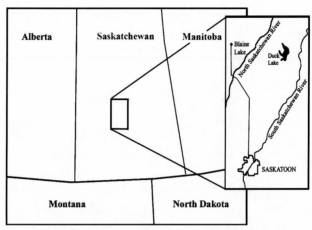

Figure 10.1. Map of Saskatchewan showing the location of Blain Lake inset. National Topographic System, Saskatchewan Index Map 1991, scale 1:1,000,000.

the landowner, had recently lost her father and wanted to commemorate his memory by honoring Doukhobor heritage and the sites that her father had protected. Through her initiative a partnership with the University of Saskatchewan's Department of Archaeology and the Blaine Lake and Saskatoon Doukhobor Societies was created. Financial support from the Saskatchewan Heritage Foundation and the Saskatchewan Archaeological Society helped to create the Doukhobor Pit House Public Archaeology Project.

The main goals of the project were to include Doukhobor voices and interpretations in the archaeological process, creating a study relevant to the community. Determining the successes, benefits, and failures of the project through participant feedback would help researchers examine how public archaeology projects can benefit communities. As a result, active participation by descendants and descendant empowerment were features of public archaeology that were important to incorporate into the project.

From its early preservation focus, characterized by Charles McGimsey's 1972 book *Public Archaeology*, public archaeology has developed into a growing endeavor, covering many different modes of public and descendant engagement. In particular projects such as the University of Calgary's Program for Public

Archaeology and those discussed by authors such as Linda Derry (1997), Ywone Edwards-Ingram (1997), Carol McDavid (1997), Adrian Praetzellis (2002), and Ian Hodder (2000) provide models for appropriate inclusion and public or descendant participation to the benefit of both archaeology and the community.

Recently, this kind of engagement with the public has begun to be discussed in terms of "social capital" and "civic engagement." Robert Putnam's 2000 book *Bowling Alone,* on the decline of social capital within the United States, brought the issue to the forefront, sparking debate and concern. Within Canada, studies have demonstrated a varied decline of trust and participation in traditional political and community forums, related to increased mobility, pressures of time and money, television and the Internet, lack of interpersonal trust, and generational changes (Barnard et al. 2003; Nevitte 2002; Young 2002).

These findings are similar to Putnam's; however, it has been shown that many Canadians do take an interest and participate in civic organizations, in ways different than the previous "civic generation" (Nevitte 2002:12; Putnam 2000:257). For example, studies of younger Canadian generations (fifteen to thirty-five years of age) demonstrate a relatively high rate of involvement in charities, volunteering, and social activities (Barnard et al. 2003). However, these generations demand more of a personal return for their involvement. They want to provide input and learn skills through involvement in community, but many feel that because of their age they are undervalued and ignored by traditional forums (Barnard et al. 2003:26–28).

Archaeology is ideal to match these interests and can play a major role in creative civic engagement. Public archaeology projects can engage individuals on a new level, providing a unique active learning experience while benefiting the community as a whole. Archaeology can also serve as a method of empowering a community. This empowerment is important within civic engagement, as it provides a group with the confidence to participate in the larger community. Within the Doukhobor community, creating this confidence was extremely important to allow increasing social capital to form bridges between communities, to the benefit of the province of Saskatchewan and Canada.

Excavation

The original intent of the excavation was to examine the visible remains of a dugout or pit house, described below, as this was the emotional focus for the local Doukhobor community. However, due to the small size and awkward location of the structure, excavation was limited and another site was added to the project. The Ospennia village, a quarter of a mile from the dugout site, had been built and inhabited by the same group. This site was easier to access, with more excavation options to accommodate the needs of the volunteers. The addition of this site to the project also provided more material for an analysis of public archaeology. The research design also included an examination of the spatial organization of the dugout. It was hoped that the sampling of both sites would contribute to current and future information about Doukhobor villages in Saskatchewan.

Excavation at both the Dugout and Ospennia sites ran for six weeks in the summer of 2004, supervised by myself. An important first step of the project was an opening day ceremony (see figure 10.2), featuring hymns and prayers performed by the local Doukhobor Church. This defined the project's commitment to giving the Doukhobor community an active voice in the archaeology of its past.

In total, thirty-six public volunteers were involved in the excavation of one or both of the sites. Volunteers were almost exclusively of Doukhobor descent, both practicing and nonpracticing. A small number of participants were spouses of descendants and members of the local community. To provide quality supervision and excavation, only six volunteers were scheduled per day. To give everyone the best opportunity to volunteer, the week was split up between the two sites. Volunteers worked individually or with another volunteer, excavating, screening, and writing their own notes, while supervised and aided by myself.

The dugout site had been constructed as a shallow pit dug into the side of a hill, as can be seen in figure 10.3. Wood walls with wooden pegging and daub formed the body of the dugout and a sod roof would have topped the structure. The local Doukhobor community tended to call these structures "caves,"

Figure 10.2. Prayers and hymns were performed at the opening day of the excavation to commemorate the sites and Doukhobor people. Photograph by Meagan Brooks.

Figure 10.3. The remains of the dugout during the fall of 2003, before excavation. Photograph by Meagan Brooks.

possibly due to the cavelike look they would have had once the sod roof grew into the surrounding hillside. At the excavation site, the wood walls remain although any trace of a roof has long since disappeared. Unfortunately the dugout site had few artifacts or features indicating spatial patterns within the structure. However, the excavation did reveal further information upon its construction with a rough wood-and-rock foundation.

Doukhobor communal villages were generally built along a specific plan, featuring a main street with identical houses facing each other (Kozakavich 1998:35). At the Ospennia site regular mounds represent the locations of houses, one of which was mechanically cleared for excavation. A clearly defined cellar pit was located late in the project. The materials from the cellar are related to the abandonment and destruction of the house. As well, articulated animal skeletons and large stones may represent postabandonment waste. Unfortunately the scheduled excavation ended before the cellar could be completely excavated, or further features and outbuildings defined. There is an opportunity for future excavations at the Ospennia site through the University of Saskatchewan or the Saskatchewan Archaeological Society. These future operations will be able to build upon the archaeological work done during the Doukhobor Pit House Public Archaeology Project, hopefully maintaining a positive relationship with the community.

Qualitative Data

While the archaeology of this project did prove fascinating to the researcher and volunteers, this project's true significance lies within the qualitative data analysis. In order to evaluate the program and determine those methods that best lead to beneficial community inclusion, analysis of data gathered through questionnaires, daily journals, and three in-depth interviews was carried out.

Although archaeologists deal with qualitative data frequently, such data are rarely singled out for analysis and their value is often misunderstood. Similarly to the archaeological process, qualitative data must be analyzed rigorously and this methodology accurately recorded in order to look beyond the researcher's assumptions (Patton 2002:434). For a project such as this, qualitative data are a necessity. They can elucidate patterns and themes of the project that have not been apparent from archaeological notes and volunteer demographics.

Methodology

The analyses of the questionnaires, daily journals, and the three interviews were very similar, each seeking to determine the successes, benefits, and problems of the project. Analysis was carried out following and adapting suggested methods from several qualitative research sources (Denzin and Lincoln 1998; Dey 1993; Huberman and Miles 2002; Seale et al. 2004); however, practical evaluation methods from Patton's *Qualitative Research and Evaluation Methods* (2002) formed the basis of the analysis.

The anonymous questionnaires, created by the researcher, asked nine questions relating to research objectives concerning the experience of the project, leaving the tenth for extra comments. The questionnaires were developed in an open-ended format, rather than a closed, multiple-choice format (Patton 2002:5). This was done to allow participants to provide full responses, demonstrating multiple ideas. The questionnaires were included in an information booklet about archaeology and the sites, which was given to the volunteers on their first day of participation. Volunteers were asked to fill it out and return it at the end of their participation in the project. Twenty-six questionnaires were returned, showing a response rate of 72 percent of the total volunteers. While this sample may seem small, it does not negate the worth of the data or the patterns that emerge.

During the project, volunteers were instructed to write journal entries, recording the day's events, finds, and any thoughts they had about their units, the sites, or the project. I intended to use the fifty-seven journals as support for the archaeological notes and analysis, separate from the qualitative data analysis. However, it was later recognized that the journals could demonstrate the volunteers' changing knowledge and perspectives about archaeology and Doukhobor heritage, as well as present more specific opinions about successful and unsuccessful aspects of the project. In order to maintain anonymity similar to that of the questionnaires, the journal entries were transcribed for analysis with all personal identification removed.

The interviews for analysis were carried out toward the end of the project with three individuals, chosen for their heavy involvement in the project. In order to help me conduct the interviews I made and followed an "interview guide." This guide listed a variety of open-ended questions regarding historical and cultural knowledge as well as opinions, feelings, and ideas about the project and the interviewee's experience (Patton 1987:111). Using the guide instead of following a strict list of identical questions ensured that I covered basic issues, while allowing the flexibility for further discussion. Although the interviews followed the same pattern, each was tailored to fit the level and nature of the individual's involvement in the project and his or her community.

The questionnaires, daily journals, and interview transcripts were read through several times before categories and types of responses were identified, creating classifications for each. This was done by the identification of "contextual keywords," words used in similar contexts throughout the data sets. As the interviews were more focused on individuals, contextual keyword counting was broadened to examine overarching meanings through the interviews. To ensure the categories and types were inclusive and exhaustive, classifications were examined and reworked several times with the aid of comments from colleagues and some of the volunteers from the project. Classification categories for the data sets covered areas such as motivation; personal and wider benefits; changing perspectives of archaeology, the sites, and community; and positive and negative aspects of the project. The final versions of the classifications were examined to elucidate correlations and patterns in responses between the data sets.

Discussion

The results of qualitative analysis can be broadly divided into three sections: information that can be applied to general applications; the process of working with an ethnic community; and benefits of the project for the community. While some patterns were expected, matching those demonstrated in other studies of archaeology's relationship with the public (McManamon 2002; Pokotylo 2002), others were more surprising with interesting applications.

General Applications

In many ways, the experience and opinions of the Doukhobor volunteers were similar to those of the general public. Common combinations of motivations for participation were an emotional interest in the sites, a desire to celebrate heritage, supporting family and community activities, and an interest in archaeology. Despite this range individuals were predominantly interested because of their heritage connection: "I became interested because of my Doukhobor background" (questionnaire response). Due to this prevalent motivation it had been expected that the majority of individuals would indicate a desire to participate in future archaeological projects only if they were personally related. Instead, it was seen that there was little correlation, positive or negative, between prior motivation and future participation. Rather, the correlation was found in responses indicating a beneficial learning experience.

Almost all individuals who filled out questionnaires and a portion who wrote in the daily journals indicated that they found "learning about archaeology" the most enjoyable and personally beneficial aspect of the project. Most volunteers indicated in the questionnaires that they would take part in another archaeology project regardless of personal involvement. This is positively linked with a detailed satisfaction with the guidance of the supervising archaeologist in providing a supportive learning environment. The positive relationship formed with the archaeologist encouraged participants to expand their knowledge of archaeology and discover ways of becoming engaged in archaeology and heritage issues in communities (figure 10.4).

Figure 10.4. Volunteers learning about archaeology by excavating and writing notes for their own units. Photograph by Meagan Brooks.

Interviews indicated similar patterns. The interviewed individuals had highly personal and emotional motivations for being involved in the project, some needing to honor ancestors and loved ones, others trying to recapture a lost past. Their responses regarding archaeology indicated a prior lack of knowledge and some concerns. In particular there was a prevalent attitude that archaeology was an endeavor only for exotic and "old" cultures.

> [The project] gave us a chance to partake. Whereas if you heard about another one, like the one at Wanuskewin [a nearby First Nations National Historic Site and heritage park], we would hear about it, but you aren't a part of it and therefore you don't walk in and say gee, I'd like to learn how. (interview response)

All the interviewees indicated that as a result of their positive experience with the project and archaeologists involved, they were able to appreciate archaeology as worthwhile and relevant to their community and province. An active learning experience as opposed to that of being a spectator was considered a great personal benefit and ensured continuing respect for the field.

> Yes I do understand archaeology better, I totally respect it. A lot of people don't understand what it all involved. So you spend a day seeing it, you respect it a little more than what it was always projected before, it was "oh so they dig and do all this stuff," but once you work with it you learn to respect the field. It's hard work. (interview response)

How much the volunteers learned about archaeology can be seen through their journal entries. The entries demonstrated an average of six appropriate descriptions of the archaeology and daily events and an average of three archaeological terms per entry. Among the entry descriptions, 23 percent even presented what I call "Above and Beyond" recording, where the volunteer demonstrated ideas and critical thinking about the sites, finds, or project. Over the course of the project, journal entries show a slight rise in the amount of archaeological descriptions and terms used. This rise was likely due to my increasing confidence in my teaching skills over the course of the project. Individuals who volunteered more than three days during the excavation also demonstrated a slight improvement in these areas.

These patterns can be interpreted to indicate that the volunteers saw their initial reasons for doing archaeology as relating only to this particular project and not to a favorable attitude about archaeology in general. Instead of even a general interest in archaeology, the personal and heritage links to the project were key to participation. Without these motivations it is unlikely that the majority of these individuals would have acquired such a complete introduction to archaeology. Participants genuinely enjoyed learning about archaeology and through encouragement in a learning environment were able to do their best. It is clear that a beneficial hands-on learning experience is more likely to increase interest, support, and future participation, regardless of heritage interests.

Working with an Ethnic Community

Archaeology within a specific ethnic community often needs different processes to ensure success. Analysis of the qualitative materials identified several of these processes that were particularly successful with the Doukhobor community. Throughout the data analysis, it became clear that the archaeologist's sensitive behavior and willingness to maintain an open dialogue were the keys to a beneficial experience for the community.

There were several concerns about the project that were unique to the Doukhobors. In particular media attention was a great concern and frustration for all members of the community. Past media attention has generally been inaccurate and biased, focusing upon the negative activities of the Sons of Freedom, a Doukhobor extremist group based in British Columbia, Canada.

> On TV and radio we always get associated with just the Sons of Freedom and the media doesn't seem to understand that there is a division here that is another group and this is us. The history follows us and maybe it hasn't all been positive but, as far as the media is concerned, must we keep saying that? (interview response)

Due to these problems with media and the past persecution and ignorance directed at the Doukhobor community, many older members were wary of institutions and public events that would draw attention to the community. Some believed that the university would use the community to gain publicity for itself. To ease these concerns, Brenda Cheveldayoff ensured that the media would be handled with strict guidelines. She did this with great skill, organizing the media at events so that crews would film and report on the community first and the archaeology second. As a result, news pieces that were positive and fair were produced, greatly increasing the comfort level of the community and participants.

Maintaining a dialogue with the volunteers was also extremely important to their comfort level. This dialogue ensured they felt engaged, involved, and valued. Part of this was the understanding that the Doukhobor community was to be given priority in the project over nondescendants and archaeological groups.

> We would be the first ones to see and hear and everything, so I think we were quite excited about that and of course we heard that others would be coming in after us to finish it and after having gone through that we felt good about that, just to be first on there was great. (interview response)

Instead of watching its past being interpreted from the sidelines, the community had the opportunity to contribute. Not only were its comments and feelings considered but its members were involved in every step of the excavation.

In this process, the archaeologist, so often the teacher, became the student. Before beginning excavation each morning, a brief explanation of archaeology, the sites, and the project was given. It was important to be very clear about my own objectives, in order to clear up misconceptions that I would be taking the artifacts and site away from the community. This was followed by a brief explanation of Doukhobor history, providing volunteers the opportunity to discuss and share stories. This dialogue continued throughout the day, as artifacts were found and each participant was encouraged to discuss his or her own interpretations and include them in the field notes: "Had some conversation about the Doukhobors, possibly what they brought with them to dig this dugout. Talked about the structure and how it could have been put together" (journal entry).

For Doukhobors in particular, finding the remains of butchered bone could be upsetting. Although most Doukhobors are no longer vegetarian, many are proud of their ancestors' convictions. The most successful policy was one of sensitivity coupled with discussion. The volunteers were encouraged to give their opinions, and as a result several valid interpretations for the presence of butchered bone were given. For example, one participant told of non-Doukhobor men working for her grandparents, who threatened to leave if they were not fed meat. As a result the workers were supplied with butchered meat, the remains of which were presumably deposited in her grandparents' midden. Future studies of Doukhobor villages and homesteads can build upon information such as this, to provide more complete interpretations of Doukhobor life. Discussing the issue helped to diffuse the tension of the volunteers, equalize the relationship with the archaeologist, and improve the quality of the archaeology.

The archaeologist's demeanor was also important to the Doukhobor community. While many Doukhobors indicated that they appreciated the archaeologist's patience and teaching skills, her professionalism had the most impact. An effort was made by myself and any visiting archaeologists to maintain sensitive and appropriate behavior at all times. This included attempting to be friendly yet neutral within the community. For example, I tried to accept invitations to some community events, such as church lunches, while politely declining others, such as political meetings with the town. Similarly, all my communication with the media was aimed at providing clear, accurate, and sensitive information about the project and encouraging the media to speak with community members on all other matters. Volunteers indicated that this professional but attentive manner helped the Doukhobors to feel comfortable with the project.

> I think what really helped us feel more relaxed is . . . when you were dealing with the children and the teachers that came out and when you explained the archaeological aspect in a professional manner all of a sudden they start viewing us in a professional manner much better than we were perceived before. (interview response)

Benefits

The benefits identified by volunteers through the questionnaires, daily journals, and interviews are both personal and community-wide. Personal benefits, such as learning about heritage and reconnecting with the community, add up to larger community benefits with long-term impacts.

The largest short-term benefit of this project has been the positive exposure the Doukhobor community has received. This exposure has generated new interest in Saskatchewan about this group, creating opportunities for tourism. The positive exposure also created a revitalization of family and heritage, hopefully for the long term.

Great exchange of ideas, from the Langham area, from the east, from Veregin, Kamsack area, etc. The phones were ringing, people were talking and the Peter's Day celebration [annual event commemorating the burning of weapons], for example, was a little bigger than usual. We are still here and people are helping us to remember and document. Maybe it helps us see what direction we are going to go in now. Because often we think, "oh the old ways are great we don't want to give those up" but then sometimes we have to and progress with time. (interview response)

Renewed discussion about heritage and the past allows more community members, young and old, to become engaged in determining the course of the future for the Doukhobors. Even disagreements, inevitable within any community, can be viewed positively because they stimulate an exchange of ideas and information needed for new growth.

Support from outside groups such as the University of Saskatchewan and the Saskatchewan government was essential to encouraging this revitalization: "The positiveness of the university people, yourself, Margaret Kennedy brought with it made it, well, we felt better about ourselves and we said we were going to do more about it now" (interview response). As Saskatchewan moves into its second century, the government is actively encouraging the maintenance and growth of communities such as this for the future of the province. This positive interaction with government officials, so different from past experiences, has created bridges for the Doukhobors to become involved in the province as a community. Far from being persecuted and ignored in the province, the community is beginning to feel it is an integral part of Saskatchewan's heritage.

There is a concern, however, that this hype will be short-lived. It will be up to the community to maintain the momentum created by the project and find long-term benefits. Archaeology's role is now to provide assistance when asked; it is the community that must take the initiative. Fortunately the Doukhobor community, through the initiative of a few, has already taken steps to create long-term benefits from the project.

In 2005, at a ceremony attended by Lynda Haverstock, the lieutenant governor of Saskatchewan, the dugout site and surrounding land were designated a Provincial Heritage Site. Government funding has been awarded for the stabilization of the site and the creation of a website. The Doukhobor Dugout House Inc., a nonprofit organization established to oversee the protection and future development of the land, has recently opened a museum at the pit house site. The Doukhobor Dugout House (www.doukhobordugouthouse.com) features tours by costumed interpreters and artifact displays from the project. It is also planning cultural Doukhobor workshops in conjunction with the Doukhobor Societies (Brenda Cheveldayoff, personal communication).

A specially made scrapbook, and a copy of the thesis created by the project, will be kept for future generations of the community and circulated within the community. It is hoped that the ties formed between archaeologists and the Doukhobor community will be maintained through future consulting and the involvement of many heritage and archaeology professionals in new plans for the sites.

Conclusion

Historical archaeology's interaction with all communities is clearly important. There are few contexts, however, in which historical archaeology can be more beneficial than with modern world immigrants. The very act of immigration begins the process of divergence from the past and traditions. These can be regained with a renewed sense of pride and empowerment through the aid of archaeology. The Doukhobor community can have a more active voice in its local communities and province, becoming civically engaged. In some aspects the Doukhobors of the Canadian West experienced the archaeology as would the general public. It is vital, however, when working with an ethnic group that archaeologists listen as well as teach. Involving the ethnic community in active participation of excavation is the first step, but without including it in the larger dialogue, this effort is wasted. The historic archaeologist has a duty to maintain this dialogue in an open but professional atmosphere. Despite the recognition of these processes, if the project is not beneficial in the short and long term it cannot be called successful. To benefit the community as a whole, to reconnect this present with its past, we must look to the future. Historical archaeology has helped to give the Doukhobors the tools and confidence to mend this break, but it is up to them to keep moving forward together with their province and country.

References Cited

Barnard, Robert, Denise Campbell, Shelley Smith, and Don Embul-
deniya
    2003   Citizen Re:Generation: Understanding Active Citizen Engage-
ment Among Canada's Information Age Generations. Electronic document, www.d-code.com, pdf file, accessed August
30, 2005.
Denzin, Norman K., and Yvonna S. Lincoln (editors)
    1998   *Collecting and Interpreting Qualitative Materials.* Sage Publica-
tions Inc., Thousand Oaks, California.
Derry, Linda
    1997   Pre-Emancipation Archaeology: Does It Play in Selma, Ala-
bama. In *Historical Archaeology* 31(3):18–26.
Dey, Ian
    1993   *Qualitative Data Analysis: A User-Friendly Guide for Social Scien-
tists.* Routledge, London.
Edwards-Ingram, Ywone
    1997   Toward "True Acts of Inclusion": The "Here" and the "Out
There" Concepts in Public Archaeology. *Historical Archaeology*
31(3):27–35.
Hodder, Ian (editor)
    2000   *Towards Reflexive Method in Archaeology: The Example of Çat-
alhöyük.* MacDonald Institute for Archaeological Research,
University of Cambridge, Cambridge.
Huberman, Michael A., and Matthew B. Miles (editors)
    2002   *The Qualitative Researcher's Companion.* Sage Publications Inc.,
Thousand Oaks, California.
Kozakavich, Stacey
    1998   A State of Change: An Historical Archaeology of Doukho-
bor Identity at Kirilovka Village Site FcNx-1. Unpublished

Master's Thesis, Department of Archaeology, University of Saskatchewan, Saskatoon.

McDavid, Carol
  1997 Descendants, Decisions, and Power: The Public Interpretation of the Archaeology of the Levi Jordan Plantation. *Historical Archaeology* 31(3):114–131.

McGimsey, Charles R. III
  1972 *Public Archaeology,* Seminar Press, New York.

McManamon, Francis P.
  2002 Heritage, History and Archaeological Educators. In *Public Benefits of Archaeology,* Barbara J. Little, editor, pp. 31–45. University Press of Florida, Gainesville.

Nevitte, Neil
  2002 Introduction: Value Change and Reorientation in Citizen-State Relations. In *Value Change and Governance in Canada,* edited by Neil Nevitte, pp. 3–35. University of Toronto Press, Toronto.

Patton, Michael Quinn
  1987 *How to Use Qualitative Methods in Evaluation.* Sage Publications Inc., Newbury Park, California.
  2002 *Qualitative Research and Evaluation Methods,* 3rd ed. Sage Publications, Thousand Oaks, California.

Pokotylo, David
  2002 Public Opinion and Canadian Archaeological Heritage: A National Perspective. *Canadian Journal of Archaeology* 26(2):88–129.

Praetzellis, Adrian
  2002 Neat Stuff and Good Stories: Interpreting Historical Archaeology in Two Local Communities. In *Public Benefits of Archaeology,* edited by Barbara J. Little, pp. 51–58. University Press of Florida, Gainesville.

Putnam, Robert D.
  2000 *Bowling Alone: The Collapse and Revival of American Community.* Simon and Schuster, New York.

Seale, Clive et al. (editors)
  2004 *Qualitative Research Practice.* Sage Publications Ltd, London.

Tracie, Carl J.
  1996 *"Toil and Peaceful Life": Doukhobor Village Settlement in Saskatchewan, 1899–1918.* Canadian Plains Research Centre, University of Regina, Regina, Saskatchewan.

Woodcock, George, and Ivan Avakumovic
  1968 *The Doukhobors.* Oxford University Press, London.

Young, Lisa
  2002 Civic Engagement, Trust and Democracy: Evidence from Alberta. In *Value Change and Governance in Canada,* edited by Niel Nevitte, pp. 107–147. University of Toronto Press, Toronto.

Chapter 11

Heritage in Hampden: A Participatory Research Design for Public Archaeology in a Working-Class Neighborhood, Baltimore, Maryland

David A. Gadsby and Robert C. Chidester

Notions of reflexivity, community collaboration, and craft have become prominent in archaeology in the last ten to fifteen years. The goal of an ongoing community-based project in the working-class neighborhood of Hampden, in Baltimore, Maryland, is to use these concepts to create an activist archaeology that works in solidarity with a contemporary community for positive social change. Our public archaeology work serves community needs by involving willing community members in the project design and execution, beginning with the very earliest stages of the research. Thus, even before creating a research design, we began our project by forging community ties through partnerships with local civic and social service organizations. More importantly, we held a series of public history workshops, conceived of as dialogues with the community, to aid in the process of research design production. Labor historians in Britain and the United States have employed such workshops as union organizing tools since at least the late 1960s, and historian James Green has most recently described their effectiveness in his book *Taking History to Heart* (2000). We see these as a crucial step in using the skills and knowledge that we as archaeologists possess and placing them at the service of community members.

As not only archaeologists but also applied anthropologists, we are consciously locating our work within a tradition of community-based research (CBR) (Austin 2004; Lamphere 2004). The key tenets of the practice of CBR are fostering collaboration with local individuals and organizations; reflective practice and reciprocal learning between the community and scholars; building the capacity to create meaningful change; the balancing of research and action; interdisciplinarity and multidisciplinarity; and the situation of problems within a context larger than that of the subject community (Austin 2004:421–422). In any context individual or corporate actors necessarily have an incomplete knowledge of all of the factors affecting a specific situation, and thus those who are able to define problems also have the power to define appropriate solutions. As scholars, it is our ethical duty to support the ownership and authority of local communities over the problems facing them (Austin 2004:420) by providing them with open access to our skills and knowledge rather than taking the power to define problems and solutions for ourselves, based on our authority as "experts." In this sense, we consider ourselves to be practitioners of what Nina Wallerstein and Bonnie Duran (2003:29–31) have termed the southern tradition of collaborative research (in the context of social approaches to health research), in which the emphasis is on fostering critical consciousness and achieving social justice rather than taking a top-down, scientific approach to problem solving.

With these goals in mind, we have identified several important components in building a viable community archaeology in Hampden:

1) Identify community members and interest groups.
2) Determine the presence of a public value for archaeology in the neighborhood.
3) Form public and community alliances and partnerships for collaborative research.
4) Ensure adequate outreach and publicity.
5) Actively seek public participation in all stages of project design and interpretation, and be willing to refine these in the light of community responses and concerns (see Menzies 2001, 2004 for a similar approach to CBR).

We used our public history workshops as a way to approach each of these components. In doing so, we have sorted out a series of issues that Hampden residents have identified as being important in their understanding of the neighborhood's history. The workshops have also enabled us to delineate the various interest groups within the neighborhood, and to tease out some of the difficulties of doing research in this participatory manner.

We will begin with a brief discussion of contemporary Hampden and its history, followed by a description of the public history workshops and the results that have come from them, including the implementation of a public heritage program in Hampden.

Contemporary Hampden

Hampden is located in central Baltimore, Maryland. The area lies in the piedmont region of central Maryland, just along the fall line to the coastal plain. It occupies a low ridge just north of and upstream from the confluence of the Jones Falls to the west and its tributary Stony Run to the east, both of which ultimately drain into the Patapsco River and the Chesapeake Bay. The community is a predominantly white, working-class urban neighborhood currently in the throes of a rapid process of gentrification.

The United States Census reports that as of the year 2000, the population of Hampden was 4,873. Just over 90 percent of those people reported themselves as being racially "white" (U.S. Census 2004). This is a notable statistic in a city with a 65 percent African American population. The neighborhood is composed largely of row homes (or town houses), some of which date from as early as the 1840s, when corporations built them as housing for workers in the textile mills that were once an important part of Hampden's economy. These worker houses are some of the archaeological sites that form the basis for our project.

With the exception of one small operation, Hampden's textile mills are gone. Much of its economic activity is now based around a series of shops and restaurants along Thirty-sixth

Street (also known as "the Avenue"), most of which sell home decorations, antiques, food, liquor, or books, as well as an assortment of convenience stores, pharmacies, hardware stores, dry cleaners, tax lawyers, and so forth. Although the Avenue has long been the commercial center of Hampden, the present businesses represent a commercial renaissance for the neighborhood that has been underway for roughly a decade.

Beginning in the 1980s, area developers began to renovate the old mill buildings as artists' studios and offices. The influx of artists, according to sociologist Sharon Zukin (1995:23), places a neighborhood squarely on the road to gentrification, and that gentrification has occurred with increasing intensity over the past several years. Housing prices are on the rise as affluent families (often referred to as "yuppies" by longtime residents) move into the area. A merchants' association, with the aid of a large federal Main Streets grant, has altered the look and character of the Avenue, installing expensive boutiques, restaurants, and bars meant to attract visiting consumers from elsewhere, while rising rents have pushed locally owned businesses to other locations. A recent issue of *National Geographic Traveler* (Stables 2005:20), which showcases Hampden as an "up and coming neighborhood," attests to the increasing draw of places like this as tourist destinations. Most recently, the Hampden Village Merchants Association has paid to have the neighborhood listed as a historic district on the National Register of Historic Places (City of Baltimore 2005).

These changes have had a powerful impact on Hampden's more traditional community. Many have expressed a sense of helplessness in the face of change, and some fear that the rising property taxes that accompany rising housing prices will force them out of homes that their families have owned for decades or generations. As one longtime resident says, "There's nothing here for us anymore" (Juanita Morris, personal communication, 2004).

Thus, Hampden has begun to transform into a caricature of itself. It has not reached the state of a fully consumption-based "pleasure citadel" (D. Harvey 1991:237) such as Baltimore's Inner Harbor (D. Harvey 1991:247–248) or New York's Times

Square (Zukin 1995:133–142). It is instead something between the "genuine article" of a working-class neighborhood—working-class people still to some extent live and shop there—and a complete fake. The direction of development seems to be headed toward the latter, however, and as developers and merchants march gentrification forward, a new symbolic economy based around the neighborhood's working-class image has begun to evolve. Public festivals, restaurants, and shops on Hampden's main street lampoon an imaginary blue-collar experience by disseminating inaccurate and cartoonlike images of working-class men and women. They capitalize on the "kitsch" of working-class lives and homes and parody the tastes and styles of working-class people in public performances. In this new Hampden, working-class people are abstracted, sketched as cartoons, and relegated to the no-man's-land of Hampden's working past. They are thus safe and unthreatening, but retain an illusion of authenticity. The commodification of Hampden's working-class heritage cannot be seen as some kind of passive process. It is detrimental to the public political voice of working people and thus has material political and economic consequences.

Zukin's 1995 analysis of urban gentrification is based on the symbolic economy, in which agents of gentrification and commerce in American cities rely on "culture" and "style," including art, heritage, and history, to create urban spaces where people can consume commodities and businesspeople can conduct their business (Zukin 1995:13). This has meant the semiprivatization of formerly public places such as parks and streets. In turn, the democratic processes that formerly governed the management of such places have been co-opted by private interests, and the voices of developers, businesspeople, and other elites are privileged over those of most citizens. Additionally, elites, under the auspices of the historic preservation movement, have taken control of the histories of those transformed places, and used those histories as tools to further gentrification (Zukin 2005:124).

History and heritage, then, become no small problem for people in Hampden. As Zukin (1995:124–125) notes, historic designations can raise the cost of living in a neighborhood dramatically. University of Texas anthropologist John Hartigan (2000:16) has written about the propensity of working-class whites to regard history in terms of people and events in the past, while middle-class whites tend to regard it as being related to material culture, particularly houses. In the second formulation, houses are of course also imbued with elevated monetary value because of their possession of (any) history. Thus what was once particular history—the history of working-class struggle, or alternately of neighborhood unity—is transformed into a generic kind of history that is assumed to exist in old houses. Places become worth something not because they are associated with a particular person or event, but because they have "something about them," a "character" or "style" that speaks to the aesthetic sensibilities of middle-class gentrifiers.

More importantly, history of this kind can be marketed, as in the case of the multimillion-dollar Clipper Mill redevelopment in the nearby neighborhood of Woodberry. Here, developers have explicitly used the heritage of a nineteenth-century foundry as a selling point for their new luxury condominiums:

> In 1853, a modest machine plant was born on Woodberry Road, just north of a nameless branch of the Jones Falls at the foot of Tempest Hill. The new plant, coined Union Machine Shops, housed Poole & Hunt's general offices, an iron foundry, erecting and pattern shops, a melting house and stables. Instantly it became the backbone of the Woodberry/Hampden community, employing thousands of men as it grew to become one of the country's largest machine manufacturing plants.[1]
>
> Today, Struever Bros., Eccles & Rouse, Inc. is redeveloping Clipper Mill, creating a new urban corporate campus and upscale residential community. (Struever Brothers, Eccles and Rouse 2005)

This kind of marketing simultaneously elides the role of working people in the creation of the neighborhood now being gentrified and hijacks their history as a history of place over people. People who live in surrounding neighborhoods—people with a stake in how redevelopment goes—are left out of the process.

The processes of gentrification are broadly overdetermined by a dizzying array of interconnected social, cultural, and economic forces, and their foundation is built upon discourse. In order to understand how hegemonic discourses are created, copied, and perpetuated, however, we must first examine them on the level of practice. In other words, we need to understand how democracy is hijacked from the bottom up and whether or not there are prospects for creating a more democratic development process. Just as Foucault (1977/1995) has suggested that understanding contemporary modes of surveillance means examining the microphysics of personal discipline, those interested in the workings of the discourses of late capitalism should seek to understand how they are "generalized" through the "regular extension, the infinitely minute" (Foucault 1977/1995:224) operation of discursive hegemony within the confines of daily life.

Pasts, both individual and collective, can alternately become an important organizing principle for political action. In Hampden, we have tried to engage community members in an exploration of the community's history, particularly its history of working-class struggle and labor heritage, in the hope that they will find grounds for a public discourse that includes all community members and that contests those discourses put forward by gentrifiers. Additionally, we attempt to foster community pride by engaging the public in an ongoing study of the archaeological remains of everyday life there.

Historical Background

The community possesses a rich social history. The neighborhood began in the early years of the nineteenth century as a series of scattered villages designed to house the labor pool for gristmills along the Jones Falls. As the mills converted to the production of cotton duck, or canvas, the early villages gradually expanded uphill, converging at the ridge top and forming the neighborhood of Hampden, a moderately sized and cohesive town community with a large, stable working population, mostly of western European descent (Beirne 1976:86–87). Originally located in Baltimore County, the neighborhood was incorporated into the City of Baltimore in 1888 (Arnold 1978).

Churches, public halls, labor halls, social clubs, and a library came to play a major part in the town's development (Bullock 1971:16). Many of these institutions, particularly the churches, are still visible on the contemporary landscape. The construction of such institutions played a major role in a paternalistic social system that enmeshed Hampden's residents and workers in a series of relations that tied them, economically and socially, to the community, and especially to the mills.

Those mills and their associated industries constitute a vital part of the Hampden story. They provided the economic incentive for migration to the area and a ready-made social and economic system for the growing village. The mill owners literally built the oldest parts of the neighborhood and had a hand in the development of much of the rest. The mills themselves constituted a source of livelihood for Hampden's residents well into the twentieth century and served as an important source of community cohesion (Hollyday 1994:101–115; Beirne 1989, 68). At the height of the industry, seven mills operated in the Jones Falls Valley. They employed three thousand people and commanded a major part of the nation's cotton production through the Second World War (Beirne 1976:90).

Labor relations played a vital role in Hampden's past. Throughout the first century of Hampden's existence, its mill owners used paternalism to establish and maintain industrial discipline in the community. Their strategies involved building housing, creating institutions, supporting churches, fostering kinship relations, and appealing to race or heritage to maintain discipline among factory workers. Historian Bill Harvey (1988:22–25) suggests that a tacit agreement existed between workers and mill owners, in which the owners agreed not to hire people of African or eastern European descent (outsiders) in exchange for worker discipline. Whether or not such an agreement ever actually existed, historical evidence indicates that Hampden's working population was politically active throughout the village's economic heyday, from the 1870s to the 1920s, and frequently established union locals and participated in organized labor actions (Chidester 2005).

Demographic stability has been a theme in Hampden's history. Generally, Hampden has drawn residents from rural parts of

Virginia, West Virginia, Maryland, and Pennsylvania (B. Harvey 1988:2–3). The boom years of the 1870s and 1880s saw a dramatic increase in migration to Hampden, but a high degree of residential stability has been present since then: families now living in Hampden may have inhabited the same house for three or four generations (Beirne 1976:84). This stability has meant much to Hampden residents who see their neighborhood as unique and traditional.

One feature of demographic stability has been the historical exclusion of outsiders. As noted, African Americans and eastern Europeans have historically been excluded from the community and from the livelihood that the mill labor allowed workers. The area remains predominantly white. As late as 1979, the Ku Klux Klan was considered a "social club" (Butler 1979) and as recently as 1990, racist groups were allowed to march in Hampden, citing it as "one of the last white neighborhoods around" (News Services and Staff Reports 1990). This perception is due in part to Hampden's resistance to the blockbusting real estate practices of the 1960s and 1970s, when speculating realtors capitalized on white working-class racism by buying houses below market value from white homeowners afraid of integrated neighborhoods and selling them at above market value to African-American families (Durr 2003). Hampden has not been as successful at resisting gentrification and the increased diversity that comes with it. While conditions seem to be changing rapidly, and diversity seems to be on the increase, it remains important for Hampden to confront its past racial difficulties.

Public History Workshops as a
Starting Point for Community Collaboration

With the aid of a small grant from the Maryland Humanities Council, the senior author organized a series of three public history workshops held in Hampden throughout the fall of 2004. The format for each of the three workshops was as follows: A speaker who was knowledgeable about some facet of Hampden history spoke for twenty to thirty minutes, and then the floor was opened to all attendees, with the speaker and David Gadsby moderating the discussion. Each workshop focused on a different topic: general Hampden history, labor history in Hampden, and archaeology in Hampden. Workshop participants were eager to participate, to hold discussions about neighborhood history, and to critique, correct, or respond to workshop leaders when they felt it necessary. Because a variety of people attended the workshops, the range of questions and comments was diverse. In large part, however, a great deal of energy was focused around the themes of old versus new, and outsiders versus insiders.

One of the key roles of scholars involved in CBR is to place local problems, whether social, economic, or other kinds, into a larger context. Anthropologist Diane Austin has pointed out that while it may be true that local people know the problems besetting their community the best, that does not necessarily mean that they know all they need to know to fix them. In most situations, local problems can be traced to larger-scale processes whose relevance may not be immediately apparent. Thus, "transferring decision making about such problems to local leaders and residents places responsibility and some control on their shoulders, but it does not grant them authority in the arenas where the decisions that create these problems are made" (Austin 2004:420). The workshops that we held were a way for us to find out not only what concerns are foremost in the minds of contemporary Hampden residents, but also the contexts in which such concerns are viewed. This, in turn, has allowed us to think about the ways in which we might be able to place these concerns within larger societal contexts.

By reviewing videotapes of the workshops, classifying responses by general theme, and applying appropriate larger contexts, we have identified four major research topics, or themes, to be addressed by public archaeology in the community. In other words, we have used these workshops to build a research model for understanding Hampden on its own terms. The chief components of this model are

Gentrification, Stability, and Social Change
Race and Racism
Class, Labor, and Paternalism
Gender, Family, and Work.

Gentrification, Stability, and Social Change

An important goal of community archaeology is to establish links between past and present—to explore ways in which contemporary conditions have been shaped by history. Taking the recent gentrification as an archaeological problem for Hampden provides an opportunity to do this. Gentrification, as a form of change, can be contrasted easily with the idea of stability, proposed as an important aspect of life in Baltimore's industrial communities by historical geographer Randall Beirne (1976, 1979a, 1979b) in the 1970s. It is important to explore ways that the archaeological record in times of change and instability contrasts with that of times of stability. In order to address the problem of gentrification, this research thus includes the most recent archaeological deposits as well as standing structures in order to illuminate gentrification as a part of a broad historical context.

Race and Racism

Hampden's character as a traditionally white community foregrounds race as a prominent feature of its history. Workshop participants frequently discussed whether or not Hampden was a racist place, how minorities were treated during the Jim Crow era, and the incipient diversity in the community. There was, however, no discussion of the black part of the neighborhood, known as Hoe's Heights.

Numerous historical archaeologists have researched issues of race and racialization, typically by employing a comparative method between the assemblages of the dominant and dominated race or ethnicity. Race and the identity of African-Americans, as explored by archaeologists such Laurie Wilkie (2000), Leland Ferguson (1992), Matthew Emerson (1988), and Mark Leone and Gladys-Marie Fry (1999), has been a major focus of such studies. However, Hampden, which has been historically conceived of as a racially homogeneous community, presents a different problem because, in theory, there should not be race-based variation in the material culture. One solution may be to do some excavating in the abovementioned Hoe's Heights for comparison. Another may be to explore various theoretical frameworks in an attempt to explain how racial ideals are constructed and maintained. Theoretical perspectives that emphasize the formation of white social identity vis-à-vis an imaginary other (e.g., Goldberg 2002; Roediger 1999; Saxton 1990) are quite useful in theorizing past and present social dynamics in Hampden. Theories around white identity that link race and class provide an avenue by which to explore their construction within specific historical contexts (Hartigan 1997:496).

Class, Labor, and Paternalism

There should be no doubt that Hampden is and has been a site of class struggle. Historically, this struggle has been carried out in the traditional form of labor's resistance to or negotiation with capital, organized or otherwise, over the terms of work, pay, and housing (Chidester 2005). Recently, however, the struggle has taken on new dimensions. Working-class people, the neighborhood's traditional inhabitants, view gentrification and the coming of middle-class people as an invasion. Conversely, the gentrifiers view their presence in the neighborhood as a force for economic revival and see little or no need to negotiate the terms of that revival with the "natives."

Class relations in company towns are of obvious importance, and they were identified repeatedly by workshop participants, particularly in conjunction with statements about contemporary class relations. The social system in Hampden was structured around the mills, and it was hierarchical, just as the mills were. Archaeologically, we can address this by exploring the domestic activity patterns of members of various social classes. Additionally, the concept of paternalism and its decline in the early twentieth century pose an opportunity for archaeological research. As workers transitioned from a system of paternalism through welfare capitalism to one of modern corporate capitalism, certain changes, such as increased diversity in consumer goods, should be evident in the material record.

Gender, Family, and Work

A fourth subject of inquiry for workshop participants was that of the role of women in family life and in the workplace. Women and their roles in the past have been a focus of archaeology since the early 1970s. Feminist archaeologists have pointed not only to the presence of women in the historical record (e.g., Conkey and Gero 1991; Gilchrist 1991) but also to their roles in creating and maintaining identities (e.g., Meskell 2001; Voss 1999). Within historical archaeology, some theorists have begun to examine working-class women's spaces such as the Boott Mills boardinghouses (Mrozowski et al. 1996) and houses of prostitution (Seifert 2005).

Workshop participants were surprised to learn that much of the mill workforce was composed of women and children, and they wanted to know what roles women played in the workforce. Archaeological explorations of worker housing at Hampden should reveal artifacts and patterns related to family life and gender. In addition, a millgirl housing complex, now dismantled, might provide an opportunity to explore the archaeology of a living space inhabited mostly by young women.

Conclusion

It is important to stress that we do not see this model as set in stone, and we can easily identify some problems with it. For instance, we are conscious that public history workshops draw from a relatively limited pool of the community's population: those interested in history and heritage. We continually attempt to broaden our audience by conducting excavation out in public, providing site tours and volunteer opportunities. Similarly, we find that we must be cognizant of our own research agendas and balance them appropriately with those of the community. This we accomplish through additional community forums such as a publicly accessible weblog, or "blog," and by keeping an open ear to feedback and criticism from community members and project participants. Additionally, while this program places archaeology at its core, it is multidisciplinary in nature. In addition to historical and archaeological research, we include oral history, ethnography, social geography, and heritage studies as integral parts of this project. Finally, we strive to continue public outreach activities as we complete research, analysis, and writing and also after these phases of the project are over by engaging in what Roger Sanjek (2004:448) has termed "third stage" activities, such as writing for a nonacademic audience and engaging the local media. We hope that these approaches to participatory research will allow and encourage a greater number of Hampden residents to learn about our project and to participate in it.

We also maintain partnerships with several community organizations, including the local high school, the Hampden Community Council, and the Hampden Main Streets Association, a local business organization. We have received funding from the city of Baltimore and are continuing to request support from local and national foundations. Ties such as these can only strengthen a community-based project. Additionally, we provide educational opportunities that redress a serious problem with the high school dropout rate in Hampden by training area high school and university students together.

Despite our faith in "history from below" and community collaboration, however, we must also be cognizant of the problems experienced by other scholars attempting similar projects. Postmodernist theory has "enshrined and positively recommended" "the principle of self-representation" (O'Hanlon and Washbrook 1992:150). Rather than positioning the scholar as the privileged interpreter of culture and history, anthropologist James Clifford has argued that we need to allow "autonomous textual space" for "indigenous statements [that] make sense in terms different from those of the arranging ethnographer" (Clifford 1988:51). In practical application, however, many such projects have optimistically proceeded without considering the power relations that are inherent in *any* scholar-subject interaction. After all, how can a textual space for indigenous or marginalized voices be truly autonomous if the privileged scholar must first offer that space? The Subaltern Studies Group of South Asian scholars, for instance, has sought to retrieve subaltern consciousness from the oppression of colonialist, national-ist, and other dominant histories (Chakrabarty 2002:chap. 1). Despite their innovative methods and epistemological position, however, the very fact that many of them have been trained in the western educational tradition puts them in a privileged position vis-à-vis the subjects of their investigations. In explor-ing the question "Can the Subaltern Speak?" literary critic and Subaltern Studies Group member Gayatri Spivak (1988) con-cluded that, in fact, regardless of whether subalterns can speak (either by themselves through the historical record or through historians), contemporary scholars, however epistemologically positioned, are incapable of hearing them. And in ethnography, attempts to allow an individual or individuals to speak for them-selves ignore the problem of positioning one or a few people to represent a much larger social group. In a critique of Subaltern Studies, South Asian historians Rosalind O'Hanlon and David Washbrook (1992:161) have pointed out "because [this approach] privileges the voices of authoritative indigenous individuals . . . [i]t is hard to see how such an approach can recognise or give ad-equate place to conflict within social contexts thus examined or to those groups or communities who may dissent very strongly from these authoritative accounts."

These theoretical obstacles are not merely flights of post-modernist fancy, as we have already learned from our interac-tion with the Hampden community. We have now completed two field seasons, excavating five domestic sites with the help of volunteers and area high school students as well as financial support from the Hampden Community Council and other or-ganizations. In addition, we have presented our work in public in various ways. These interactions have taught us that scholars are not the only ones who are having a hard time reenvision-ing our roles in relation to those whom we study. For instance, in separate letters to the authors thanking us for sharing our research as part of a speaker series at a local retirement com-munity, the program coordinator wrote that we "have a lot to offer the people of Hampden about their past" (Scieszka 2005). The idea that we, as "experts," have the authority (or even the right) to give Hampden's history to its people is a frustrating one that we must work to overcome by showing people not only that the community's history belongs to them, but that they can use lessons from the past to help them confront contemporary problems.

Can we find ways to circumvent these obstacles and create a truly democratic project that will allow every resident of Hampden to have a say, should they want one? And can we simultaneously use our project to address the very real social problems facing the community today? The only way to test any of this is to continue to go out and dig, and to ensure that community members are intimately involved in the dig, interpretation efforts, and other aspects of the project. While the collaborative and public aspects of our project may not have been as successful during the first two seasons as we had originally hoped or gone exactly as we had planned, these experiences have now given us a much better idea of what further steps must be taken in the future to build a truly strong, democratic, and civically vital public archaeology program in which some or all of the various interest groups in Hampden have a stake *and* a voice.

Note

1. The characterization of the Poole and Hunt Shop as the "backbone" of the community, as well as the statistic of "thousands of men," are highly suspect, since the foundry was one of several mills in the neighborhood, which during the boom years of the 1870s and 1880s employed roughly three thousand people all together.

References Cited

Arnold, Joseph L.
  1978 Suburban Growth and Municipal Annexation, 1745–1918. *Maryland Historical Magazine* 73(2):109–128.
Austin, Diane E.
  2004 Partnerships, Not Projects! Improving the Environment through Collaborative Research and Action. *Human Organization* 63(4):419–430.

Beirne, D. Randall
    1976   Steadfast Americans: Residential Stability Among Workers in
            Baltimore, 1880–1930. Unpublished Ph.D. dissertation, Uni-
            versity of Maryland, College Park.
    1979a   Residential Growth and Stability in the Baltimore Industrial
            Community of Canton During the Late Nineteenth Century.
            Maryland Historical Magazine 74(1):39–51.
    1979b   Residential Stability Among Urban Workers: Industrial
            Linkage in Hampden-Woodberry, Baltimore, 1880–1930.
            In *Geographical Perspectives on Maryland's Past,* edited by
            Robert D. Mitchell and Edward K. Miller, pp. 168–187.
            Occasional Paper No. 4, Department of Geography, Uni-
            versity of Maryland, College Park.
    1989   Hampden. In *North Baltimore: From Estate to Development,* by
            Karen Lewand. Baltimore City Department of Planning and
            the University of Baltimore.
Bullock, James G., Jr.
    1971   *A Brief History of Textile Manufacturing along Jones Falls.* 2nd ed.
            Mt. Vernon Mills, Baltimore.
Butler, Luther
    1979   *Interview with Luther Butler.* Conducted by Susan Hawes, Tran-
            scribed by John Brockenwich. Manuscript on file, Baltimore
            Neighborhood Heritage Project Archive, Special Collections,
            University of Baltimore Langsdale Library.
Chakrabarty, Dipesh
    2002   *Habitations of Modernity: Essays in the Wake of Subaltern Studies.*
            University of Chicago Press, Chicago.
Chidester, Robert C.
    2005   Forgetting Which Past? The Mt. Vernon–Woodberry Mills
            Strike of 1923 and Public Memory in Hampden, Baltimore.
            Unpublished manuscript in possession of the authors.
City of Baltimore
    2005   Good News: Applications for Historic Designation Pay Off.
            Electronic document, http://www.ci.baltimore.md.us/neigh-
            borhoods/nnf/050121.html, accessed May 3, 2005.
Clifford, James
    1988   *The Predicament of Culture: Twentieth-Century Ethnography,
            Literature, and Art.* Harvard University Press, Cambridge,
            Massachusetts.
Conkey, Margaret W., and Joan M. Gero
    1991   Tensions, Pluralities, and Engendering Archaeology: An Intro-

duction to Women and Prehistory. In *Engendering Archaeology: Women and Prehistory*, edited by Joan M. Gero and Margaret W. Conkey, pp. 3–30. Blackwell, Oxford.

Durr, Kenneth D.
    2003   *Behind the Backlash: White Working-Class Politics in Baltimore, 1940–1980*. University of North Carolina Press, Chapel Hill.

Emerson, Matthew
    1988   *Decorated Clay Pipes from the Chesapeake*. University Microfilms, Ann Arbor.

Epperson, Terrence W.
    1999   The Global Importance of African Diaspora Archaeology in the Analysis and Abolition of Whiteness. Paper presented at the Fourth World Archaeological Congress, Cape Town, South Africa.

Ferguson, Leland G.
    1992   *Uncommon Ground: Archaeology and Early African America, 1650–1800*. Smithsonian Institution Press, Washington, D.C.

Foucault, Michel
    1995   [1977] *Discipline and Punish: The Birth of the Prison*. Vintage, New York.

Gilchrist, Roberta
    1991   Women's Archaeology? Political Feminism, Gender Theory and Historical Revision. *Antiquity* 65(248):495–501.

Goldberg, David Theo
    2002   *The Racial State*. Blackwell, Malden, Massachusetts.

Green, James
    2000   *Taking History to Heart: The Power of the Past in Building Social Movements*. University of Massachusetts Press, Amherst.

Hartigan, John
    1997   Establishing the Fact of Whiteness. *American Anthropologist* 99(3):495–505.
    2000   Remembering White Detroit: Whiteness in the Mix of History and Memory. *City and Society* 7(2):11–34.

Harvey, Bill
    1988   *The People Is Grass: A History of Hampden-Woodberry, 1802–1945*. Della Press, Baltimore.

Harvey, David
    1991   The View from Federal Hill. In *The Baltimore Book: New Views of Local History*, edited by Elizabeth Fee, Linda Shopes, and Linda Zeidman, pp. 227–249. Temple University Press, Philadelphia.

Hollyday, Guy
    1994   *Stone Hill: The People and Their Stories.* Privately published, Baltimore.
Lamphere, Louise
    2004   The Convergence of Applied, Practicing, and Public Anthropology in the 21st Century. *Human Organization* 63(4):431–443.
Leone, Mark P. and Gladys-Marie Fry
    1999   Conjuring in the Big House Kitchen: An Interpretation of African American Belief Systems, Based on the Uses of Archaeology and Folklore Sources. *Journal of American Folklore* 112:372–403.
Menzies, Charles
    2001   Reflections on Research with, for, and among Indigenous Peoples. *Canadian Journal of Native Education* 25:19–36.
    2004   Putting Words into Action: Negotiating Collaborative Research in Gitkxaala. *Canadian Journal of Native Education* 28:15–32.
Meskell, Lynn
    2001   Archaeologies of Identity. In *Archaeological Theory Today,* edited by Ian Hodder, pp. 187–213. Polity Press, Cambridge.
Mrozowski, Steven A., Grace H. Ziesing, and Mary C. Beaudry
    1996   *Living on the Boott: Historical Archaeology at the Boott Mills Boardinghouses, Lowell, Massachusetts.* University of Massachusetts Press, Amherst.
News Services and Staff Reports
    1990   Skinheads Delay Baltimore March in Route Dispute. *Washington Post* 7 June:D4.
O'Hanlon, Rosalind, and David Washbrook
    1992   After Orientalism: Culture, Criticism and Politics in the Third World. *Comparative Studies in Society and History* 34:141–184.
Roediger, David
    1999   [1991] *The Wages of Whiteness: Race and the Making of the American Working Class.* Verso, New York.
Saxton, Alexander
    1990   *The Rise and Fall of the White Republic: Class Politics and Mass Culture in the Nineteenth Century.* Verso, New York.
Sanjek, Roger
    2004   Going Public: Responsibilities and Strategies in the Aftermath of Ethnography. *Human Organization* 63(4):444–456.
Scieszka, Beverly
    2005   Letters to David Gadsby and Robert Chidester, 29 June. In possession of the authors.

Seifert, Donna (editor)
   2005   Sin City. *Historical Archaeology* 39(1).
Spivak, Gayatri Chakravorty
   1988   Can the Subaltern Speak? In *Marxism and the Interpretation of Culture*, edited by Cary Nelson and Lawrence Grossberg, pp. 271–313. University of Illinois Press, Urbana.
Stables, Eleanor
   2005   [Neighborhood Watch] Hampden, Baltimore, MD. *National Geographic Traveler* 22(3):20.
Struever Brothers, Eccles and Rouse
   2005   Clipper Mill. Electronic document, http://www.sber.com/project_detail.asp?ProjectID=165, accessed May 3, 2005.
U.S. Census
   2004   *Race Alone or in Combination (table).* Electronic document, http://factfinder.census.gov/servlet/QTTable?_   bm=y &-geo_id=86000US21211&-qr_name=DEC_2000_   SF1_U_ QTP5&-ds_name=DEC_2000_SF1_U&-_lang=en&-_sse=on, accessed April 28, 2004.
Voss, Barbara L.
   1999   Feminisms, Queer Theories, and the Archaeological Study of Past Sexualities. *World Archaeology* 32(2):180–192.
Wallerstein, Nina, and Bonnie Duran
   2003   The Conceptual, Historical, and Practice Roots of Community Based Participatory Research and Related Participatory Traditions. In *Community-Based Participatory Research for Health*, edited by Meredith Minkler and Nina Wallerstein, pp. 27–52. Jossey-Bass, San Francisco.
Wilkie, Laurie A.
   2000   *Creating Freedom: Material Culture and African American Identity at Oakley Plantation, Louisiana, 1840–1950.* Louisiana State University Press, Baton Rouge.
Zukin, Sharon
   1995   *The Cultures of Cities.* Blackwell, Malden, Massachusetts.

Chapter 12

Civic Engagement and Social Justice: Race on the Illinois Frontier

Paul A. Shackel

Some historic sites are becoming significant central places where citizens come to understand the relationship between past and contemporary social and political issues. Making these links between the past and the present can facilitate an exploration of both historic and contemporary concerns related to social justice (American Association of Museums [AAM] 2002). Recently, the American Association of Museums has made a tremendous effort to promote civic engagement, and I believe that archaeology can also play a role in this movement. Archaeology can help foster a dialogue that examines the history of social, economic, religious, gender, and racial inequalities and their relationship to contemporary society. I believe it is important to know how these injustices developed and to realize why they exist today. In turn, this knowledge can inspire social consciousness and give citizens the option to act.

In 2002 I became involved in the New Philadelphia archaeology project, a partnership between the University of Maryland, the University of Illinois, the Illinois State Museum, and the New Philadelphia Association. With the aid of a National Science Foundation Research Experiences for Undergraduates (NSF-REU) grant we had the opportunity to recruit a diverse body of undergraduate students and create a learning experience for both the students and the local community. Our goal was to engage these groups in as many aspects of the project as possible, and have them contribute to exploration of community heritage. We encouraged student and community interaction while making both groups more aware of the historical issues related to race and racism. We also wanted to explore with them the construction of race in a very white community, in a region that has been known to be hostile toward African Americans (Loewen 2005). We believed that perhaps we could help foster the changing attitude of inclusion already being encouraged in the New Philadelphia Association—a small nonprofit group created to help preserve the memory of Frank McWorter and New Philadelphia.

The Development of New Philadelphia

New Philadelphia is located about twenty-five miles east of the Mississippi River and developed as a small multiracial rural community from 1836. It is the earliest known town legally founded by a free African American, Frank McWorter (Walker 1983). McWorter platted the town with 144 lots, each measuring 60 x 120 ft. There were two main thoroughfares, Broad Way and Main Street, each 80 ft. wide; secondary streets were 60 ft. wide; and alleys measured 15 ft. wide (figure 12.1).

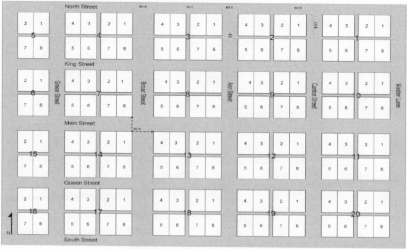

Figure 12.1. Map of New Philadelphia showing blocks, lots, streets, and alleys. Drawn by Christopher Valvano.

From the beginning of the town, both whites and blacks purchased town lots, and the place attracted craftsmen, merchants, and laborers. The 1855 Illinois state census lists 58 people living in New Philadelphia (Walker 1983). The town's population peaked in 1865 with about 160 residents. Four years later the railroad bypassed the town by about a mile, and people began to leave for cities like Chicago and St. Louis as well as to migrate west of the Mississippi. About eight households and a blacksmith remained in 1900 and by the 1930s it was virtually abandoned. Throughout the town's history, from the 1850s through the 1920s, the African American population fluctuated between 25 and 35 percent, significantly higher when compared to the township, county, and state (King 2006).

The story of New Philadelphia has never completely vanished from the memory of the local community. The New Philadelphia schoolhouse, built across the road from the town, operated from about 1874 until the 1940s with both white and black students. It served as a social center where community members gathered for festivals, funerals, and meetings. In the 1960s Grace Matteson began to gather stories of the town. She described a multiracial town and noted that many of the families "were a mixed race: some of them were part French, some part Indian, some Irish, and many of them part Caucasian. It will be recalled that Free Frank himself was described as 'a yellow man'" (Matteson 1964:20–21). She also wrote that the whites and the black families lived in harmony with each other in the community (Matteson 1964:21). Less than two decades later Helen McWorter Simpson (1981), great-granddaughter of Frank McWorter, wrote about her family members and described life in New Philadelphia. Soon afterward, Juliet Walker (1983) published a biography of Frank McWorter, which covers his early days of enslavement in the Carolinas and in Kentucky, to his founding of the town of New Philadelphia. Today, only planted fields and a few foundations exist, and the McWorters and other town descendants with at least 120 different surnames are scattered throughout the country.

When we arrived at the site in 2002, the community knew of the general location of the town site, and a sign explaining the significance of the place stood at a two-car parking area off of a country road known as the Baylis blacktop. However, people's recollection of the location of the town's center varied. Local land surveyors Marvin and Tom Likes of Likes Land Surveyors, Inc. of Barry, Illinois, donating their time, located the original town plat and imposed the town plan over the existing topography, marking the boundaries of the town, blocks, and lots. The Likeses then produced a map, which was overlaid on an existing aerial photograph, which then guided our initial archaeological survey in the fall of 2002 and the spring of 2003 (Gwaltney 2004).

New Philadelphia is about forty-two acres, and our walkover survey located and identified artifacts on the surface, allowing the team to determine which areas were settled within the town proper. In general, the clustering of artifacts shows distinct patterns and indicates that there are large concentrations of artifacts found within the lots bordering the town's two main streets (figure 12.2). These artifacts are mostly kitchenwares, such as ceramics and bottle glass, indicating that these lots served domestic purposes, rather than being craft or industrial sites. It appears that the town's businesses, like blacksmithing, occupied the town's edge (Gwaltney 2004).

In 2004 we received a three-year National Science Foundation Research Experiences for Undergraduates grant (Grant #0353550) to train students in archaeological techniques. Our goal was to recruit a diverse student body to work on understanding the history of the entire town. We developed research goals and realized that this multiracial town could serve as a case study examining consumerism, diet, and community layout and interaction. We questioned whether consumer differences could be a matter of access to markets, and we wanted to find out if racism could have affected these choices. While we explored these questions we always kept the students and community involved, and we kept the issue of past and present racism alive in the everyday dialogue of our project.

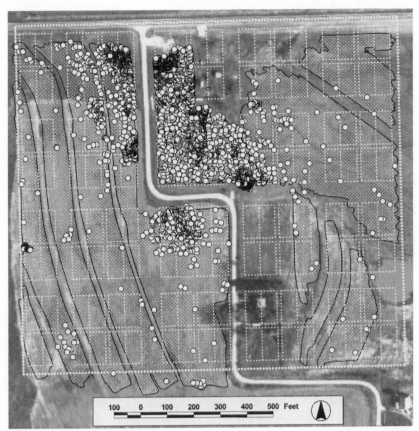

Figure 12.2. The results of the walkover survey showing the concentration of artifacts along Broad Way (running north-south) and Main Street (running east-west) (Gwaltney 2004).

A Call for an Archaeology of Civic Engagement and Social Justice

I have worked mostly in areas of the archaeology of race and labor, and I want to include a few thoughts on how to make an archaeology project more socially relevant and make practitioners and the public aware of issues of justice. First, archaeologists need to critically analyze and expose racism in the past and present and to dismantle the structures of oppression where we can. We need to recognize race and provide a historical perspective of racism when telling the story. Second, we need to explore diversity in the past and to promote it in the present. Racism is not dismantled if you have only like-minded people participating in the project. Third, it is important to build a multicultural organization. We need to explore and identify the dividing walls, in the past and in the present. I hope that by building a more inclusive discipline our efforts will help build diversity in the field and in interpretations. The story is not complete without a variety of perspectives. Fourth, we should create a color-conscious past rather than a color-blind past. It is important to recognize cultural and ethnic differences in order to provide a richer perspective of the past and the future.

Introducing traditionally muted viewpoints to an archaeology project has made the discipline much more complicated. In local, state, and federally owned parks it is a difficult task to counter the status quo and do a different kind of archaeology. Based on my personal experience I can suggest that change only occurs with persistence, partnerships, and public outreach, and sometimes it takes what may seem like a long time. Archaeologists have the potential of telling a much broader and inclusive story that makes connections to the past and the present. Answering the call for social justice can be appealing to a wider audience, and we need to assert our findings to the public and seek to incorporate them into the public memory.

Archaeology can place contemporary problems in a historic context and show that these concerns are not new, and that people have faced them for a long time. Archaeologists can address issues of a diverse past and real-world problem solving (see Bender and Smith 2000). It is important to motivate students and practitioners of archaeology to convince stakeholders and decision makers that we can make these contributions.

The Challenge of
Many Stakeholders and Many Histories

The archaeology of peripheralized groups is not always part of our national public memory (LaRoche and Blakey 1997; Little

1994). In the case of the archaeology of African American life, for a long time research has focused on plantation life and bondage, and these studies continue to be prevalent today. Recently, there has been a new emphasis on archaeological explorations that focus on social uplift and achievement, themes that are becoming more prominent in our national public memory. These stories include the archaeology of the Underground Railroad (Levine et al. 2005) as well as survival and prospering in an racialized and segregated society (Mullins 2004). These types of stories appear to have greater public support from the descendant communities (Leone et al. 2005).

The story of New Philadelphia also fits into this new genre; however, when dealing with many different stakeholders, it is sometimes difficult to establish a coherent message for the place. Trying to change the way people view the history of any place does not come quickly, nor does it come easily. When I first became interested in the New Philadelphia project many community members referred to the place as an all-black town. Despite Matteson's (1964) accounting of the town as "mixed race" and as a place where both blacks and whites lived, Walker's (1983) accounting of the early settlement of the place, where she demonstrates the multiracial composition of the town, and oral histories that recalled both whites and blacks living in the town in the early twentieth century, the myth prevailed. When we presented our census data research in 2003 (see King 2006) and claimed that only about one-third of the town's population was African American at any one time, some stakeholders were surprised, and some were very doubtful and challenged our findings.

At this point we realized that because of the many interest groups and the different perceptions of the past, we had to try to reach out to all of the interested communities. It would be best to democratize all of our data and research. Therefore, we began to post all of our work on the Internet (www.heritage.umd.edu; follow the links to New Philadelphia) and challenged the public to make their own conclusions from our data and research. This type of transparency allows others to see how we make our conclusions from data about the site, and it also allows people to challenge our interpretations. It demonstrates to the local community that we are not sweeping into a community, taking data, and waiting to publish them at some future date. Rather, we are sharing our findings as soon as they develop. This interaction helps facilitate a much smoother dialog with all interested parties.

However, despite our best efforts to be transparent, differences still remain between our academic research and the memory of some of the stakeholders. In the New Philadelphia community it seems that forgetting about a past may be a lot easier than remembering all of the details of the past. For a long time local citizens and many descendants have understood the history of New Philadelphia as one of unique success in interracial living. After all, Matteson (1964) wrote in 1964 that it was a place of harmony, and this story has carried forward into the twenty-first century. The New Philadelphia Association web page states that it was a place "where black and white Americans lived together peacefully on the antebellum Illinois frontier" (New Philadelphia Association 2006). Even though the New Philadelphia Association has been a big supporter of our archaeology project, it is difficult for me to support its interpretation of frontier Illinois history. After all, when Illinois became a state in 1818, its constitution stated that enslaved persons owned by French citizens could be retained in bondage. The state constitution allowed indentured servitude, whereby African Americans were contracted to work for decades. The offspring of indentured servants had to serve until they became twenty-one years of age for males, and eighteen years of age for females. Enslaved people could also be brought into the salines region in southern Illinois for the production of salt until 1825 (Davis 1998:165). Black Codes passed in 1819 and 1829 restricted the rights of African Americans and discouraged their settlement in the state (Simeone 2000:157).

Free African Americans in southern and central Illinois met some resistance from the local populations. For instance, about fifty miles south of New Philadelphia in Alton, Illinois, Elijah Lovejoy ran his abolitionist newspaper and founded the Illinois Anti-Slavery Society. An angry mob attacked his newspaper in 1837, one year after the founding of New Philadelphia. They killed Lovejoy while he tried to protect his press (Beecher 1838;

Dillon 1961; Tanner 1881). Only thirteen miles east of New Philadelphia in the town of Griggsville, violence broke out after an 1838 antislavery meeting (Chapman 1880:516).

The Underground Railroad thrived in communities surrounding New Philadelphia in places like Quincy, Pittsfield, and Jacksonville. There are also family accounts that the McWorters participated in the Underground Railroad (Walker 1983). The 1845 Illinois Supreme Court decision of *Jarrot v. Jarrot* terminated the institution of slavery in Illinois for all time. However, this decision did not stop slave trackers from dragging away suspected bystanders and at times capturing innocent and free African Americans to transport them down south for sale into bondage. Illinois did not resist the Fugitive Slave Act of 1850 like other northern states by passing personal liberties laws (Davis 1998:289). Free African Americans were not on equal footing with whites, and they were not allowed to vote.

Many new immigrants came to the Illinois frontier, including "Dutch, Germans, Swiss, Yankees, Irish, Scotch, a few English, and a number from more southern states," like Kentucky and Tennessee (Oliver 1924:68). The growing diversity in frontier Illinois also meant that no single interest group could dominate the social and political scene. People had to work with each other for consensus, although the Black Codes also meant that African Americans were often left out of this consensus building. While Illinois was considered a free state and all forms of legal slavery had died by 1845, state delegates voted 137 to 7 to deny suffrage to blacks. In addition, Article XIV directed the General Assembly to pass laws prohibiting the immigration of blacks to Illinois. While Illinois opposed slavery, it refused equality to African Americans (Davis 1998:413). So while neighbors had to coexist in order to survive on the frontier, racism still affected those blacks that settled in Illinois, including New Philadelphia.

Our field school addresses the historic and contemporary issue of race and racism in the local community. There are newspaper and several oral accounts of Ku Klux Klan disturbances in the post–World War I era. While these stories are known, some members of the local community prefer to only tell the story of peaceful coexistence and honor the African American individual who founded the town. At the same time an African American descendant and member of the New Philadelphia Association is quite clear about the stories of racism that his family endured while living in the town. There are oral traditions that surrounding communities became sundown towns—meaning African Americans were not allowed in the community after the sun set (Loewen 2005; Shackel 2005). Calhoun County, which lies immediately south of Pike County (where New Philadelphia is situated), was a sundown county. Local residents told me that into the 1970s a sign was posted on a bridge entering the county seat that said "Don't let the sun go down on you"—with the understanding that everyone, especially African Americans, knew the meaning of the message. An oral history also referred to the McWorters not being welcome after sunset in the town of Barry, the closest town to New Philadelphia.

The history of racism on the landscape is obvious. When I asked Pike County residents how many blacks lived in the county, most counted the number on one hand. The 1990 U.S. Federal Census indicates that 6 African Americans claimed Pike County as their home in a county with about 17,000 people. When I mentioned this figure to some longtime residents, they thought that this number might be too high. No African Americans live in Calhoun County. The 2000 U.S. Federal Census lists 260 African Americans in Pike County; however, this dramatic increase is attributed to a new federal correctional facility in the county. Almost all African Americans listed (256) are over eighteen years of age. These stories are on our web page (www.heritage.umd.edu; follow the links to New Philadelphia) and we will continue to make public the town's stories in the years ahead.

Surely, having students of different ethnic backgrounds enter the very white community of Pike County changed the community's complexion for a few weeks during field school. One local community member explained, "When you are a stranger, every head turns." The member explained that while she has not heard of any negative comments about the racial makeup of the students, "I suspect there are some racial comments floating around."

I spoke to a local community organization (on June 11, 2004) about race being a historical construction and I told them that there was no relationship between race and biology. When I discussed racism with this all-white audience, most of their eyes looked down and away from me. I wondered, were they uninterested, or were they not willing to face a racist past? Several people in the audience commented that they did not experience racism in the local community. Whenever members of the organization spoke about African Americans they sometimes used a patronizing tone. People made comments to me after my lecture such as "They were good, nice and hard working," as well as "I think they are a lot smarter than people give them credit." One student who lived in rural Illinois in an all-white area explained that she was never aware of racism since it was not part of her daily experience, especially in a place where no blacks lived. In much the same way, I believe that the evening's audience probably did not explicitly experience racism because no blacks lived in the area. However, African Americans did live in Pike County and surrounding areas at one time, but during the Jim Crow era left for larger towns or moved to the West.

We had an open dialogue with the field school students and the local community and addressed issues of race and racism. The community was invited, along with the students, to view in three parts a 2003 PBS special on race titled *Race: The Power of Illusion*. The film dismantles the myths associated with the construction of race. In an open conversation, one white student from the region expressed amazement that blacks did not have an extra muscle in their legs that allowed them to run faster. An African American student told of his experiences being profiled and harassed by St. Louis city police on several occasions. While we created a productive dialogue we were also able to imagine similar stereotypes and physical assaults in a historic context when peace supposedly existed between people of different colors.

Students expressed their anger that racism existed in the past and that it still exists today. Several students approached me after the second episode of the video and told me that they were mad that racism still exists and that they believed that racism should be combated in the school systems. This was a teachable moment and we discussed ways in which they could make a difference. "How do you do this?" I responded. One student explained very carefully that racism can only change if individuals worked on it on a case-by-case basis. You need to change the world one person at a time. The other student responded that we needed more government legislation to help even the playing field as well as more antidiscrimination laws. According to the student, the safety net that helped minorities to gain an equal footing began to disappear during the Reagan administration, and during the George W. Bush administration it is even more difficult for minorities to gain an equal footing. Minorities tend to be poorer than whites and they tend to have jobs that pay minimum wage. The students created an action plan and a call for justice. They stated that they needed to deal with this issue on an individual level and make issues related to race and racism part of the school curriculum. Their goal was to help create a color-conscious society rather than a color-blind society.

Gerald McWorter, head of the African American Studies program at the University of Toledo, and a fifth-generation descendant of Frank McWorter, interacted with our students during our movie discussion in 2006. Professor McWorter launched into a passionate call for activism. He longed for the civil rights movement when people came together and fought the system for equal rights. He pointed our attention to the current administration's repeated attempts to continually strangle urban areas, areas that are predominantly black and brown. When there are cuts in education, welfare, and Medicare, the majority of people being hurt are those who are poor and middle class, and who belong to minority groups. The wealth gap increases in the United States and it is important that we turn this situation around by working hard in our everyday lives as well as in our scholarship. We all agreed at the end of the evening that the work at New Philadelphia could make a difference in the way people look at the past and act in the present.

When I first started to help develop the archaeology program at New Philadelphia I told community leaders that I thought that it would be important to make issues of race and racism part of the agenda for the archaeology program. Many of the community leaders who invited us to participate in the project thought that this would be an important approach to the research project.

However, one community leader told me that she was reluctant to support this program since there were many other urgent social justice causes, like helping the poor and underprivileged in the slums of Chicago. At the end of the 2006 field season, the same community leader came up to me and said that while she was originally reluctant to support the project, she now saw the importance of the archaeology program. Racism has created tremendous inequities in this country and it is probably one of the leading causes of poverty and inadequate health care in this nation. She recognized that if we could continue to make the story of race and racism part of the New Philadelphia story, it could enlighten people about the current inequities in society, and perhaps it might make a change in the way they live and perceive others.

Other community members have told me that they are now committed to developing a multicultural past in order to help promote a multicultural present. For instance, descendants, local community members, and members of the New Philadelphia research team gathered at a church supper during the annual Barry Apple festival in 2004. We discussed the redistribution of power in order to allow for real-world multivocality. Access and inclusion are a social responsibility in this process, and the New Philadelphia Association affirmed that all of the stakeholders should be invited to participate in the change. In 2005 the New Philadelphia Association asked members of the McWorter family to be on the association's governing board. Some members of the governing board are very eager to discuss the tough issues that come with overseeing the preservation and interpretation of a multiracial town in a racist society.

In the summer of 2005 the McWorter family held part of their family reunion at New Philadelphia. Members of the New Philadelphia Association cooked burgers and pork and had a selection of homemade pies, all within view of the archaeology site. After lunch family members took tours of the site, and students explained to the family the archaeology of the place and shared with them their experiences as archaeologists. The McWorters saw features being excavated and we told them of the importance of the site and its place in the national public memory. They also visited the family cemetery in a nearby overgrown area. Many McWorter descendants have become partners in the project and are now taking charge of the cleaning and restoration of the town's African American cemetery.

In 2005 the New Philadelphia town site was placed on the National Register of Historic Places because the place has information that contributes to our understanding of human history and the information is considered important (Criterion D). A detailed analysis of artifacts and faunal materials also helps provide a foundation for additional interpretations of the lifeways of the residents of New Philadelphia. In 1988 Juliet Walker successfully placed Frank McWorter's grave site on the National Register of Historic Places.

A New Perspective

The democratization of knowledge in research, practice, and teaching is an important part of our project. Our work is also challenging some of the traditional perceptions of New Philadelphia found in the local and descendant communities. First, many stakeholders referred to the place as an all-black town. However, in-depth census data research shows that both blacks and whites lived within the town from the 1850s through the 1920s and that African Americans made up about one-third of the population (King 2006). Second, there is also the story that the town died soon after the railroad bypassed it in 1869. Our archaeology shows that while the town's population continued to decrease, some residents invested significant amounts of money to build dwellings in the town as late as the early twentieth century. Some have greeted our conclusion with surprise, and others with anger, because they had always believed that the town disappeared shortly after the railroad was routed to the north of the town.

Third, when comparing sites from the early nineteenth century in Illinois many forms of material culture become homogenized and earlier cultural differences are indistinguishable (Mazrim 2002:268). A review of the material goods uncovered through our archaeology shows that there is little difference in the types of material culture found at sites inhabited by different ethnic groups or people from different regions. All of the residents of New Philadelphia have the same types of material culture and can access local merchants for consumer goods, such as refined earthenwares. What distinguishes the different households from each other appears to be their dietary habits. Households from the Upland South (Tennessee, Kentucky, and South Carolina) maintain a high proportion of pork and wild game in their diet. Residents from Ohio, New York, and Massachusetts tend to have a higher proportion of cow in their diet, a pattern often referred to as a Yankee tradition. It seems like the New Philadelphia residents brought with them traditions that are most commonly found in their former homeland regions. However, it is also important to realize that dietary preferences may be more complex than maintaining tradition. Lack of access to some markets, because of economics, transportation, and/or racial discrimination, may have encouraged some families to continue the tradition of raising their own hogs and relying on foraging and hunting for a substantial amount of their protein intake (Shackel 2006). In all cases we have taken a comparative approach that includes different households in the entire town, and the data from which we draw our conclusions are on our websites. This action allows all of the stakeholders the opportunity to observe and challenge our ideas.

Gerald McWorter spoke to the students and the community in 2005 and commented on the archaeology project. He told us that he thought that the memory of Frank McWorter was important, and that family legend always reinforced the idea that the story of freedom and his commitment to freedom were the cornerstone to their family's history. Because of this legacy Gerald McWorter felt the weight of history to promote the story of freedom. "He [Frank McWorter] was a leader of an integrated community" (Gerald McWorter, personal communication, June 23, 2005). His family always told him about the story of freedom, and the New Philadelphia archaeology project is a way of keeping the word alive. He is very supportive of the program and he hopes to create a larger umbrella of supporters for the larger New Philadelphia project. Meanwhile, because our goal is to promote the entire town's history, other family members have accused us of promoting a revisionist history that slights the importance of the town's founder. This input is valuable in understanding how the different communities view the project and see the importance of our archaeology.

Currently, the larger stories about racism on the Illinois frontier are now being incorporated into the public memory of the local community, although we are explicit about this message in our public and academic presentations. Making people aware of the racism that existed in Illinois is an important part of New Philadelphia's story. It is imperative that we consider John Hope Franklin's words. He explains, "The places that commemorate sad history are not places in which we wallow, or wallow in remorse, but instead places in which we may be moved to a new resolve, to be better citizens. . . . Explaining history from a variety of angles makes it not only more interesting, but more true. When it is more true, more people come to feel that they have a part in it. That is where patriotism and loyalty intersect with truth" (National Park Service 2000). In other words, we need to think twice about what we choose to remember and we should also think hard about what histories we are ignoring. We need to think of ways to use archaeology to challenge consensus histories, confront the way these histories have been created, and understand why they exist in the first place. Placing the story of New Philadelphia within the larger context of race and racism on the Illinois frontier makes it an even more interesting and valuable story for our nation's public memory.

Many McWorter family members see our archaeology project as a way to promote and preserve the story of this very important town. Other family members do not feel that we are accurately representing what they feel is the most important story of the place, the founder of the town. The desires of the local and descendant communities for preserving the site are truly varied. But there is a common ground to start from—we all believe that it is important to save and remember the place and we will work toward building consensus.

Places of the past are one venue for civic engagement and addressing matters of social justice. The foundation of civic engagement is a commitment to building and sustaining relationships with neighbors and communities of interest. The American Association of Museums (AAM 2002) calls for museums to take a more active role in creating a community dialogue to provide leadership in this movement. If we want to be part of important national dialogues, we need to think about how we can make our discipline relevant to the larger community. Archaeology can be part of creating a more relevant and inclusive story, and it can be a touchstone for a dialogue that can be placed in the broader conversation of the past. Following the lead of the movement in the museum world that is being encouraged by the American Association of Museums, archaeologists need to think about how to make their work more civically engaged. One way is to look at the historical development of labor, race, class, and gender and the impact of industrialization on work, domestic lifestyles, and health conditions. Framing these historical concerns in a modern context and making them part of our research designs can help our discipline become relevant to our contemporary and diverse society.

Acknowledgment

This material is based upon work supported by the National Foundation under Grant No. 0353550. Any opinions, findings, and conclusions or recommendations expressed in this material are those of the author and do not necessarily reflect the views of the National Science Foundation.

References Cited

American Association of Museums (AAM)
  2002   *Mastering Civic Engagement: A Challenge to Museums.* American Association of Museums, Washington, D.C. (no editor is listed)
Beecher, Edward
  1838   *Narratives of the Riots at Alton: In Connection with the Death of Rev. Elijah P. Lovejoy.* George Holton, Alton, Illinois.

Bender, Susan J., and George S. Smith (editors)
  2000   *Teaching Archaeology in the Twenty-First Century.* Society for
          American Archaeology, Washington, D.C.
Chapman, Charles C.
  1880   *History of Pike County, Illinois.* C. C. Chapman, Chicago.
Davis, James E.
  1998   *Frontier Illinois.* Indiana University Press, Bloomington.
Dillon, Merton L.
  1961   *Elijah P. Lovejoy: Abolitionist Editor.* University of Illinois Press,
          Urbana.
Gwaltney, Thomas
  2004   New Philadelphia Project Pedestrian Survey: Final Report
          and Catalog. Phase I Archeology at the Historic Town of New
          Philadelphia, Illinois. ArGIS Consultants, LLC, Bethesda,
          Maryland. Electronic document, http://www.heritage.umd.
          edu/CHRSWeb/New%20Philadelphia/NP_Final_Report_
          View.pdf, accessed January 17, 2007.
King, Charlotte
  2006   New Philadelphia Census Data. Electronic document, http://
          www.heritage.umd.edu/CHRSWeb/New%20Philadelphia/
          censusfiles/CensusDataMenu.htm, accessed July 22, 2006.
LaRoche, Cheryl J., and Michael L. Blakey.
  1997   Seizing Intellectual Power: The Dialogue at the New York Af-
          rican Burial Ground. *Historical Archaeology* 31:84–106.
Leone, Mark P., Cheryl Janifer LaRoche, and Jennifer Babiarz
  2005   The Archaeology of Black Americans in Recent Times. *Annual
          Review of Anthropology* 34(1): 575–598.
Levine, Mary Ann, Kelly M. Britt, and James A. Delle
  2005   Heritage Tourism and Community Outreach: Public Archae-
          ology at the Thaddeus Stevens and Lydia Hamilton Smith
          Site in Lancaster, Pennsylvania, USA. *International Journal of
          Heritage Studies* 11(5):399–414.
Little, Barbara J.
  1994   People with History: An Update on Historical Archaeology in
          the United States. *Journal of Archaeological Method and Theory*
          1:5–40.
  1999   Nominating Archaeological Sites to the National Register of
          Historic Places: What's the Point? *SAA Bulletin* 17(4):19.
Loewen, James
  2005   *Sundowner Towns: A Hidden Dimension of American Racism.*
          New Press, New York.

Matteson, Grace
    1964   "Free Frank" McWorter and the "Ghost Town" of New Phila-
            delphia, Pike County, Illinois. Pike County Historical Society,
            Pittsfield, Illinois.
Mazrim, Robert
    2002   *"Now Quite Out of Society": Archaeology and Frontier Illinois. Es-
            says and Excavation Reports.* Illinois Transportation Archaelogi-
            cal Research Program, Transportation Archaeological Bulletins
            No.1. Illinois Department of Transportation, Department of
            Anthropology, University of Illinois at Urbana-Champaign.
Mullins, Paul
    2004   African-American Heritage in a Multicultural Community: An
            Archaeology of Race, Culture, and Consumption. In *Places in
            Mind: Public Archaeology as Applied Anthropology,* edited by Paul
            A. Shackel and Erve J. Chambers, pp. 57–69. Routledge, New
            York.
National Park Service
    2000   Civic Engagement. Electronic document, www.nps.gov/civic,
            accessed April 13, 2005.
New Philadelphia Association
    2006   New Philadelphia: A Pioneer Town. Electronic document,
            http://www.newphiladelphiail.org, accessed August 24, 2006.
Oliver, William
    1924   *Eight Months in Illinois.* Walter M. Hill, Chicago.
Shackel, Paul A.
    2005   Memory, Civic Engagement and the Public Meaning of Ar-
            chaeological Heritage. *SAA Archaeological Record* 5(2): 24–27.
    2006   New Philadelphia Archaeology Report. Electronic docu-
            ment, http://www.heritage.umd.edu/chrsweb/New%20
            Philadelphia/2006report/2006menu.htm, accessed August
            27, 2006.
Simeone, James
    2000   *Democracy and Slavery in Frontier Illinois: The Bottomland Repub-
            lic.* Northern Illinois University Press, DeKalb.
Simpson, Helen McWorter
    1981   *Makers of History.* Laddie B. Warren, Evansville, Indiana.
Tanner, Henry
    1881   *The Martyrdom of Lovejoy—An Account of the Life, Trials, and
            Perils of Rev. Elijah P. Lovejoy Who was Killed by a Pro-Slavery
            Mob at Alton, Illinois the Night of November 7, 1838.* Fergus,
            Chicago.

Walker, Juliet E. K.
   1983   *Free Frank: A Black Pioneer on the Antebellum Frontier.* University Press of Kentucky, Lexington.

Chapter 13

Learning through Visitors: Exhibits as a Tool for Encouraging Civic Engagement through Archaeology

Teresa S. Moyer

Museums and archaeology have historically held the shared goal of engaging public interest through the presentation of artifacts in order to interpret the past. Practitioners in both professions have recently asked questions about the relevance of their work to contemporary society. These questions have led to a jointly held belief in socially and politically involved participatory approaches. In this chapter, I urge archaeologists to consider the potential of museum exhibits as a tool for civic engagement. I also encourage archaeologists to consider using their anthropological and ethnographic skills to learn about museumgoers. I build on the experiences of several museums that have become more knowledgeable about their visitors, enabling them to create informed, responsive, and interpretive products that relate to the world beyond the institution.

By "museums," I mean any cultural institution that uses archaeology in its presentations to the public, including national and state parks, museums, living history sites, and historical societies. The public primarily encounters archaeology in such places and sees its applicability outside of academia. Exhibits serve as a translator between what curators and archaeologists want the public to know and how visitors understand, relate to, and apply this information. In this way, exhibits can play an important role in encouraging civic engagement by showing connections between archaeological materials and ideas relevant to visitors, thus encouraging them to apply their curiosity about other people to activism in the world beyond the museum.

This chapter begins with several case studies of history museums that demonstrate issues associated with community engagement. I then discuss visitors' encounters with archaeological exhibits to show that the promotion of activism beyond the institution requires a different approach. Following that, I offer alternative frameworks for approaching exhibits and civic engagement with visitor use in mind that have developed through museum evaluation and anthropological techniques. I conclude with a discussion of the importance of why archaeologists need to consider such approaches in their civic engagement work. Overall, I argue that museums, archaeology, and archaeologists have a responsibility to the public to make their work useful and relevant.

Models from History Museums

The search for contemporary uses for archaeology shows that it provides a safe space in which to discuss controversial or difficult topics. Museums offer structure to these conversations; archaeology contributes the media, such as artifacts and oral histories. The ability to synthesize the resources of the two fields offers opportunities for discussing social issues in a way that encourages action. The critical analysis of what museums mean to communities has resulted in a number of paradigms for conceptualizing these sites. Nancy J. Fuller (1992:328) describes the "ecomuseum" as

> based on the belief that museums and communities should be related to the whole of life. They are concerned with integrating the family home with other aspects of the community, such as the natural environment, economics, and social relationships. Ecomuseums are community learning centers that link the past with the present as a strategy to deal with the future needs of that particular society. . . . Rather than serving as a storehouse or a temple, both of which isolate objects from ordi-

nary people and require professional assistance for access and understanding, an ecomuseum recognizes the importance of culture in the development of self-identity and its role in helping a community adjust to rapid change. The ecomuseum thus becomes a tool for the economic, social, and political growth and development of the society from which it springs.

Many history museums have begun to make over their exhibits to address "long neglected versions of history and culture, thereby giving voice to the perspectives of laborers, women, and other underrepresented groups" (Roberts 1997:70). They have begun, as well, to accept "the entry of other noncuratorial, nonscientific meanings into the interpretive domain" through accepting that visitors find their own significance in objects despite curators' guiding efforts (Roberts 1997:70). Curators and archaeologists can set the groundwork for visitors to find meanings and channel these into an ethic for activism.

A number of history museums have begun asking the difficult questions, particularly about sensitive topics like the role of "otherness" and ethnicity in American society. For instance, environmental historian Patricia Nelson Limerick has researched the history of Chinese immigrant railroad workers in environmental change and California's economic development. She notes that often the role of the Chinese is characterized as "contributing" to the overall story, despite the major role they actually played. Dolores Hayden comments on her findings, "One could add that coming to terms with ethnic history in the landscape requires engaging with such bitter experiences, as well as the indifference and denial surrounding them" (Hayden 1995:22). History museums offer a "safe space" for groups to confront historical injustices, as in the racism against Asians in California in the nineteenth century. An exhibit might address the minimization of the role of Chinese workers, a fact that underscored anti-Asian racism in California society in history. Across the United States, the Museum of Chinese in the Americas in Manhattan's Chinatown reclaims, interprets, and explores the Chinese American cultural experiences. Exhibits in this museum address issues such as the reception of Asian immigrants by the United States, culture clash, maintenance and disassembly of traditional familial structures, and the relationship of Chinatown to other neighborhoods on the Lower East Side (Tchen 1992). A pervading theme is the dissonance of Chinese communities' internal identity from their perception by the cities around them. To promote the telling of stories by firsthand witnesses, the museum solicits the community for help in putting together artifacts and cultural perspectives for its exhibits (See the Museum of Chinese in the Americas website at www.moca-nyc.org). The museum shares its building with community action and social groups. This proximal relationship offers potential for future collaborative and anthropological work.

Other civic engagement projects are based in community education, but reshape residents' understanding of their role in a larger scheme of society. In the Cincinnati Neighborhood Studies Project, which also updated the Works Progress Administration architectural guide to the city, professional historians and community residents researched the history of their city in terms of "regular" people. They focused in particular on asking locals to rethink their role in history (Giglierano et al. 1988:182). Conversations with participants revealed useful insights into the relationship between past and present, individual and society that could influence the scope of future applied history projects in Cincinnati. When first contacted for assistance on the project, locals could not understand historians' interest in their neighborhoods (Giglierano et al. 1988:178). To them, history consisted only of long-past "significant events" which happened to "important" people (Giglierano et al. 1988:179). Noting the reactions of community members helped shape historians' approach to working with the neighborhoods to write a history. In a larger sense, this reaction suggests issues for civic dialogue such as "What is the role of neighborhoods or individuals in society?" "Who makes history?" and even "What makes a person important?" Such questions address the relationship between citizens and the world around them and bring attention to the significant role citizens can play in what we will eventually see as history.

Museums like the Tenement House Museum on the Lower East Side of Manhattan, New York, employ anthropologists who attend community meetings and volunteer in local events as part of their staff of museum educators and exhibit developers. They consider participation in neighborhood activities to be part of their job description. Since the museum's mission includes using the tenements' history to engage in social action, staff members benefit from hearing locals' civic concerns and can use these issues in the development of responsive programming and exhibit development (Tenement House Museum staff, personal communication, 2001). Being visible to local groups and being a part of discussions on civic issues and concerns enables museums to be better informed about the kinds of programs and exhibits to develop.

Museums offer a place for visitors to learn about how archaeologists decipher the types and contexts of artifacts and sites. Exhibits can frame objects, particularly curious ones like those recovered in archaeological investigations, to emphasize that real people lived in the past and that they, too, experienced prejudice, a feeling of difference or insecurity, and a sense of community. Archaeological excavations behind the tenement recovered artifacts that point to the culture of the poor and working class living on the Lower East Side in the nineteenth and twentieth centuries (http://www.tenement.org/research_collections.html). The bulk of the museum's collection, however, consists of objects found inside the building and donated materials related to the history of the site. These artifacts provide a tangible link between their original users and contemporary visitors, illuminating the continuing concerns of democratic societies, such as power and change. Exhibits offer objects to focus on and text to get conversation started, and for these reasons they can serve a civic purpose. Successful museums committed to civic engagement create exhibits that respond to information gained through interaction with the community, look at the past to make obvious hierarchical structures of power, and offer the stories and views of communities from the inside. They provide a space for visitors to practice activism, as through encouraging discussion or offering activities that mime engagement, and they model behaviors and ethics for citizens to emulate.

Visitors and Exhibits

What does the public typically perceive about archaeology through the help of museums? Many places hook their audience by exploiting the romantic caricature of the mysterious archaeologist digging for objects left by people who lived long ago and far away. Hollywood representations may inspire some of the most memorable heuristics about archaeology. But what does this approach do for visitors? It is telling, for example, that the Smithsonian Institution National Museum of American History rarely includes archaeological materials in its exhibits, but has Indiana Jones's leather jacket and fedora on display alongside Dorothy's ruby slippers, the Lone Ranger's mask, and Mr. Spock's phaser.

The display of archaeology as pop culture betrays a reluctance to present difficult topics because they are seen as politically risky and not visitor friendly. But this fear of confrontation prevents museums from acting on their full potential. Susan Pearce (1990:158) writes about the relationship between archaeology, exhibitions, and the public:

> It follows that exhibitions are perpetually involved in the past through a series of persuasive presentations grounded in the present; but because exhibitions have to be intelligible to the visitors in the most basic sense, that is to say they have to be close enough to general experiences and assumptions to "make sense," they tend to take a comfortable choice from the range of contemporary options, and to include ideas about moral progress and the absolute value of technological change. In this way, exhibitions usually end up preserving a stereotyped idea of the past, and confirming a particular point of view of the nature of the present. The designing of an exhibition is an act of interpretation, which opens up meaning, and in a political world this is a political act, which needs to be handled with great care.

Lisa C. Roberts (1997:74–75) writes in a chapter about education as empowerment in her book *Knowledge to Narrative: Educators and the Changing Museum* that "the very nature of museums' exhibit function has been altered. Once a seemingly straightforward matter of displaying collections, exhibition can now be viewed as an eminently interpretive endeavor: not just that the information exhibits present is subject to multiple interpretations, but the very act of presentation is fundamentally interpretive." Roberts advocates maximizing the skills of museum educators to develop meaning in exhibits; I read this as support of an anthropology of museum visitors in order to make museums more relevant to their everyday experiences. Exhibits do not have to be passive; rather they can lead visitors to make connections between the displays and to ask questions that encourage critical perspectives.

A different tack from the traditional show-and-tell style is necessary for exhibits with a purpose rooted in civic engagement. Techniques from museum evaluation and anthropology include tracking a visitor's path using a stopwatch, observation of behavior, participant observation, exit and telephone interviews, assessment of the amount of "correct" information taken away according to the designers' and curators' plan, listening in on visitors' conversations, and counting on a regular schedule the visitors clustered at exhibit nodes. Currently, museums rarely use their archaeology to teach approaches relevant in contemporary society, but research from the aforementioned studies can help designers and archaeologists understand which elements encourage people to consider the past as inspiration for future activism.

The typical label-and-tell approach of archaeological exhibits does not inspire dialogue and critical thinking in visitors. Many archaeological exhibits contain information important for archaeologists, but it is not necessarily accessible or meaningful to a layperson. For example, visitors have difficulty deciphering the typical artifact label that lists typology, date, dimensions, and a vague reference to a culture because they do not have the archaeological training to interpret this coded information. Such exhibits perpetuate the opacity of professional archaeology by offering information that is primarily important in an archaeological ordering of the past. Exhibits often contain text panels as well, filled with details on the processes of archaeology rather than reasons to care about history and its interpretation. Visitors to such exhibits tend to move quickly: their eyes slide over text, settle on the objects for a time, and move on. Visitors tend not to progress through exhibits in the comprehensive, systematic, linear fashion exhibit planners imagine, and rarely discuss the material while in front of it. Tracking studies show that visitors tend to view only 20–40 percent of an exhibition in most fields.

Audience research at the Minnesota Historical Society resulted in changes to its approach to exhibits. The exhibit staff listened to their audience to learn more about traditional and nontraditional visitors to the history center. The information gleaned from interviews informed exhibit development by shattering institutional assumptions about what visitors knew and were interested to know. The research project helped tailor the tone of subsequent exhibits. These countered the characterization of history as dry, serious, and impersonal by communicating the opposite. The researchers found that people did not necessarily believe that there was a single version of history and that they preferred to see exhibits about everyday life (Franco 1994:160). Audience research also mirrored findings around the nation that while historians and curators see time as a continuum, the general public lacks the sense of connections between long-past and recent history. These shifts in design help to accommodate such differences between professional familiarity with the nuances of history and visitors encountering it for the first time. Barbara Franco (1994:161), who worked at the Minnesota Historical Society at the time of the study, writes that

> this distinction helps explain the success of certain ways of learning history—first-person interpretation, a dramatic presentation, what your grandmother tells you, a historic site, real objects. . . . With this knowledge, the Minnesota Historical Society has been able to articulate that the overall goal of the exhibits program is to enable visitors to connect their experiences with the experiences of people in the past. Rather than a traditional timeline approach to history, the exhibitions in the history center approach history from the standpoint of common human experiences of family, work, community, and sense of place. Emotional engagement, active participation,

and first-person narratives of real people are some of the ways that our exhibits help visitors connect their individual experiences to the experiences of people in the past.

Museums are a powerful influence on the public's conception of the past and its relevance to contemporary society. The goal of encouraging public activism beyond the museum requires techniques in exhibits that go beyond the label-and-tell approach. If exhibits are to be a training ground for real-world situations, their design should incorporate opportunities for practicing the kinds of skills necessary for activism when visitors return to their everyday lives. Civic engagement requires skills such as the ability to become informed about issues through research and reading and the ability to talk about issues and understand situations from multiple angles. In an archaeological exhibit, these skills can be practiced through a shift in design oriented toward encouraging internal and conversational dialogue. This can happen by posing direct questions, using objects that relate to larger experiences and events in newspapers and historical accounts, and presenting information interpretively rather than directly. Visitors tend to hover the longest in front of dioramas, object-filled cases, and quotes from real people in history. This tendency makes these places ideal ones to insert creative approaches to skill building, and the message that involving oneself in the world is important can be inserted into displays like these. Using a story approach teaches skills such as creativity in considering problems and using data to interpret a situation. Story and context also help nonarchaeologists wade through technical material, and explain why they should care about the materials laid before them.

A Shift in Approach

Civic engagement in exhibits combines artifactual reminders of past peoples with interpretation that teaches skills and cultivates an ethic in contemporary viewers for community activism. Exhibits with this agenda address the meanings of the past in visitors' own lives. The materials that characterize archaeology, like artifacts and documentary records, already draw visitors' attention. Archaeologists can take advantage of the "hook" of the public's curiosity by integrating the ethic of community activism into exhibits. Seen in this way, archaeology can give people perspective on modern events that are sensitive, difficult, or personal, and that happened relatively recently in history. This is not to say that interpretation and agenda should trump data, but rather that archaeology can have powerful applications as a medium to encourage critical thinking.

If traditional label-and-tell exhibits do not grab visitors' attention, and furthermore seem to perpetuate an object-based look at the past rather than providing insight into meaning, then perhaps archaeologists should consider a different approach. Exhibits with social or political themes require additional attention to address particular topics in appropriate ways without dumbing down or desensitizing the material. Barbara Franco of the Minnesota Historical Society asks a question of historians that is also relevant to archaeologists: "How might the work of historians change if communication were taken as seriously as research and analysis?" (Franco 1994:157). Looking at exhibits this way demonstrates that traditional exhibit designs may run counter to the goals of civic engagement, as they often create a hierarchy of materials displayed and a jargon-oriented narrative that separates visitor from archaeologist and material.

Museums increasingly understand their responsibility to a wider-than-traditional audience, as well as the value of including educational and interpretive staff in exhibit development. When this staff is involved with exhibitions, they incorporate the experiences of their daily anthropology of their interactions with visitors. "Formal tours are giving way to informal programs that stress exploration; cognitive learning objectives are being replaced by affective learning; school tours are supplemented by programs for families and adults" (Franco 1994:155–156). This helps to ensure that exhibits become learning environments with opportunities for self-directed learning, addressing visitors' emotions and minds, a contemporary trend in museums' communication to their audience.

Museum anthropology can be a useful framework for integrating an ethic of civic engagement into exhibits. Recent models that define museums, theories of learning, and approaches to interpretation offer help in conceptualizing the intellectual shape exhibits can take, the ways people typically relate to them, and the influences that help a person see in a new way. The results reach across disciplines, showing that investigating people's preconceived ideas about the past brings insight into myths that need to be dispelled, or new ideas that need to be brought forth.

Approaches: Theory and Method

Questions about the teaching abilities of traditional exhibits lead to insights into how people operate in museum environments. Eileen Hooper-Greenhill (1994:140, 145) finds that people learn best when they interact with educators and exhibits by handling objects or talking about them. Beyond education, she believes museums can act as forces for change in modern cultural shifts (Hooper-Greenhill 1994:6). Jay Rounds identifies several heuristics that may help bridge the gap between what curators want visitors to know and what visitors can absorb. Visitor mechanisms include being attracted to high-interest areas, scanning for points of particular interest, and identifying where other people have already gathered, signaling something of interest to see (Rounds 2004). He suggests an ecological approach to understanding the curiosity-driven visitor, a visitor who engages in exhibits according to what catches his or her eye and attention. This approach describes a more typical visitor experience than that often described by evaluations, and suggests elements that will help people think more deeply.

Research and observation find that people are willing to connect emotionally with resources, and that when they do, they become more open to analyzing information and using it to understand their present-day experiences. National Park Service interpreters find that the incorporation of emotion, empathy, and personal connections into exhibits creates a greater sense of caring for resources among visitors. Interpretation guru Freeman

Tilden shaped NPS interpretation with his in-park research into the relationships between national park resources and the public. In forming his view, Tilden (1957/1977:32–33) argued that

> in the field of Interpretation, whether of the National Park System or other institutions, the activity is not instruction so much as what we may call provocation. It is true that the visitors to these preserves frequently desire straight information, which may be called instruction, and a good interpreter will always be able to teach when called upon. But the purpose of Interpretation is to stimulate the reader or hearer toward a desire to widen his horizon of interests and knowledge, and to gain an understanding of the greater truths that lie behind any statements of fact.

Recent initiatives in melding archaeology and interpretation by the National Park Service have resulted in *Module 440: Effective Interpretation of Archeological Resources,* a joint project between the Archeology Program, Southeast Archeological Center, and the Interpretive Division. Two online distance learning guides, *Archeology for Interpreters: A Guide to Knowledge of the Resource* (www. cr.nps.gov/archeology/afori/index.htm) and *Interpretation for Archeologists: A Guide to Increasing Knowledge, Skills, and Abilities* (www.cr.nps.gov/archeology/ifora/index.htm), were written by anthropologists with specialties in archaeology and museology. As a result, these guides were developed with the assumption that anthropologically informed interpretation can both create more effective programs and offer applications for archaeological resources beyond the institution. Archaeologists tend to shy away from interpretation, a phenomenon not unique to their field. Often, professionals are unwilling to utilize emotion in engaging audiences with the past because they are "afraid of compromising their scholarly objectivity" (Franco 1994:162). Other times, archaeologists presume, without asking, to know what the public cares about and wants to know about archaeology, a problem that pervades many exhibits and makes them ineffective in reaching visitors or the issues they care about in everyday life.

The Archaeology in Annapolis program was an experiment in public archaeology that applied critical theory to the excavations, education program, and overall interpretation of Annapolis, Maryland. Critical archaeology examines current versions of history that continue the process of reinforcing ideology, in order to unmask these ideological versions of the past in a public way (Potter 1992:123). The critically informed tours run by Archaeology in Annapolis were evaluated over several seasons by the use of one-page questionnaires, which asked visitors what they learned about archaeology that they did not know prior to visiting the sites, and what connection they saw between the site and everyday modern life. What Potter found, however, was that only 5–10 percent of visitors showed they had learned that archaeology has modern relevance according to his standards, but more than half had learned something about archaeological procedures and techniques. Others responded in a way completely at odds with the archaeologists' hopes (Potter 1992:124). Anthropological approaches to visitor experiences and integration of political consciousness into interpretation may not meet archaeologists' expectations, but this does not mean that they should not try. Mark Leone has written with regard to the project at Annapolis that "once one sees that the production of material forms is productive of society, then it is possible to see that the material forms which an archaeologist makes may also have a shaping purpose or result" (Leone 1992). Anthropological studies of visitors to Archaeology in Annapolis demonstrated the distance between what archaeologists want nonarchaeologists to glean from their interpretations and what they actually do. Its attention to teaching critical theory as a new way for visitors to approach the past and present and its evaluation of the approach shows how interpretation to the public is today part of the archaeology package. Archaeologists can be powerful in shaping the public's view of the world.

Conclusion: Why Not?

James Deetz once reflected that "if I have any conclusion, it relates to our duty as custodians of that which we, as a species, have stacked on this planet. We must not only preserve it but also find reasonably imaginative and creative ways to share it with other people. This is what I think the museum business is about" (Deetz 1981:34). Deetz probably was not talking specifically about civic engagement, but I think he is right. Archaeologists do have the responsibility of being productive agents in contemporary society by working with the public, but some of the nation's most well-visited historical institutions fail to do so. Although Indy's jacket is a familiar icon of American pop culture, it is troubling that a museum like the Smithsonian that promotes some of the most important themes of America's democratic development does not connect archaeology to promotion of democratic action by everyday people.

No matter how idealistic it sounds, I reject the excuses museums make to stay out of civic issues. Museums must use their resources to get people talking. Many of our largest federal institutions and parks fail to communicate that it is essential for people to be involved in their communities and country in order for democracy to work. It seems to me that archaeology can humanize the past to motivate people to engage with the present and not take hard-won rights for granted. In a wider view, our recent political history emphasizes that museums, as educational resources for the public, should be using as many of their resources as possible to encourage democratic action and critical thinking with the past as a point of reference. It does not work to be disengaged from the public as an archaeologist, and not solely because public interest keeps archaeology from being a self-perpetuating discipline. Using archaeology as a way to motivate people to talk about the tough topics, I believe, is why we do what we do. Yet, museums in general need to do a better job of drawing on their archaeological resources—be they artifacts or people—to own up to their responsibility as facilitators in this discussion.

References Cited

Deetz, James
   1981   The Link from Object to Person to Concept. In *Museums, Adults, and the Humanities: A Guide for Educational Programming,* edited by Zipporah W. Collins, pp. 24–34. American Association of Museums, Washington, D.C.

Franco, Barbara
   1994   The Communication Conundrum: What Is the Message? Who
          Is Listening? *Journal of American History* 81(1):151–163.
Fuller, Nancy J.
   1992   The Museum as Vehicle for Community Empowerment: The
          Ak-Chin Indian Community Ecomuseum Project. In *Museums
          and Communities: The Politics of Public Culture,* edited by Ivan
          Karp, Christine Mullen Kreamer, and Steven D. Lavine, pp.
          327–366. Smithsonian Institution Press, Washington, D.C.
Giglierano, Geoffrey J., Deborah A. Overmyer, and Frederic L. Propas
   1988   *The Bicentennial Guide to Greater Cincinnati: A Portrait of Two
          Hundred Years.* The Cincinnati Historical Society, Cincinnati.
Hayden, Dolores
   1995   *The Power of Place.* MIT Press, Cambridge.
Hooper-Greenhill, Eilean
   1994   *Museums and Their Visitors.* Routledge, London.
Leone, Mark P.
   1992   Epilogue: The Productive Nature of Material Culture and Ar-
          chaeology. *Historical Archaeology* 26(3):130–133.
Pearce, Susan M.
   1990   *Archaeological Curatorship.* Leicester University Press, Leicester.
Potter, Parker B., Jr.
   1992   Critical Archaeology: In the Ground and on the Street. *Histori-
          cal Archaeology* 26(3):117–129.
Roberts, Lisa C.
   1997   *From Knowledge to Narrative: Educators and the Changing Mu-
          seum.* Smithsonian Institution Press, Washington, D.C.
Rounds, Jay
   2004   Strategies for the Curiosity-Driven Museum Visitor. *Curator*
          47(4):389–412.
Tchen, John Kuo Wei
   1992   Creating a Dialogic Museum: The Chinatown History Mu-
          seum. In *Museums and Communities: The Politics of Public
          Culture,* edited by Ivan Karp, Christine Mullen Kreamer, and
          Steven D. Lavine, pp. 285–326. Smithsonian Institution Press,
          Washington, D.C.
Tilden, Freeman.
   1977   [1957] *Interpreting Our Heritage,* 3rd ed., University of North
          Carolina Press, Chapel Hill.

Index

About the Contributors

Kelly M. Britt is a Ph.D. candidate in anthropology at Columbia University and an adjunct instructor in American Studies at Lebanon Valley College in Annville, Pennsylvania. She has published in the *International Journal of Heritage Studies, Anthropology News,* and the *Society for American Archaeology Archaeological Record.*

Meagan Brooks received her Master's in Archaeology from the University of Saskatchewan in 2006. She is currently working in Canadian public and historic archaeology.

Robert C. Chidester is a candidate in the doctoral program in anthropology and history at the University of Michigan, and holds a Master of Applied Anthropology degree from the University of Maryland. He is codirector of the Hampden Community Archaeology Project in Baltimore.

Chip Colwell-Chanthaphonh is based out of Santa Fe, New Mexico, as the Project Director for Anthropological Research, LLC. He is the author of *Massacre at Camp Grant: Forgetting and Remembering Apache History (2007)* and *History Is in the Land: Multivocal Tribal Traditions in Arizona's San Pedro Valley* (with T. J. Ferguson, 2006), and editor of *Archaeological Ethics* (with Karen D. Vitelli, 2006), among other publications.

David A. Gadsby holds a Masters of Applied Anthropology from the University of Maryland and is currently a doctoral student at American University in Washington, D.C. A working archaeologist for over a decade, Gadsby is currently codirector of the Hampden Community Archaeology Project.

Martin D. Gallivan received his Ph.D. from the University of Virginia and is currently assistant professor in the William & Mary Department of Anthropology. He is the author of *James River Chiefdoms: The Rise of Social Inequality in the Chesapeake* (2003) and director of archaeological research at the Werowocomoco site in Tidewater Virginia.

Patrice L. Jeppson earned her Ph.D. degree in the Program in Historical Archaeology at the University of Pennsylvania. Between 2003 and 2006, she served as the historical and public archaeology consultant to the Benjamin Franklin Tercentenary Commission.

Barbara J. Little is the author of *Historical Archaeology: Why the Past Matters* (2007) and co-author with Donald Hardesty of *Assessing Site Significance: A Guide for Archaeologists and Historians* (2000). She is especially interested in the ways that people value and use history, archaeology, and historic places.

Carol McDavid's training (Ph.D., Archaeology, Cambridge) and subsequent research focuses on how archaeologists can make archaeology more usable by multiple publics as a tool for community collaboration and reform. Her work focuses on the public contexts surrounding the historical archaeology of the African Diaspora, and she now teaches and directs a community archaeology project in Freedmen's Town, Houston, Texas.

Danielle Moretti-Langholtz received her Ph.D. from the University of Oklahoma. She is the coauthor of *We're Still Here: Contemporary Virginia Indians Tell Their Stories* (2000) and the director of the American Indian Resource Center at the College of William & Mary.

Teresa S. Moyer holds a Masters of Applied Anthropology degree from the University of Maryland and is currently a Ph.D candidate in American Studies. She has worked for the National Park Service, the Smithsonian Institution, and a variety of local history museums and organizations.

Paul R. Mullins is chair and associate professor of anthropology at Indiana University-Purdue University, Indianapolis. He is the author of *Race and Affluence: An Archaeology of Consumer Culture* (1999).

Adrian Praetzellis is professor of anthropology at Sonoma State University. In addition to the usual academic stuff, he is the perpetrator of two archaeology textbook/mystery novels: *Death By Theory* (2000) and *Dug To Death* (2003).

Mary Praetzellis is associate director at the Anthropological Studies Center, Sonoma State University. Her arrest at a sit-in at Sproul Hall at the University of California, Berkeley, in 1968 is no longer on her permanent record.

Paul A. Shackel is professor of anthropology and director of the Center for Heritage Resource Studies at the University of Maryland. He has written, coauthored, and edited twelve books related to issues of heritage and the representation of race and labor in public memory.

Lori C. Stahlgren is a staff archaeologist with the Kentucky Archaeological Survey and the Kentucky Heritage Council. She holds a law degree from the University of Louisville and an MA in Anthropology from Northern Arizona University and is a Ph.D candidate at Syracuse University.

M. Jay Stottman is a staff archaeologist at the Kentucky Archaeological Survey and holds an MA from the University of Kentucky and is currently enrolled in its doctoral program. He specializes in historical, urban, and public archaeology, and developed the Building Blocks of History archaeology education program at Riverside, the Farnsley-Moremen Landing.

Thad Van Bueren has worked as a professional archaeologist since 1978. In his guise as a California Department of Transportation archaeologist he regularly engages descendent communities and has published scholarly volumes on work camps and utopian communities.